My LIFE in

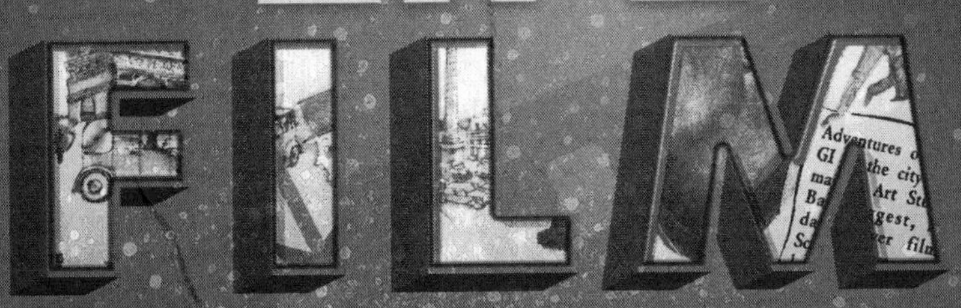

HOW THE *Movies* SHAPED MY *Soul*

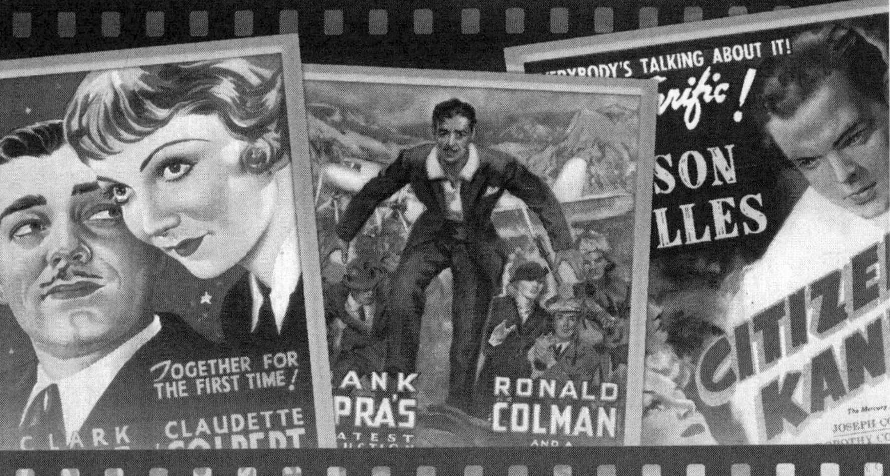

LOUIS MARKOS

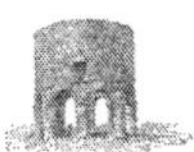

STONE TOWER PRESS

My Life in Film: How the Movies Shaped My Soul

Stone Tower Press
7 Ellen Rd.
Middletown, RI 02842
stonetowerpress.com

ISBN: 979-8-9894008-2-9

Formatting and cover design by Amy Cole, JPL Design Solutions

Printed in the United States of America

CONTENTS

For Bill Brewer

With good memories of three decades of
Film, Food, and Friendship

INTRODUCTION

Film is the defining genre of the last century. Film's unique ability to combine all the arts—from drama to painting to music to dance to photography—allows it to offer the fullest, most immersive of all aesthetic experiences. To watch a movie, to *really* watch a movie, is to be drawn into another world, into another life. Those who truly give themselves to a great film will be changed by the encounter.

Many, perhaps most, people watch films passively, just for entertainment or to pass the time. I have not watched them so. The best films, the true and enduring classics, have transformed me as a person, allowing me to see the world afresh from new eyes and from a new perspective. They have challenged me to reassess my beliefs and values, to reorder my priorities and obligations, and to rethink my goals and choices. Nearly all of them have, in some way or another, called me to recommit myself to a life of virtue.

That does not mean that the movies that have changed my life are didactic. Far from it! Their message is absorbed fully into the cinematic experience: into the decisions and motivations of the characters, the twists and turns of the plot, even, and especially, the editing, lighting, and camera work. Most of the twenty films that I will be discussing in this book are not specifically religious; yet, they have all touched me on a deeply spiritual level where issues of purpose and of worth, of repentance and renewal, of mercy and love mingle and join.

I will be inviting you to watch these films over my shoulder, to experience them as I have experienced them, as life-changing pilgrimages. For the sake of focus, and because I want to challenge my contemporary readers to revisit the Golden Age of Hollywood, I will confine myself to the great American films of the 1930s and 40s, though I will bend that rule slightly to take in one film from the early 50s. The timeless classics I will consider are *Casablanca* and *Citizen Kane, Mr. Smith Goes to Washington* and *It's a Wonderful Life, Queen Christina* and *San Francisco, The Wizard of Oz* and *Wuthering Heights, The Maltese Falcon* and *The Grapes of Wrath, Rebecca* and *Meet Me in St. Louis, The Palm Beach Story* and *The Philadelphia Story, Love Me Tonight* and *42nd Street, Top Hat* and *It Happened One Night, Lost Horizon,* and, from 1951, *An American in Paris.*

What I love about these films is their genius for being both artistic and accessible. They speak to all people in a direct, human way, while also providing multiple levels of meaning for those who wish to go deeper. They are like the people we associate with in our daily lives. They have a simple persona, a surface-level personality that we can become acquainted with after a brief conversation, while yet possessing unique quirks and idiosyncrasies, hidden gifts and talents, and deeply personal losses and triumphs that we could spend a lifetime getting to know.

Indeed, one of the things that draws me to these films, and others like them, is their unique ability to condense a person's entire life—with all its desires and fears, triumphs and failures, agonies and ecstasies—into the space of two short hours. Through experiencing nearly four thousand of these condensed lives, I have gained a special kind of wisdom: a wisdom that senses how futility and purpose are woven together in our world; a wisdom that comes when we understand the full implication of mortality and the synergy between our choices and our destinies, our abilities and our limitations.

I am not ashamed to confess that I cry a great deal when I watch old films, and not just at the sad parts. I find that in the presence of beauty, of elegance, of class I am often moved to tears. When I watch a scene that is just so "right," it triggers something inside of me, a yearning for a sense of wholeness and proportion. According to Aristotle, great art takes a world that is arbitrary and haphazard and molds and re-shapes it into a more perfect world that runs in accordance with higher laws of balance and harmony and necessity. In the world of the classic film, everything—love and hate, life and death, cowardice and sacrifice—happens as it should.

I am also not ashamed to admit to my enduring love for the magic of movies, for the way they break down time and space, now condensing, now expanding, zeroing in on a face and then pulling back to embrace the horizon. Movies release us from the tyranny of those spatiotemporal limits that control our lives. The camera can go anywhere, see anything; it is not bound by geographical rigidity or historical progression.

And one more thing that must be clearly stated at the outset. If I had never seen *Casablanca* or *Citizen Kane, The Grapes of Wrath* or *Wuthering Heights,* I would be a different person: maybe not a less virtuous person in the strict sense of the word, but certainly a lesser human being. Those films have formed much of my character, have altered my perceptions, dreams, and desires in a thousand subtle ways.

So take care, dear reader. Although I will end each chapter with a catalog of "fun facts for the fans" and with annotated lists of other films to watch that feature the same actor or actress or director or theme, my main business will be to delve deeply into each of my chosen films to unlock their cinematic wisdom. Or, to put it another way, though the chapters will be generously sprinkled with film trivia, the book will not be trivial. It will call upon you to extend to these classic films what the Romantic poet Coleridge called the willing suspension of disbelief. Please do not allow self-protective cynicism to shield you from the non-didactic-but-life-changing lessons these films would teach you.

The curtain is about to go up. It is time to shed yourself of your adult skepticism and recall the innocent wonder of your childhood. For movies *are* magic; they are, to quote Shakespeare by way of *The Maltese Falcon,* "the stuff that dreams are made of."

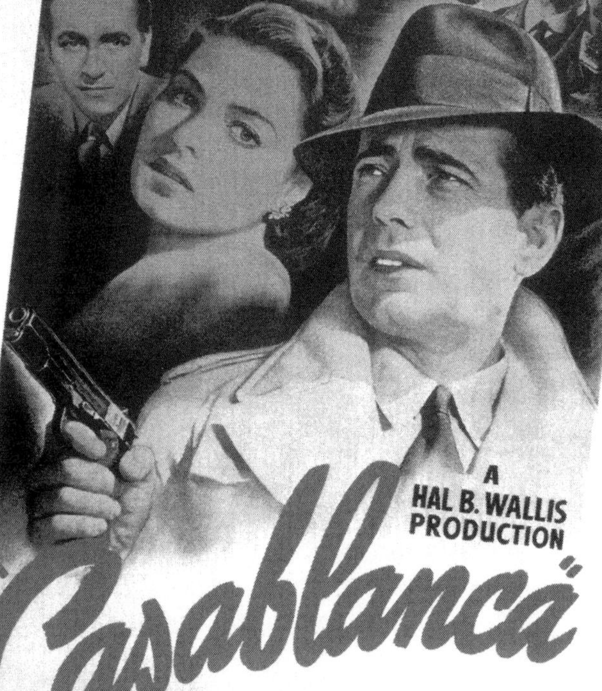
Humphrey
BOGART · Ingrid
BERGMAN · Paul
HENREID
A
HAL B. WALLIS
PRODUCTION
"Casablanca"
CLAUDE
RAINS · CONRAD
VEIDT · SYDNEY
GREENSTREET · PETER
LORRE
Directed by MICHAEL CURTIZ

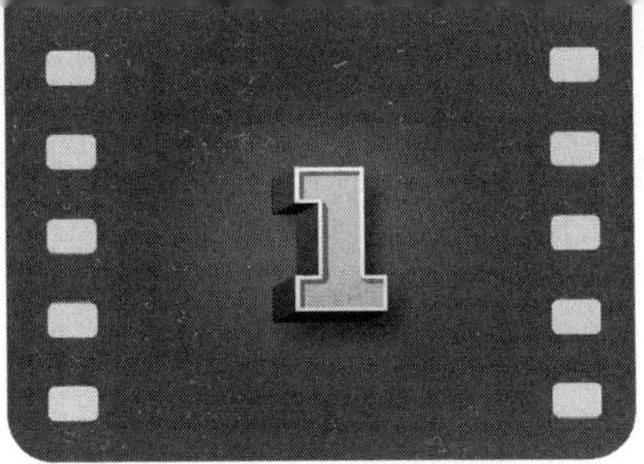

CASABLANCA

(WB; 1942; MICHAEL CURTIZ)

Most film critics and movie lovers will not hesitate to put *Casablanca* on their top-ten list. It certainly holds a secure place in my own personal top five. That is because *Casablanca* is more than a movie. It is a journey, a journey into the dark night of the soul, into fear and regret, into the loss of hope, purpose, and self identity.

Although the film boasts one of the most perfect ensemble casts ever assembled, we experience the movie through the eyes of Rick Blaine, played to perfection by Humphrey Bogart. Rick is an expatriate American living in Morocco, a self-exile with a shady past who is neither a paragon of virtue nor a hero willing to sacrifice himself for others. He runs a popular nightclub named after himself to which refugees from across Europe and North Africa are drawn. They know Rick to be a tough customer who never drinks with his guests and who does not hesitate to toss out Nazi collaborators, no matter the size of their wallets.

Rick is an enigma, a man who has long been carrying out an internal wrestling match with his own goodness and decency. Despite his outward cynicism, he possesses an innate sense of right and wrong that manifests itself in his willingness to fight on the side of the underdog. In 1935, he ran guns into Africa to help the Ethiopians resist the exploitation of the fascist Mussolini. In the following year, he fought in Spain on the loyalist side, resisting another fascist dictator named Franco.

But that was five years ago. Something has happened to our enigmatic anti-hero since then, something that has made him abandon both past and future to live in a perpetual present—not the hopeful present of faith and love, but the existential present of apathy and despair. The first time we meet Rick, he is signing a line of credit. At first all we see is his hand writing the words, "OK, Rick." Then his hand takes up a cigarette and draws it toward his face. Here is a man going through the motions, trapped in a world of his own making.

Casablanca was filmed in black and white for a reason. It is a movie of shadows and smoke, of dark alleys and crowded bazaars. Its characters live and move in those shadows, afraid to face the sun, to be exposed by its searing light. The camera moves swiftly from scene to scene and locale to locale, scarcely allowing us to catch our breath. But it never breaks free of the circuitous alleys and labyrinthine bazaars. Every time the camera turns to another corner of the *Casablanca* world, it runs into another character or conflict or encounter. The camera is restless, like the desperate refugees waiting for their exit visas, but it cannot escape. It, like the people, is trapped in a city of frustrated dreams, repressed fears, and dark intrigues. It is always catching sight of figures looking out of windows or enclosed by some kind of arch or frame; even when it shows us a flying airplane, it gives us no sense of the freedom of flight.

It may sound like I am describing a horror film, but I am not. *Casablanca* is, rather, a psychological, Jungian film where one is ever likely to bump into his alter-ego, his shadow. As in a good Shakespearean tragedy, Rick is surrounded by four foils, each of whom brings out a different aspect of his complex character.

First there is Ugarte, played by a memorably sniveling, self-deprecating Peter Lorre. Ugarte is a resourceful-but-somehow-pathetic trafficker in stolen goods who has just obtained, by murdering two German couriers, exit visas that he wants Rick to hide for him. Rick lives in the same world as Ugarte and is more than willing to tamper with the roulette wheel in his gambling room, but he refuses to stoop to Ugarte's parasitic level. He thinks he can live like Ugarte without sacrificing his integrity and self-respect.

Then there is Louie Renault (Claude Rains), the French prefect of police who is not above using his position to obtain sexual favors and to line his own pockets. He has, deep down, the heart of a French patriot, but it has been covered over by layers and layers of graft, favor-currying, and passive collaboration. Like Rick, he has learned how to look out for number one. Louie is Rick's closest friend, and the two men do what they can to help each other—but Rick lives by a more refined code. He does not exploit women the way Louie does, and he shields his workers the best he can.

The most corrupt figure of all is Señor Ferrari (Sydney Greenstreet); he is the proprietor of the Blue Parrot, but he makes the bulk of his money by running the black market and orchestrating all illegal activity in Casablanca. Like Rick, he is a successful businessman, but he will do things that Rick, even in his darkest moments, will not—namely, buy and sell human flesh.

Ugarte, Louie, and Ferrari all dwell on a lower ethical rung than Rick; in their own way, each threatens to pull him down into the moral morass that is Casablanca. But there is a fourth foil who embodies all that is most noble, fearless, and self-sacrificing in humanity: the Czechoslovakian freedom fighter Victor Lazlo (played with great dignity by Paul Henreid). Having escaped from a concentration camp, Lazlo has come to Casablanca to seek passage to Portugal—by way of Ugarte's stolen exit visas—and from there to America. He needs to do this, not only so he can save his life, but so he can continue his work of stirring up the free peoples of the world to resist fascism. In the film, he represents all those lost causes that the younger Rick had once fought for.

Simple, it seems. Surely the presence of Lazlo will wake up Rick's sleeping conscience and bring him back on to the side of the angels. But there is a problem. Lazlo is married to Ilsa Lund (played by a luminous Ingrid Bergman), the only woman Rick has ever loved. Ilsa is like the shafts of light from the ever-present searchlights that stab at the characters and then disappear into the fog.

Ilsa had appeared out of nowhere when Rick was living in Paris. The two fell in love just as the world was going mad around them. As Rick's armor fell off chink by chink and he threw open his once barricaded heart to love's transforming power, the Germans moved ever closer to their conquest of France. Rick and Ilsa were to leave Paris together on the night train to find freedom and a life together, but Ilsa had proven false.

Rick was left alone in the rain on a dilapidated railway station platform, his hand clutching Ilsa's cryptic goodbye letter as the raindrops mercilessly tear at the fading ink. That forlorn image, that silent tableau of pain has been etched in my mind ever since I first found my way into the shadowy, black-and-white world of *Casablanca*. As for Rick, since that terrible night his soul has stagnated. He is alive without being alive, moving like a shadow through the alleys and bazaars.

And then, as if out of a dark and gloomy dream, she emerges again. Rick will not be allowed to remain in his self-protective world. He must face his demons, must be shaken out of his sloth. As he waits in his empty saloon with the film's fifth foil, the ever faithful, no-nonsense, piano-playing Sam (Dooley Wilson) who stands by his boss no matter the darkness of his moods, Rick asks a simple question. "It's December 1941 in Casablanca. What time is it in New York?"

Sam has no answer, but we in the audience, if we are paying attention, suddenly realize that this film is taking place just a few days before Pearl Harbor. In a few days, the events of December 7, 1941, will catapult isolationist America into the Second World War. What that means is that Rick himself is America, a sleeping giant about to be roused. Rick, like America, is on a collision course with destiny. If he wakes and does what he must, the world will be saved from tyranny. If he does not, if he refuses to rise up to meet his destiny, then, as Lazlo explains to Rick, the world will die. Rick must make the choice for all of us.

The first time I saw *Casablanca* was at a film society showing at my graduate alma mater, the University of Michigan. Unfortunately, my enjoyment of the film was marred by the presence of a large group of politically-correct philistines who seemed to have nothing better to do than to laugh scornfully at any line in the film that they considered sexist, racist, or "unenlightened." At one point they smugly mocked what is arguably the most important line in the film.

After Ilsa explains to Rick the true reason why she abandoned him at the train station—she had thought Lazlo had been killed in a concentration camp but then had learned he was alive and calling for her—Rick tells her that their story is still in need of an ending. Will she remain with him in Casablanca or go to America with Lazlo? In response, the distraught, emotionally confused Ilsa tells Rick that she no longer knows what is right and wrong, that he must do the thinking for both of them. The thought that a woman would call on a man to do the thinking for her is what set off the scoffers, but their adolescent jeers caused them to miss Ilsa's full speech. "You'll have to do the thinking for both of us," she says, and then adds: "for all of us." "All right," Rick responds quietly, "I will."

In the kind of tight, Aristotelian plotting that distinguishes the Golden Age of Hollywood, key lines like that are never spoken and then dropped. They always return, both as a way of giving unity to beginning, middle, and end, and as a way of offering closure, resolution, and enlightenment. In the climax of the movie, filmed in a dark, claustrophobic runway that seems too small to allow an airplane to take off into the air of liberation and freedom, Ilsa thinks that she and Rick will be getting on the plane to Lisbon. But she is wrong.

Rick is staying behind with Louie and allowing Ilsa to leave with her husband. Why? Because Rick has remembered who he is. He has come to realize that Lazlo is fighting the same fight that he once fought (and will now fight again!) and that Ilsa is an essential part of Lazlo's work. He will not put his own personal happiness above the larger goal of freeing the world from totalitarianism.

"Last night," he reminds Ilsa, "you said I was to do the thinking for both of us. Well, I've done a lot of it since then, and it all adds up to one thing. You're getting on that plane with Victor where you belong." He has indeed done a lot of thinking. He has searched his crippled heart and soul and discovered reserves of strength and faith and courage that he thought had been depleted.

In that last scene, which plays out at least four times a year in the movie theater of my mind, Rick taught me that one man *can* make a difference, that the decisions of individuals can affect the world. Human beings, Rick helped me to understand, can make noble, even altruistic choices, can be driven by things higher than lust, greed, and self-preservation. *Casablanca,* while looking directly into the face of evil, ennobles our fallen but still God-breathed humanity. Despite the machinations of evil men, there are yet things worth fighting for, suffering for, even dying for.

As Rick nears the climax of his final speech to Ilsa, his embrace of self-sacrifice reaches so exalted a height that he finds himself, perhaps unconsciously, paraphrasing the words of Christ (John 13:36): "But I've got a job to do, too. Where I'm going you can't follow. What I've got to do, you can't be any part of. Ilsa, I'm no good at being noble, but it doesn't take much to see that the problems of three little people don't amount to a hill o'beans in this crazy world of ours."

Odd, is it not, that one of the most romantic movies ever made should end with the boy losing the girl! But that is at it should be, as it must be. In another time and place, Rick and Ilsa might walk off together, hand in hand, into the sunset. But not in this time and this place. There is too much at stake.

Still, the film offers abundant recompense. As Ilsa and Victor fly off to continue their work, Rick and Louie head off into the night to fight in the French resistance. Love between the sexes gives way to a vigorous male friendship with the power to break the chains of tyranny and to bring back joy and camaraderie to a world in pain.

Fun Facts for the Fans

- Though *Casablanca* was released in 1942, it won the best picture Oscar for 1943; it also won Oscars for direction and script and nominations for Bogart, Rains, photography (Arthur Edeson), music (Max Steiner), and editing (Owen Marks).

- The script, by Julius J. & Philip G. Epstein and Howard Koch, was based on an unproduced play, *Everybody Comes to Rick's*, by Murray Burnett & Joan Alison.

- No one had any idea they were making a classic American film; it was meant to be a fairly routine war film with Ronald Reagan in the role of Rick.

- The script was written as they went along: no one knew until the end of the film whether Ilsa would end up with Rick or Lazlo, thus forcing Bergman to show real love for both of her male co-stars.
- Though critics often analyze films as the creation of a single creative mind, usually the director (French critics call this the auteur theory), *Casablanca* shows the studio system at its collaborative best.
- *Casablanca* embodies to perfection the tough, gritty, proletarian focus of its studio, Warner Brothers, known for its gangster films (*Little Caesar, G-Men, Public Enemy*) and it unglamorous, blue-collar, backstage musicals (*42nd Street, The Gold Diggers of 1933, Footlight Parade*).
- Warner Brothers often claimed that its films were "Torn from Today's Headlines," as in *Confessions of a Nazi Spy*.

Other Films to Watch

Best films of Humphrey Bogart: As second lead in the role of a nasty gangster: *Dead End, Angels with Dirty Faces, The Roaring Twenties*. As lead: *The Maltese Falcon* (as Sam Spade), *Across the Pacific* (fights Japanese spies), *Sahara* (World War II actioner), *To Have and Have Not* (based on Hemingway; his first film with Lauren Bacall), *The Big Sleep* (as Philip Marlowe), *The Treasure of the Sierra Madre* (in an unattractive role), *Key Largo* (fights last of the gangsters), *The African Queen* (a second unattractive role that angered many of his fans; acted alongside Katherine Hepburn and won his only Oscar), *The Caine Mutiny* (as Captain Queeg), *Sabrina* (uncharacteristic romantic role), *The Desperate Hours* (nasty gangster again).

Different perspectives on World War II: *Across the Pacific, Sahara* (see above), *All Through the Night* (Bogie + gangsters foil Nazis), *Confessions of a Nazi Spy* (first Hollywood film to attack the Nazis), *The 49th Parallel* (British film about Nazis in Canada), *Desperate Journey* (silly propaganda but great fun), *The Mortal Storm* (Nazis corrupt Germany), *Foreign*

Correspondent (Hitchcock's call to America to join the war), *Arise My Love* (romance, but calls on America to join war), *So Proudly We Hail* (about a group of army nurses), Mrs. Miniver (effect of war on British civilians), *Bridge on the River Kwai* (Asian front), *Twelve O'Clock High* (Battle of Britain), *Why We Fight* (series of documentary propaganda films by Frank Capra), *Lifeboat* (Hitchcock), *To Be or Not to Be* (satiric look at Nazis), *The Great Dictator* (Chaplin's satire on Hitler), *The Desert Fox* (positive study of Rommel), *Guns of Navarone* (heroic commando raid), *The Dirty Dozen* (anti-heroic commando raid), *Five Graves to Cairo* (spy romance), *Stalag 17* (inspiration for *Hogan's Heroes*), *In Which We Serve* (about the crew of a British boat), *Patton* (best picture of 1970), *The Longest Day* (recreation of the Battle of Normandy).

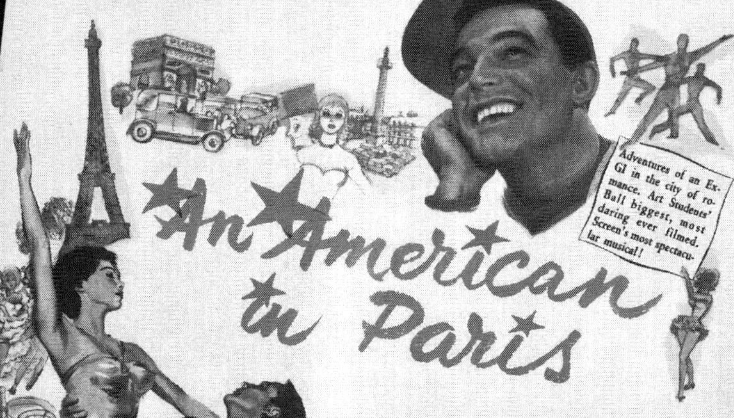
What a joy to see M·G·M's
Color by Technicolor musical!
Adventures of an Ex-GI in the city of romance. Art Students' Ball biggest, most daring ever filmed. Screen's most spectacular musical!
An American in Paris
To the Music of
GEORGE GERSHWIN
Starring
GENE KELLY
and Introducing
LESLIE CARON
with
OSCAR LEVANT
GEORGES GUETARY
NINA FOCH
Hear the stars sing the hits in the M-G-M Records album
Story and Screen Play by ALAN JAY LERNER
Lyrics by IRA GERSHWIN
Directed by VINCENTE MINNELLI ★ Produced by ARTHUR FREED
A Metro-Goldwyn-Mayer Picture

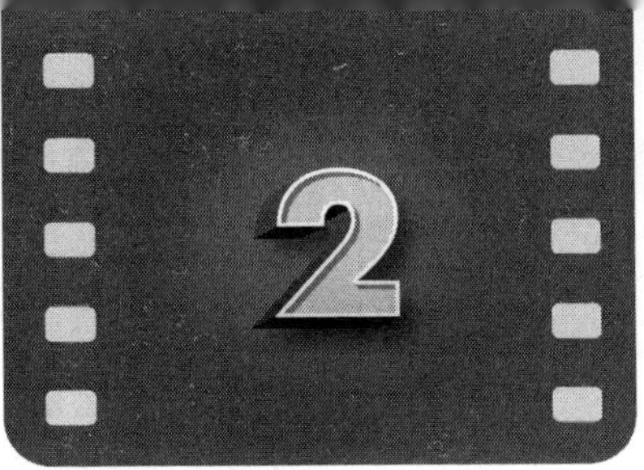

AN AMERICAN IN PARIS

(MGM; 1951; VINCENTE MINNELLI)

Although *An American in Paris* won the Oscar for best picture only eight years after *Casablanca* took the same award, the two films couldn't be more different. When the latter film was being made, America was embroiled in World War II and the future looked dark and uncertain. By 1951, however, the war was fast becoming a memory, and American was basking in the sunny optimism of post-war prosperity.

The shadowy, paranoid, black-and-white world of Morocco has given way to a gleaming Paris of the imagination, bathed in light and shot in glorious Technicolor. Of course, both movies were filmed entirely on sound stages in Hollywood, but that only adds to the artistic control that makes each Oscar winner a window into a different world, a different mood, a different soul.

I needed, and continue to need, both films, for there are some days when I interact with the world like Rick Blaine—desiring to do great deeds but lonely, cautious, and self-protective—and others when I look out upon the world through the twinkling eye of Jerry Mulligan. Jerry, an American GI who stayed on in Paris after the end of the war to become a painter, is the brash, ebullient hero of *An American in Paris*; he is played by the equally brash and ebullient Gene Kelly.

Since I was nine or ten, Kelly has been one of my most enduring heroes. He taught me to face the world with a wink and a smile and to always sing the loudest when the rain is falling the heaviest. While Fred

Astaire, of whom I will have much to say in a later chapter, danced for the aristocracy, Kelly danced for the proletariat: for the sailors and the stunt doubles and the little guys from the little towns. Throughout most of *An American in Paris,* he walks the sidewalks of the Champs-Élysées with a bounce to his step that I find myself imitating on a regular basis. Why walk, after all, when you can skip and glide along the surface of the pavement.

Like *Casablanca, An American in Paris* features a love triangle in which a young woman, Lise (played beguilingly by the nineteen-year-old Leslie Caron), must choose between the young Jerry whom she loves passionately and an older man, her fiancée Henri (George Gauteray), whom she respects and to whom she owes a debt of gratitude. Indeed, when Lise explains to Jerry her relationship with Henri, she uses words that are almost identical to those used by Ilsa when she explains to Rick her relationship with Victor Lazlo. Both Lise and Ilsa were orphans in the storm, taken in, protected, and partially raised by the at-first parental Henri/Victor.

The parallel between the two films is intensified by the fact that Jerry is involved in his own love triangle with an older woman, Milo (Nina Foch), who is patronizing his artistic career. Had the movie been made in 1942, Jerry and Lise might have chosen duty over passion and said goodbye in a dark, foggy airport, but it was 1951, America felt happy and satisfied, and so, in the closing frames of the film, the two lovers go off hand-in-hand into the brightly lit world of Paris.

So, who am I? Am I Jerry dancing off with Lise, or Rick giving up the girl? I am both, for the times are ever changing, and if I am to be a man of virtue and integrity, I must, to co-opt a line from *The Lord of the Rings,* make the proper use of the time that has been given to me. From Rick, I learned how one rises above the pain of loss and betrayal; from Jerry, I learned what it means to live the life of the imagination.

More than any other film, it was *An American in Paris* that introduced me to what the world could be like were it perceived through the enchanted eyes of an artist: not the tormented artist drinking himself into oblivion while alienating all his friends, but the hopeful artist who finds magic in the most ordinary of things.

The film begins with Jerry speaking to us in a fervent voice over while the camera sweeps along the fountains and boulevards of Paris. He immediately transports us, as he has transported himself, to his adopted home: "here on this star called Paris." That beautiful phrase is quite literal, for the Paris street system is laid out like a series of stars radiating out from circular plazas—not so much for aesthetic reasons as to prevent revolutionaries from setting up barricades in the streets, as they did again and again from the dawn of the French Revolution through the middle of the nineteenth century.

But, of course, the phrase is more than literal. Jerry has found a world of ethereal beauty which one gazes on through a lovely cloud of fairy dust. And that world is both the Champs-Élysées—French for Elysian Fields, the place where the brave and righteous go in Greek mythology to stroll along the green grass and converse about beauty and virtue—and the back lot of Metro Goldwyn Mayer—that blessed place where there were, so MGM proudly claimed, more stars than there are in the heavens.

After introducing us to Paris, Jerry and the camera take us up into the tiny garret of the starving artist. Amazingly, the garret really *is* small, not like the attic where the Jewish refuges hide for safety in Hollywood's *The Diary of Anne Frank* (1959), which appears to be bigger than a four-bedroom house! No, Jerry's attic is quite tiny ... and yet, he has used his creativity and his skill to open it up into a palace of art.

No sooner does Jerry rise from his slumbers than he pulls his bed up, via ropes and pulleys, into the ceiling, and whisks his table and chair out of the closet and into the one room of his efficiency garret. He opens his French doors to breathe in the morning air and retrieve his fruit and milk from their "refrigerator" on the balcony. In a graceful, effortless dance, Jerry continues to move objects with his feet and smack gears and levers with his hands, transforming his cramped apartment into a spacious home.

In one scene of the film, he goes down a flight of stairs to visit his friend Adam (played with grumpy charm by Oscar Levant), a starving musician whose piano fills up half his room. But that doesn't stop Jerry from doing an energetic dance to "Tra-La-La." As he revs himself up in to a tap-dancing frenzy, he kicks door jams and piano legs and narrow corridor walls with such wild abandon that he seems to stretch out the space by sheer will power.

In another scene, Jerry, Adam, and Henri perform "By Strauss" downstairs in the crowded parlor. In the wink of an eye, the grubby parlor expands into a showroom, but without ever losing its simple humanity. At one point, Jerry dances with a little old lady, and the chubby proprietor finds himself raised up to the status of an emperor. Yet the place never ceases to be what it is. There is no "instrumental" magic here, just the power of song and dance and imagination to exalt the meek and make the humble sublime.

In yet another scene, Jerry and Henri sing "'S Wonderful" to an adoring crowd outside the parlor. Musicals are famous—to some people, notorious—for having characters burst into song at the drop of a hat; they do that here, but in such a way that the onlookers and passersby are drawn in to the infectious spell. As the two finish their song, they step further and further away from each other as the camera pulls up and up. By the end of the number, they have stretched out the crowded street to the farthest it can go, with our two characters in opposite corners of the frame. But the frame does not break. It holds within it all the life and joy and dreamy wonder that two men in love can contain within their nearly-bursting hearts.

But the best scene of all, the one that makes me smile if I merely think about it while fighting my way home through Houston traffic, concerns a love-struck Jerry and a group of American-loving Parisian children. Jerry does not merely sing "I've Got Rhythm" to them; he teaches it to them and gets them to join along. Song doesn't just lift up Jerry; it transforms the wide-eyed children into cowboys and pilots, train conductors and Charlie Chaplins. No matter the hardship or the sorrow, rhythm and music have the power to chase away old man trouble and replace him with daisies and green pastures.

While all the numbers that include Jerry partake of this same infectious joy and exuberance, the one song Henri performs by himself ("I'll Build a Stairway to Paradise") is both meticulously staged and performed *on* a stage. It is a wonderful number, but it is, by its very nature, less vital and spontaneous. In sharp contrast, when Jerry and Lise dance to "Love Is Here to Stay" along the Seine, they act out their courtship with such poignant immediacy that the two seem to be making up the steps as they go. That is why Henri must finally surrender Lise to Jerry: in this film, in this incarnation of the human spirit, the bohemian life of the imagination must win out in the end.

Though I am, myself, of the bourgeois persuasion, I thrill each time I hear Jerry say, in his opening voice over, that if an artist can't make it in Paris, he might as well give up and marry the boss's daughter. Adam, in his opening voice over, tells us that he once got a real job, but he stopped it to go back to the piano since he found he was enjoying working too much! In his own way, Richard Blain has also run away from small-town, middle-class America, but into the darkness of Casablanca rather than into the light of Paris.

But there is a difference. Jerry is not hiding; he is living now, in the moment, as Jesus himself tells us we all should live (Mathew 6:34). True, there are many movies about artists that show the painter or musician or writer falling in to a life of hedonism or sloth or self-destructive rebellion. But that is not what *An American in Paris* is about.

Jerry tells Milo that it is hard for an artist to sell one of his paintings. When a writer sells his book, he can always buy a copy from a bookstore. For the artist, however, the original is everything; once he sells it, it is out of his life forever. Life itself is like that. It needs to be lived now, with the same kind of innocent, grateful spontaneity out of which the film's best musical numbers spring.

Lise embodies exactly that innocent, grateful spontaneity. We first "meet" her in a magic mirror as Henri tries to explain to Adam exactly what Lise is like. In a series of vignettes that all come together in the finale to fill the mirror almost to bursting, Lise dances her various moods and personality traits to the haunting tune of "Embraceable You." She is a fairy, a creature out of myth, to some extent a male fantasy, but she is as real as are her longings for a life of joy and authenticity.

Even were it shorn of its epic, fifteen-minute dream ballet choreographed to Gershwin's jazzy orchestral piece that shares its name with the film, *An American in Paris* would be a great movie, a paean to those four words that sum up the creed of the characters in Baz Luhrmann's 2001 homage to the Paris-that-was, *Moulin Rouge*: Love, Beauty, Freedom, Truth. With the ballet, it moves into the realm of cinematic classic. For although, in terms of the plot, it is Henri's overhearing of Lise's confession of love to Jerry that leads to the happy ending, what really unites the lovers is the ballet itself, in which they pursue and court, lose and gain each other through a kaleidoscope of Parisian cityscapes as envisioned by the painters who knew and loved Paris best: Dufy, Manet, Renoir, Utrillo, Rousseau, Van Gogh, and Toulouse-Lautrec.

Before the ballet begins, Jerry and Lise (overheard by Henri) say goodbye to each other as Lise prepares to leave for America with Henri. Lise promises Jerry that Paris will help him to forget her, but he says it will not: "It is too real and too beautiful. It never lets you forget anything. It reaches in and opens you wide, and you stay that way." Though Jerry loves Paris, it is no longer enough for him, "because the more beautiful everything is, the more it will hurt without you." Lise begs Jerry not to let her leave him this way, but Jerry can say nothing else.

Indeed, Lise's plea marks the last line of dialogue in the film. After this moment there will be only the ballet and the final embrace that occurs after Henri stops the taxi and motions for Lise to go back to Jerry. Jerry and Lise will run to each other from the top and bottom of a long stair case, meeting in the middle. There they will remain, in that liminal space, that threshold world of art and beauty and love.

But before that, there is the dance, the incarnation of their love, of their desire to remain within the realm of the imagination. When Lise leaves him to go to Henri, Jerry takes a black and white charcoal sketch he has made of the Place de l'Etoile, tears it in half, and throws it off the balcony. But Paris has some magic up her sleeve. A burst of wind blows the pieces together to form a sketchy background, as one might see in a number from the Ziegfeld Follies. Suddenly a red rose, shimmering against the black and white background, appears on the ground, followed by Jerry himself in black. He picks up the rose, turns toward the sketch, and the world bursts into color and music.

I could spend many pages describing the sequences of the ballet, but the words would fail me. It needs to be seen in all its glory, for only then can one enter into it as Jerry does. The dream ballet is cinema at its most pure, where anything is possible and where the emotions one feels on the inside are projected onto richly painted sets and costumes and brought to life by floating camera movements, revolving mirrors, colored steam, and a host of dancing figures.

The message is not that one should live in a fantasy world, but that life is filled with magic and beauty and love—if only we will have eyes to see it. In that sense, the life of the imagination touches, if tenuously, on the spiritual life, and the famous words of Julian of Norwich, that all will be well and all will be well and all manner of thing will be well, call out to us in the midst of a world where there seems to be neither life nor hope.

Fun Facts for the Fans

- *An American in Paris* won Oscars for best picture, screenplay, photography, art direction (Cedric Gibbons & Preston Ames), musical arrangement, and costumes. It was nominated for director (Vincente Minnelli) and editing.
- Minnelli spent fully 1/5 of the budget on the dream ballet.
- Before moving to Hollywood, Minnelli designed store window and backdrops for musical shows; these prepared him to create the eye-popping sets for the ballet.
- The original screenplay was written by Alan Jay Lerner, who would later go on to write the book and lyrics for five classic musicals: *My Fair Lady, Camelot, Gigi, Brigadoon,* and *Paint Your Wagon.* All were made into films, with *Gigi* starting its life as a film musical and then later becoming a stage musical.
- Lerner was allowed to use any songs he wanted from the Gershwin song book.

- The song that Kelly sings to Caron along the Seine, "Love Is Here to Stay," was the last song George wrote before he died. Ira wrote the lyrics later to express the love he felt for his brother.
- Maurice Chevalier was originally slated to play Henri, but he turned it down because he didn't get the girl. Sadly, this delayed Chevalier's return to Hollywood until he starred in *Gigi*, another MGM award-winning musical written by Lerner and directed by Minnelli.
- Although the film is supposed to take place after World War II, the setting is really post-World War I Paris, the Jazz Age made famous by Hemingway and Fitzgerald. At one point, Adam starts playing a 1920s Gershwin jazz song ("Fascinating Rhythm"), and Henri tells him that he prefers Viennese waltzes to this *new*, upstart jazz.
- Oscar Levant was a personal friend of George Gershwin and looked to him as a role model. In the biopic of Gershwin, *Rhapsody in Blue*, Levant plays himself!
- In the original cut of the film, Milo gives a sad monologue and Henri sings "But Not for Me" after they lose Jerry/Lise, but they were deleted because they detracted from the happy ending.

Other Films to Watch

Under the MGM production unit of Arthur Freed, Vincenti Minnelli also made these classic musicals: *Cabin in the Sky* (all-black fantasy musical of good vs. evil), *Meet Me in St. Louis* (see chapter 16), *The Band Wagon* (great routines in great color, danced by Fred Astaire and Cyd Charisse), *Brigadoon* (Kelly and Charisse dance in a magic Scottish town), *Gigi* (the height of class with a beguiling Caron returning to Paris).

Without Minnelli, Gene Kelly made many fine musicals: *For Me and My Gal* (his first film, with Judy Garland), *Cover Girl* (with Rita Hayworth, who began her career as a dancer), *Anchors Aweigh* (Kelly and Frank Sinatra as loveable sailors; includes Kelly dancing with an animated Jerry the Mouse), *The Pirate* (with Garland again), *Take Me Out to the Ball Game* (now Kelly and Sinatra are baseball players), *On the Town* (his third and final outing with Sinatra), *Summer Stock* (lesser film with Garland, but some great numbers), *Singin' in the Rain* (perhaps the best musical ever made, with witty dialogue to match its unforgettable numbers), *It's Always Fair Weather* (a sort of sequel to *On the Town* that has a serious, even bitter edge to it), *Invitation to the Dance* (an experimental series of three stories told through ballet).

Four great MGM musicals starring Howard Keel: *Annie Get Your Gun* (from the Irving Berlin musical), *Showboat* (remake of an older black-and-white version, starring a lovely Ava Gardner), *Kiss Me Kate* (Cole Porter's musical reworking of *The Taming of the Shrew*), *Seven Brides for Seven Brothers* (based on the Rape of the Sabine Women!)

SAN FRANCISCO

Clark
GABLE

Jeanette
MAC DONALD

SPENCER TRACY
JACK HOLT
JESSIE RALPH

REGI: W. S. VAN DYKE

Metro Goldwyn Mayer

SAN FRANCISCO

(MGM; 1936; W. S. VAN DYKE)

At the core of both *Casablanca* and *An American in Paris* is a love triangle in which the heroine must choose, not only between two different men whom she loves, but between two different value systems and potential futures. In the former, Ilsa must choose either to stay with Victor and the path of duty or to run off with Rick in pursuit of passion and romantic love. In the latter, Lise must choose either to marry Henri and live a safe life in America as the wife of a successful stage singer or risk everything to live a life of love, beauty, and freedom with a struggling artist who has himself chosen love over the security offered by a rich patroness who wants to possess him.

In *San Francisco,* Mary Blake (Jeanette MacDonald), the innocent, devout daughter of a country parson, has come to the Barbary Coast in hopes of becoming a singer. As the story progresses, she finds herself torn between Blackie Norton (Clark Gable), the rough-and-tumble owner of San Francisco's infamous Paradise saloon, and Jack Burley (Jack Holt), a rich society man from the snobby, sophisticated Nob Hill.

This love triangle, however, is complicated by a second one that the film layers on top of the first. Blackie has long been best friends with Father Tim Mullin (Spencer Tracy), though he has never really understood why his one-time drinking and brawling partner found religion and became a priest. As Mary struggles to choose between Blackie and Burley, she must also choose between her heart, which belongs to the heathen Blackie, and her soul, which belongs to the Christian faith of Father Tim.

On the surface, it would seem that Blackie is a simple villain and Mary should and must resolve her dual love triangle by rejecting him in favor of Burley and Tim. But life is rarely that simple. Blackie, played with overwhelming masculine charm by MGM's reigning king, is more than a man: he is a summation of all the good and evil in human nature, particularly all the good and evil of that glorious, pre-1906 San Francisco that the opening title card of the film describes as "splendid and sensuous, vulgar and magnificent." And, behind that, all the good and evil of Hollywood's Golden Age!

As Gable was the King of Hollywood, so Blackie is the King of the Barbary Coast. The San Francisco of Blackie, like the Los Angeles of Gable, is, in many ways, Sin City, the Babylon of the West. According to Tim, San Francisco is "the wickedest, most corrupt, most godless city in America," and yet, it has such heart, such generosity, such untapped potential for honor and nobility. Blackie, Tim tells Mary, is "as ashamed of his good deeds as other people are of their sins," a statement backed up by the revelation that Blackie anonymously donated $4000 to build an organ for Tim's church.

Don't be fooled. Blackie is a dangerous man whom one must be careful not to cross. He is, Tim warns Mary, "as unscrupulous with women as he is ruthless with men." He grew up on the streets, and he knows how to survive. He is not against religion, but he dismisses it as just another racket to pull in the suckers. Nietzsche light, we might say, except for the fact that there is a door that opens on to Blackie's well-protected soul. That door is music, and Mary possesses the key. Tim, who has been trying, unsuccessfully, for the last twenty years to reform his friend, wonders if Mary and her music might not succeed where he has failed.

Blackie, like Rick, has always lived by a code. He may be ruthless when it comes to protecting his Paradise, but he has never lied, cheated, or been really underhanded. Like Rick, he does not buy and sell human beings, nor does he bow down before the phonies and the snobs. Though he uses emotional pressure to keep Mary singing in his saloon, he does offer to let her out of her contract with no strings attached if she truly wants to be free. It's finally Burley who thinks that he can buy and own Mary, who hides a Mephistophelian mind under his veneer of charm, who works with the opera, not because the music lifts his soul, but because it gives him the respectability, social clout, and power he lusts for.

Blackie, in contrast, embodies the old proverb that music calms the savage beast. At first he thinks that opera, like religion, is just another racket, and insists that Mary stick to the jazzy, honky-tonk music of the Paradise. The kid from the streets feels threatened by the highbrow music of Nob Hill and closes his ears to it. Then he hears Mary singing at Burley's opera house, and a new, more expansive world opens before him. Burley, like the Pharisees who rejected Jesus, remains closed to the holiness of the Temple of Art he has built to stroke his ego, while Blackie, like the prostitutes and tax collectors who flocked to the carpenter from Nazareth, perceives in Mary's singing a goodness, truth, and beauty he has never known.

It was *San Francisco*, and other movies like it, that helped teach me to look deeper, as Jesus did when he spoke to the Samaritan woman at the well (John 4). While the outside world saw only a pathetic outcast who had been married five times and was now living with a sixth man, Jesus saw a daughter of God yearning for love, acceptance, and intimacy. That is why, rather than condemn her, he offers her living water that she might quench her God-given thirst in a manner that is neither sinful nor self-destructive.

As surprising as it may seem to modern readers, MGM's big, splashy, expensive epic is, at its heart, a conversion story. But that conversion will be hard won. At one point in the picture, Mary has a conversation with Burley's mother (Jessie Ralph). Mrs. Burley, as it turns out, was a washer-woman before she married the man who ushered her into the Nob Hill aristocracy. That marriage pulled her out of poverty and gave her the chance to be a pillar in her community, but it almost didn't happen. Like Mary, she had once been in love with "a selfish, sinful, adorable scoundrel" like Blackie. But she turned him down in the end, for, as she confesses sadly, he was killing her soul.

Mary knows Mrs. Burley is correct, that if she marries Blackie, he will drag her down to his level. Tim warns her of this as well, a warning that takes on flesh when Tim tries to convince Mary to leave her job at the Paradise and Blackie punches him in the nose. No, Mary cannot give herself to this man and retain her faith, calling, and identity. And so Burley will get the girl, even after Mary has caught a glimpse of his dark side.

And then it happens. What happens? If you were reading carefully above, you will have noted that *San Francisco* takes place in 1906, the year of the great earthquake.

I grew up in the 1970s when theaters across America were overrun with disaster movies. From *Airport* to *The Poseidon Adventure, Earthquake* to *The Towering Inferno,* these visceral films promised viewers an all-star ensemble cast whose lives and loves all intertwine during a freak natural disaster. *San Francisco* arguably marks the premier embodiment of this questionable genre, but with two important differences. First, rather than give us a smorgasbord of cardboard characters in clichéd situations, *San Francisco* focuses in tightly on a small group of characters for whom we care deeply. Second, and this rises up out of the first, we become so engrossed in the relationships between those characters that, when the disaster comes, we have completely forgotten it was coming.

That forgetting happens to me every time I watch the movie: not just because I am living the loves and struggles of Blackie and Tim, Mary and Burley, but because the earthquake rises up *out* of the plot rather than being tacked on to it as a way of increasing box office revenues. Blackie, Burley, and the Barbary Coast are on a collision course with the apocalypse, and when it comes, all of their lives are changed utterly. The two opposing worlds of San Francisco and Nob Hill are equally affected by the earthquake, as fire and destruction rage across the coast. Both will be bombed to stop the spread of the fire; both will be incorporated into the new city that will be built out of the old.

The special effects used to convey the awesome power and terror of the earthquake are impressive even by today's standards. More than the burning set pieces themselves, it is the quick editing and the disorienting camera angles, the bursting pipes, crumbling statues, and wheels spinning out of control that capture the full destructive force of the tremor.

As we watch with bated breath, Blackie makes his way through a lurid nightmare city that recalls the burning ruins of Troy that Virgil depicts so unforgettably in Book II of the *Aeneid*.

As Blackie watches people searching desperately for their family members, he realizes how deeply and truly he loves Mary. The first time he sees a man praying, he yells at him to "stop that drivel," but as the chaos and the pressing human need overwhelm him, he begins to sense his own need for God. He, the King of the Barbary Coast, is as helpless as the people around him. As he watches one of his friends die, he hears him confess that "it took an earthquake to get me." He also meets Mrs. Burley, who weeps but who has resigned herself to the loss of her son and her home, both of which have fallen victim to the quake.

Just when he is about to give up all hope of finding Mary, Blackie looks up to discover her singing the hymn "Nearer My God to Thee" (the same hymn that the orchestra of the Titanic would play as the ship sank into the ocean). Humbled and grateful, he tells Tim that he wants to thank God but does not know how. Tim tells him to just say what's in his heart. Blackie kneels and speaks, even though the words feel strange and uncomfortable on his lips: "thank you God, thank you; I really mean it." As he does so, Mary turns and sees him. The sight fills her with joy, and the two are reunited in a deep and lasting bond that can now weather any storm.

As Blackie, Mary, and Tim march forward with the other survivors, they sing "Glory, Glory Hallelujah," an apocalyptic song from the Civil War that looks ahead to the return of the Messiah. Suddenly, in the midst of their song, the news reaches them that the fire has been put out. San Francisco will not suffer the fate of Sodom and Gomorra; she will rise again, will be born anew out of the ashes like the mythical phoenix.

Every time I watch that closing scene, each time with moist eyes and an exultant heart, I am reminded that Jesus did not preach the good news until John the Baptist came and preached the bad news. No one, after all, goes looking for a savior unless he thinks he needs to be saved from something. Most of us, I've come to realize over the years, are like Blackie. We think that we have it all figured out, that we are self-reliant and don't need anyone's charity. Religion is ok in its place, but it really is for the suckers, the losers who can't take care of themselves.

And then the personal earthquake hits, and we realize that all that self-reliance stuff is an illusion. The road to Easter Sunday runs straight through Good Friday; to rise again, one must first die to the old life of sin and shame, fear and regret. Only when I watched the film a second time did I notice the cross stitch in Father Tim's room, the one that reads "I am the Resurrection and the Life," the very words Jesus spoke before he raised Lazarus from the dead (John 11).

The earthquake robs Blackie of his beloved Paradise, but it wins him Mary, she whom the Church Fathers often referred to as the second Eve. Paradise lost and regained; a man and a city reborn out of the ashes of their own despair. Not a bad message for a "secular" Hollywood blockbuster! Truly the kind of movie they don't make any more.

Fun Facts for the Fans

- *San Francisco* earned Oscar nominations for picture, director, story, and Tracy.
- The same team that made *King Kong* in 1933 produced a disaster film in 1935, *The Last Days of Pompeii,* that ends with a spectacular eruption of Mt. Vesuvius.
- Gable did not want to make *San Francisco* because he did not want to be sung at by Jeanette MacDonald; luckily, MGM forced him to do it, as they also forced him to do two other pictures, *Mutiny on the Bounty* and *Gone with the Wind*!
- Gable had an out-of-wedlock daughter with Loretta Young, whose highly virtuous on-screen image caused the child's paternity to be kept secret for decades.
- In *San Francisco,* we not only see the struggle between Nob Hill and Blackie's Paradise, but between MGM's mogul Louis B. Mayer, who had a love for opera and upper middle class family values, and his boy

wonder chief of production Irving Thalberg, who liked the grittier world of Gable's dangerous man.

- Though not directly overseen by Thalberg, *San Francisco* is solidly in the line of the kind of Prestige Picture he liked and was responsible for producing at MGM.
- As the producer, rather than the director, was king at MGM, the film's highly capable and prolific director is far less known than other Golden Age directors.
- MacDonald's screen image was sexier at Paramount; MGM/Mayer toned it down.

Other Films to Watch

Here are some other MGM/Thalberg Prestige Pictures: the silent *Ben-Hur, The Big Parade* (epic silent film about World War I), *Mutiny on the Bounty* (with Gable as Mr. Christian and Charles Laughton as Captain Bly; won best picture), *The Good Earth* (with Paul Muni and Luise Rainer as Chinese peasants), *Camille* (with Greta Garbo as a courtesan with a heart of gold), *Romeo and Juliet* (well acted, but with too-old stars), *The Barretts of Wimpole Street* (tells true love story of Robert Browning and Elizabeth Barrett), *Dinner at Eight* and *Grand Hotel* (both featuring all-star casts; second won best picture).

In addition to winning back-to-back Oscars for Manuel the fisherman in *Captains Courageous* and Father Flanagan in *Boy's Town,* Tracy portrayed a man falsely accused of murder in *Fury,* a newspaperman in *Libeled Lady,* an explorer in *Northwest Passage,* and the title roles in *Edison the Man* and *Father of the Bride.* Later roles include *Bad Day at Black Rock, The Last Hurrah, Inherit the Wind,* and *Judgment at Nuremberg.*

CLAUDETTE
COLBERT
and
JOEL
McCREA

THE
Palm
Beach
Story

Written and
Directed by
PRESTON
STURGES

with
MARY ASTOR RUDY VALLEE

a
Paramount
Picture

THE PALM BEACH STORY

(PARAMOUNT; 1942; PRESTON STURGES)

Thus far, we have looked at one film from Warner Brothers (WB) and two from MGM; in the chapters to come, we will consider many more. On the one hand, I have always been drawn to the glamor, opulence, and star power of MGM; on the other, I have always loved to root for those tough, dispossessed, proletarian WB underdogs. But there was a third major studio that made films that fit neither category, but which played a decisive role in the formation of my character. I speak of Paramount, home of a kind of sexy, effervescent, European wit and charm that has always spoken to a part of my soul.

While MGM worshipped the rich and WB hated them, Paramount took the stance that I have always preferred: she laughed at them, but without ever getting bitter. MGM gravitated to the right and WB to the left, but Paramount remained politically neutral. When you watch Paramount's signature films of the 1930s and 40s, you'd never know there was a Depression or a war going on. Those blessed films floated above everything. They were all about money; yet, money never really mattered in the end. It wasn't star power or gutsy determination that made you a Paramount hero; it was the ability to laugh at your own cockeyed craziness, to let down your hair and enjoy life.

If truth be told, Paramount films are all about sex, not the sublimated, Freudian kind on display at MGM or the primal, Darwinian kind favored by WB, but the Cole Porter kind—where the phrase "making love" has more to do with wooing than with intercourse. The real game is in the seduction and the intimacy, in the making oneself vulnerable to the other sex. If I wanted love among the high and mighty, I turned to MGM; if I wanted a secret rendezvous with desperate lovers stealing kisses in the dark, I turned to WB. But if I wanted to take a trip to the moon on gossamer wings, then it was Paramount that delivered the goods.

During America's first year in the war, while WB's Rick was learning to sacrifice love for duty, Preston Sturges, the maddest of all the madcaps at Paramount, offered his beleaguered countrymen an escape from all that. True, his cinematic world would be as arbitrary and unpredictable as that of *Casablanca*, but it would be a zany, freewheeling kind of unpredictability where fate and luck favor those who put their trust in love, joy, and sex. The hero and heroine will not be orphans in the storm but children of fortune; they will make mistake after mistake but there will, somehow, be no consequences.

The Palm Beach Story offers us a Cinderella story upside down. It begins where most romantic comedies end, with our stars getting married and a title card announcing that they lived happily ever after. But then those fairy-tale words fade out to be replaced by three more: "or did they?" Five years fly by, and we discover that the marriage of Tom Jeffers (Joel McCrea) and Gerry Jeffers (Claudette Colbert) is most definitely on the rocks. As Tom confesses to Gerry—yes, they are named after MGM's animated cat and mouse—"we don't love each anymore; we're just habits."

Although the film begins with Gerry running away, the real one at fault in this loveable farce is Tom. He could be a very successful inventor and businessman, but his pride prevents him from allowing his wife to help him fulfill his dreams. With her sexy, yet somehow innocent charm, she can convince any rich man to back her husband's risky schemes, but, again, he won't let her do so. She tries to explain to him that she can help him without compromising herself or their vows in any way: "You have no idea what a long-legged gal can do without doing anything." But he will have none of it.

Tom is not only too stubborn; he is too idealistic. His wife is far more practical and level-headed than he is. She knows far better than her husband how to have fun, but she also knows far better than he how to survive. When Tom keeps carrying on, Gerry doesn't tell him he is being tyrannical or foolish; she simply says: "You're such a child."

One year earlier, Sturges had made a film with Joel McCrea (*Sullivan's Travels*) in which he played an idealistic director of comedies who has grown tired of making sexy, fluffy Paramount pictures and wants to make a socially-conscious film about the Depression that he plans to call "O Brother, Where Art Thou?" (Yes, that is the source of the peculiar title of the Coen brothers hilarious cinematic reworking of the *Odyssey*.)

With impassioned voice, Sullivan tries to explain to the studio executive his vision for the film: "I want this picture to be a commentary on modern conditions. Stark realism. The problems that confront the average man." Without missing a beat, the exec adds in a po-faced monotone: "But with a little sex." That is not only one of the best bits of repartee in cinema history; it sums up perfectly the ethos of Paramount—an ethos that is not as hedonistic and "un-Christian" as it may at first appear.

Watch *Sullivan's Travels* and you'll discover that the shrewd exec turns out to be more right than the idealistic director. Through a series of mishaps that are as hilarious as they are terrifying, Sullivan's attempts to make "O Brother, Where Art Thou?" land him in a prison chain gang. In the midst of his despair and near total loss of hope, Sullivan and his gang are led to a church, not for a prayer meeting but to allow them to watch a Disney short on a makeshift screen. As the cartoon proceeds, the hard, joyless faces of the convicts suddenly soften, and they all burst into laughter. Sullivan looks around in revelatory wonder and then joins them in their raucous chorus.

This being a Sturges films, Sullivan is eventually released and returns to the studio. The studio bosses all expect that Sullivan, having now experienced sorrow, pain, and injustice, will push even harder to make his WB-type film. But they are wrong. The chastened Sullivan explains to them that he is too happy now to make that film, and that, in any case, he hasn't suffered enough to make it. No, his next picture will be a comedy.

As the bosses stare at him with shocked expressions, Sullivan speaks the closing lines of the film: "There's a lot to be said for making people laugh. Did you know that's all some people have? It isn't much, but it's better than nothing in this cockeyed caravan." As he speaks those glorious words, the camera dissolves, and we are back in the church watching the convicts laughing in abandoned, heartfelt glee.

Neither *Sullivan's Travels* nor *The Palm Beach Story* is a Christian film in the strict sense of the word, but from them, and from the other Sturges films, I have learned a great biblical lesson about the need for balance in life. According to the wisest man who ever lived, there is a time for everything under the sun (Ecclesiastes 3)—and that includes movies from MGM, WB, and, yes, Paramount.

But the lesson goes deeper than that. It's not just that we need laughter as much as tears, dancing as much as mourning. Laughter and dancing teach us to let go, to be vulnerable and trusting and grateful in a way that tears and mourning do not. Tom Jeffers just doesn't realize what he has in Gerry. Rather than accept the grace of her beauty, her charm, and her fervent, addictive love of life, he wants to be a rugged WB individualist living by an inflated MGM sense of propriety that is more stiff-necked than truly pious. He's going to have to be taken down a notch or two.

While Tom thrashes around desperately trying to preserve his self-respect and his self-control, Gerry throws dignity to the wind and trusts herself to fortune. When she sneaks back into their apartment to get something, she learns that it has been put up for sale and is forced to hide out in the shower. There, she is discovered by the very old, very rich, very deaf Weenie King (Robert Dudley) who plans to buy out the lease. He is instantly charmed by the loveable Gerry and decides to help her in her plight. As it turns out, this upside down Cinderella story will be aided along, not by a fairy godmother, but by a fairy godfather.

When Tom learns that Gerry was able to pay off their rent with the money given her by the Weenie King, he says, accusingly, "I suppose sex had nothing to do with it." Gerry responds, "Of course it did!"—not because she slept with the old man, but because beauty *does* have power and because everything in the world of Paramount is a form of seduction.

Tom's stubbornness convinces Gerry she must leave. He says she won't get far without money, but she charms everyone she meets, including the Ale & Quail club, who take her on as their mascot, but whose train car is derailed by the conductor when they get drunk and, in a scene of controlled/out-of-control lunacy, shoot it full of holes.

In the end, Gerry makes her way down to Palm Beach, where she meets and wins the heart of the immensely rich J. D. Hackensacker III (a wonderful caricature of John D. Rockefeller, played by the crooner Rudy Vallee). By uniting herself with the sweet but feckless Hackensacker, Gerry hopes to get him to finance one of Tom's grand business schemes. All is working smoothly until Tom, financed himself by the Weenie King, shows up and Gerry has to make believe he is her brother.

In the film's funniest and most characteristic scene, Hackensacker tells Gerry to open up all the windows in her room so that he can serenade her with a song ("Goodnight Sweetheart"). As he does so, his lilting voice floating romantically in the evening breeze, Tom enters Gerry's room. Gerry tries to resist her overwhelming attraction to Tom, but Hackensacker's self-defeating song ironically breaks down her defenses. In a vain attempt to silence the music, she closes all of her windows one by one, but it floods in nevertheless, insisting that she forget all about her practical plans and give in to her heart.

As the song reaches a crescendo, and Gerry, no longer able to fight her passion, is about to yield to Tom's kiss, she whispers sadly: "I hope you realize this is costing us millions." Now it's Gerry's turn to learn to be vulnerable, to trust to love even if it means putting all her best laid schemes in jeopardy.

In the end, husband and wife are reunited ... and they get the money, too! This is Paramount after all. Sturges even finds a way to let Hackensacker get the desires of his heart—a way that is so absolutely and delightfully absurd that I won't spoil it for you. Watch the movie yourself and find out how freeing a thing it can be to cast off your pride and self-sufficiency and give yourself over to the graceful and gracious tide of love.

I promise you it'll do you good.

Fun Facts for the Fans

- Preston Sturges grew up all over Europe with his eccentric mother who was a personal friend of the scandalous dancer Isabella Duncan.
- As a young man, Sturges invented a kiss-proof lipstick; he also had the fortune, or misfortune, to marry (and divorce) two heiresses, with one of whom he eloped.
- Unlike MGM and WB, who kept their writing and directing departments separate, Paramount encouraged creative writer-directors like Sturges and Billy Wilder.
- In the film, Hackensacker has a zany sister played by Mary Astor; in contrast, MGM cast Astor as the perfect bourgeois mother in *Meet Me in St. Louis,* while WB cast her as a cold-hearted, manipulative femme fatale in *The Maltese Falcon.*
- Sturges's subtle interweaving of verbal comedy and pratfalls owes a great deal to the Marx Brothers; that same unique blend appears in the *Road* pictures of Bob Hope and Bing Crosby, who spent the 1940s traveling, with Dorothy Lamour in tow, on the Road to Singapore Zanzibar, Morocco, Utopia, and Rio.
- In one scene, the scrawny Hackensacker laments: "That's one of the tragedies of this life, that the men most in need of a beating up are always enormous."
- In another, a policeman gives Tom and Gerry this wise marital advice: "Why don't you two learn to get along together; I had to."
- When the American Film Institute released its list of the 100 best films, Steven Spielberg asked that one of his films be taken off to make room for a Sturges film.

Other Films to Watch

Writer-director Sturges made a successful string of classic comedies at Paramount; all of them are parodies of one sort or another that are populated by colorful character actors and that tend to spiral out of control. Here they are in chronological order: *The Great McGinty* (about crooked politicians); *Christmas in July* (a send up of the American dream); *Sullivan's Travels; The Lady Eve* (card shark Barbara Stanwyck swindles and then falls for a naive Henry Fonda); *The Miracle of Morgan's Creek* (after Betty Hutton gets pregnant by a soldier whose name she can't remember, Eddie Bracken comes to the rescue; this one parodies every single American institution); *Hail the Conquering Hero* (army-reject Bracken is mistaken for a war hero).

The Marx Brothers (Groucho, Chico, Harpo, and Zeppo) made 5 films at Paramount of ascending brilliance and lunacy: *The Cocoanuts* (in a hotel), *Animal Crackers* (in high society), *Monkey Business* (stowaways on a ship), *Horse Feathers* (at a university), and *Duck Soup* (in a country at war that unintentionally parodies the rise of Hitler and the Nazis). The boys, minus Zeppo, later left for MGM where Irving Thalberg smacked them into shape and their madness slowly ebbed. Still, the MGM films are all worth watching (especially the first and the last): *A Night at the Opera, A Day at the Races, Room Service, At the Circus, Go West, The Big Store, A Night in Casablanca.*

After Sturges's talent dried up, the romantic-comedy torch passed down to another writer-turned-director, Billy Wilder, who began at Paramount and then went independent. His best in this genre are *The Major and the Minor, Foreign Affair, Sabrina, Love in the Afternoon, Some Like it Hot, The Apartment, Irma La Douce,* and *Avanti.*

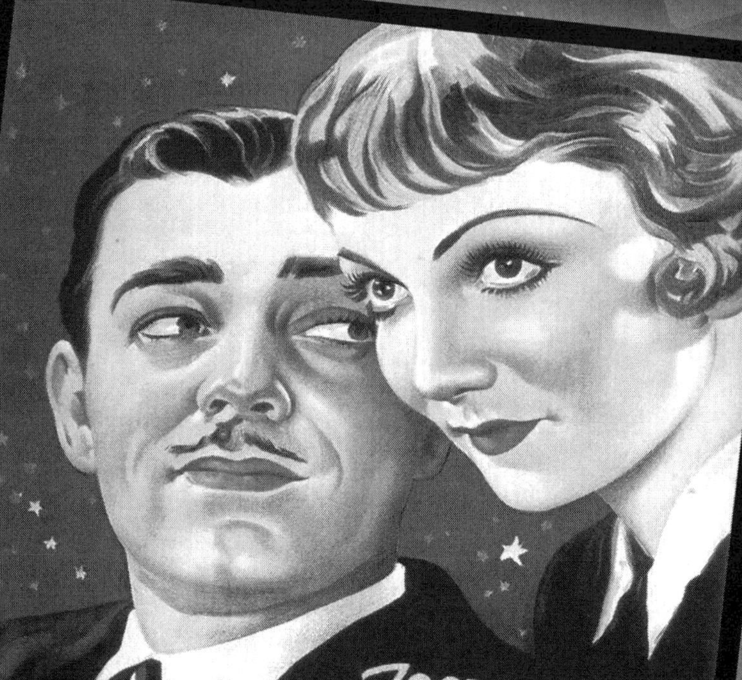
TOGETHER FOR
THE FIRST TIME!
CLARK
GABLE and CLAUDETTE
COLBERT
IN
"It Happened One Night"
with WALTER CONNOLLY · ROSCOE KARNS
From the Cosmopolitan Magazine story by SAMUEL HOPKINS ADAMS · Screen play by ROBERT RISKIN
a FRANK CAPRA PRODUCTION
A
COLUMBIA
PICTURE

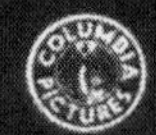
COLUMBIA
PICTURES

IT HAPPENED ONE NIGHT

(COLUMBIA; 1934; FRANK CAPRA)

In chapter three, we met Clark Gable in MGM's *San Francisco*; in chapter four, we met Claudette Colbert in Paramount's *The Palm Beach Story*. Now it's time to bring them together into a most unlikely movie. Filmed in Poverty Row at the stubbornly low-budget Columbia, Frank Capra's *It Happened One Night* won Oscars for Gable and Colbert (not to mention the script, the director, and the film itself), cementing their careers for good and drawing out their light, humorous side. It's one of those unlikely Hollywood success stories that no one could have predicted.

The story is simple. Gable is Peter Warne, a WB-style down-and-out newspaper reporter looking for a hot story that will free him from debt and from his editor. Colbert is Ellie Andrews, a Paramount-style spoiled heiress who escapes from her father's yacht so that she can marry her good-for-nothing rich playboy suitor, King Westley (Jameson Thomas). The two meet up at a bus station and form an alliance: Peter will help Ellie get across the country, on a very tight budget, to Westley in exchange for the exclusive story. Needless to say, the two start out despising each other, but end up, after many mishaps, falling in love.

It Happened One Night kicked off a genre that has played a major role in my emotional and spiritual development, particularly in my understanding of the perennial battle of the sexes. Living as we now do in an age of gender confusion where the very notion of masculinity and femininity is under attack, it might be thought that the battle of the sexes is a social-political-economic term. It is not. It refers not to the fight for jobs or political power or educational opportunities, but to the radically different ways that men and woman communicate, prioritize, perceive, and interact with themselves, with the other sex, and with the world.

Starting with *It Happened One Night* in 1934 and stretching on until 1942, when the seriousness of World War II turned the focus away from lighthearted romance, Hollywood produced a long string of what came to be known as screwball comedies. In these blessed films, the rules and dynamics of seduction and courtship were laid out in such a way as to promote real understanding between the sexes. They did so by allowing men and women, first to laugh at the opposite sex, then to laugh at themselves, and finally to learn from each other in a complementary way.

Modern films on the whole offer little insight into the complementary nature of masculinity and femininity. While the true masculine is caricatured or atrophied, the unique views, perceptions, needs, and contributions of the feminine are reduced to social constructs or simply disappear. Films that focus on graphic sex and violence either turn women into victims or, in an increasing modern fantasy, turn them into greater sexual predators and killers than the men.

Things were quite different in the screwball comedies of the 1930s. Instead of a brutally masculine world where women are either irrelevant or transformed into men with breasts, *It Happened One Night* invited me into a relational world where both hero and heroine must learn to get in touch with themselves and their feelings. Since the feminine tends to be more open to these virtues, it is more often than not the women who drive these films. Indeed, they often become the pursuer, not because they are trying to co-opt the male initiative, but because they are more willing to explore their inner desires.

Sexism has always told men that they cannot be vulnerable; modern feminism, alas, has extended that artificial constraint to women. Screwball comedies force men and women alike to be vulnerable, a process that generally calls for one or both of them to be struck on the head and have their world turned upside down. Only after a hilarious string of unpredictable screwball situations force the hero and the heroine to drop their guard are they able to realize that they are, in fact, fitted for one another, that they need, to quote the biblical definition of marriage, to become one flesh.

Screwball comedies are too wise and knowing about the nature of masculinity and femininity to fool themselves into believing the modern, Marxist-inspired delusion that men and women are essentially the same. As any impartial parent who has raised a boy and a girl can tell you, men and women are different from birth, and, as the French say, vive la difference. The goal of marriage is not sameness but a rich complementarity that transcends mere social or business relationships to touch on something deeper and more mystical. It is that moment when the boy and the girl realize that they are not independent of each other, that they need the other to help shape and soften them.

The goal of screwball comedy is to break down all the barriers, not only those between the sexes, but those between the classes as well. The genre was born out of the Great Depression, when the whole country, from rich to poor, was thrown into a crisis of identity. Nothing seemed sure anymore; all the foundations had been shaken. Movies like *It Happened one Night* shook things up even more, but only so that Humpty Dumpty could be put back together again in a stronger, more integrated, more human way.

Screwball comedies are to the history of film what Carnival—that is, Mardis Gras or Fat Tuesday—is to the sacred calendar. Carnival, which means "farewell to flesh," serves the purpose of preparing the soul for the rigors of Lent through a last hurrah of divine revelry. It is the madness that restores sanity, the madcap masking that leads to the tearing down of all masks and the revelation of the true person within.

I can always tell when two of my college students are falling in love, for they both start acting like idiots. I'm not just being facetious here. When love hits us so hard that it shatters all of our defenses, it makes us, temporarily at least, unafraid to drop the façade and be ourselves. For a season, we do not care if we are conforming to societal images and conventions. In the end, of course, we must, and should, return to the basic rules of the community, but with a renewed sense of inner-joy, self-worth and self-identity. (The cross-dressing at Carnival is not meant to promote a transgender life style, but to provide a kind of safety valve to let off societal steam and thereby restore and strengthen a more positive and integrated masculinity and femininity.)

In keeping with the screwball comedies that would follow, *It Happened One Night* begins with Peter and Ellie throwing off their old roles and setting out on their own. In a sense, both assert their freedom from dad, for the editor from whom Peter breaks is, like Ellie's rich patriarch, a seemingly stern and inflexible father figure. As in *The Palm Beach Story*, both hero and heroine must have their pride and dignity stripped away from them by a series of comic mishaps.

At first, Ellie is the helpless one, for she has no experience of surviving in a tough world without a wad of cash in her purse. Again and again, Peter calls her to account for her snobbish, pampered life. To be honest, Ellie, though likeable, is a spoiled brat who needs to be taken down a few pegs, and the audience is on Peter's side when he does it. At one point, Peter makes fun of Ellie for thinking she knows the proper way to give or receive a piggyback ride—as if rich people have any conception of how to do such humble things! To punctuate his point, Peter, while carrying Ellie on his back across a river, asks her to hold her suitcase for a moment … and then promptly smacks her on the butt. Everyone in the audience wants to do the same.

But Peter, for all his self-confidence and devil-may-care charm is not as much in control as he would like Ellie, or the audience, to think. Stranded on the side of the road without money or transportation, Peter brags to Ellie that he is an expert on hitchhiking and will hail them a car in no time at all. Indeed, he begins his cocky boast by listing for her three different techniques for thumbing a ride. Needless to say, all three of his techniques turn out to be grand failures as one car after another speeds by him.

Finally, Ellie, who has had all she can stand of the smart-alecky, know-it-all Peter, stands up and tells him, simply and calmly, that she will get them a ride, and she won't use her thumb to do it. As Peter, and the audience, look on with growing astonishment, she walks to the side of the road and, when she sees a car approaching, hikes up her skirt to reveal her shapely leg. The car screeches to a halt, and, in the next scene, we see an elated Ellie sitting in the back seat of a jalopy next to a dejected Peter.

As Ellie learns that she can't buy everything she wants or get it by throwing a tantrum, so Peter learns that his hard-boiled view of the world is frequently soft boiled. Several times in the film, as he regales Ellie with his various systems for hitching or piggybacking, dunking donuts or undressing, Peter proclaims with brash overconfidence that he should write a book on the subject. In fact, as it turns out, Peter has just as much to learn about himself and the world around him as Ellie. They need each other, as we all need others who can show us our shortcomings and share with us their strengths.

The journey that Peter and Ellie go on together begins at a bus stop, a purposely neutral starting place that puts them on something of a level playing field. From this point, they will need to remake themselves and learn to work together in a distinctly American classless society where they can't hide behind the self-defining masks of rich and poor. Amidst the grit and poverty of the Depression landscape through which the bus moves, the film interjects a brief pastoral interlude in which our would-be lovers spend the night in a haystack. It's a lovely scene and even makes use of soft-focus photography to convince us of Ellie's true inner beauty, but the film won't let us stay there. They will need to find a place for themselves in the real world of Depression America.

Since this is a comedy, reconciliation is found in great part because the two distant patriarchs of the film turn out to be kind at heart. Ellie's father, far from being a snobbish member of the idle rich, is a hard worker who recognizes Peter's integrity and prefers it to the lazy, gigolo nature of King Westley. Peter's editor, meanwhile, proves to have a sentimental streak and changes his tune when he perceives that his rebellious reporter is desperately in love with Ellie. Change is possible, the film assures us, both on the personal and the societal level, but it takes the magic of love to bring down the walls.

In the film, that wall-tumbling is even made visual in two of the most fondly remembered scenes from the Golden Age of Hollywood.

Because they are on a tight budget, Peter and Ellie have to masquerade as a married couple and share a cabin. To ensure that she will feel safe and he won't be tempted, Peter strings a rope across the center of the room and hangs a blanket over it. He then dubs the blanket the Walls of Jericho and swears that he and Ellie will remain on opposite sides. At that point in the film, it seems that that wall will be permanent, not only for our lovers but for America.

That is, until the final scene, when Peter and Ellie, now married, stop at the same hotel and string up the Walls of Jericho as before. This time, however, we hear a trumpet sound and watch the blanket come a'tumblin' down. This being a 1934 film, we don't see the lovers cross over into a single bed, but we don't have to. The walls have come down, and the lovers can make their way into their new Promised Land.

So what did *It Happened One Night* teach me? Simply this: that for the sake of personal and societal reconciliation, men and women shall relinquish their half lives, phony masks, and artificial barriers and cleave unto one another and become one flesh.

Fun Facts for the Fans

- *It Happened One Night* was the first film to win the big five Oscars (picture, director, actor, actress, script). Only two others have done so since: *One Flew Over the Cuckoo's Nest* (1975) and *The Silence of the Lambs* (1991).
- Though Frank Capra made a number of period films, after *It Happened One Night*, all of his movies were given contemporary American settings.
- Capra made this film quickly, pinning his Oscar hopes on *Lady for a Day*, which was nominated for best picture, director, actress, and script, but did not win any.
- MGM forced Gable to make the film as a way of punishing him for asking for a higher salary; ironically, his success in the film forced MGM to increase his pay.

- This is the only film where Gable's humorous side was allowed fully to emerge; an image of him chewing on a carrot was the inspiration for Bugs Bunny!
- When Gable begins to undress before Colbert in the Walls of Jericho scene, audiences were shocked to discover he was not wearing an undershirt; the revelation caused undershirt sales to plummet across the country.
- Before the film, Colbert played sexy seductresses in Cecil B. DeMille's *Cleopatra* and *Sign of the Cross*; after it, she played mostly lighthearted romantic leads.
- The man who plays the driver who picks up the hitchhiking Peter and Ellie is Alan Hale; he is the father of, and resembles strongly, Alan Hale Jr., most famous for playing the skipper on *Gilligan's Island*.
- One of the best screwball comedies, *Bringing up Baby*, sums up well the ethos of the genre: "The love impulse in man frequently reveals itself in terms of conflict."

Other Films to Watch

Here is a list of must-see screwball comedies: *20th Century* (monomaniacal Broadway producer John Barrymore battles it out with star actress Carole Lombard), *Libeled Lady* (hysterical showdown between reporters and spoiled heiress), *My Man Godfrey* (rich William Powell masquerades as butler to zany heiress Lombard), *Easy Living* (secretary Jean Arthur thrown into world of idle rich), *Nothing Sacred* (skewering of press as reporter Fredric March tries to capitalize on supposedly dying Lombard), *Bringing Up Baby* (uninhibited Katharine Hepburn sets her eye on staid scientist Cary Grant and wins him over by sheer persistence), *His Girl Friday* (editor Grant battles it out with his top female reporter/ex-wife), and Sturges's *The Palm Beach Story* and *The Lady Eve*.

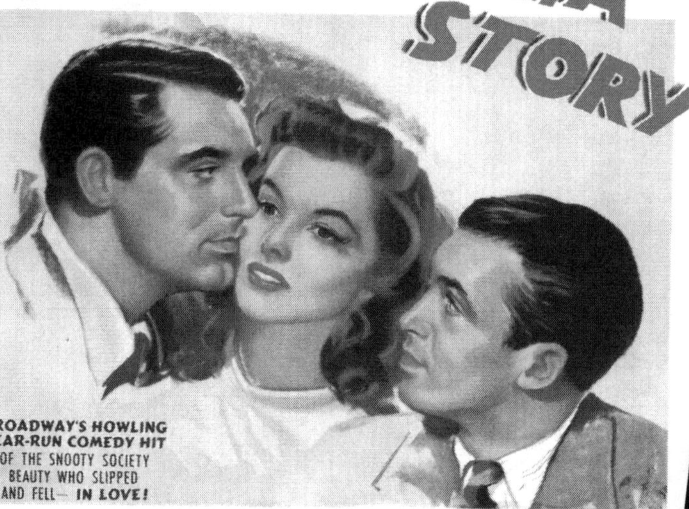
Cary GRANT
Katharine HEPBURN
James STEWART
The PHILADELPHIA STORY
BROADWAY'S HOWLING YEAR-RUN COMEDY HIT OF THE SNOOTY SOCIETY BEAUTY WHO SLIPPED AND FELL— IN LOVE!
with Ruth HUSSEY
John HOWARD Roland YOUNG
John HALLIDAY Mary NASH
Virginia WEIDLER
A Metro-Goldwyn-Mayer PICTURE
Directed by GEORGE CUKOR · Produced by JOSEPH L. MANKIEWICZ

THE PHILADELPHIA STORY

(MGM; 1940; GEORGE CUKOR)

In the previous chapter, I shared my love of screwball comedies and what they taught me about the battle of the sexes. But there was another set of comedies made between 1934 and 1942 that, though similar in many ways to the screwballs, were less physical than verbal, less zany than witty. If nearly every screwball comedy can be traced back, in one way or another, to *The Taming of the Shrew* and/or *A Midsummer's Night Dream*, then nearly every romantic comedy finds its source in *Pride and Prejudice*.

The former, as in the Shakespeare plays, brings about the happy ending by throwing the lovers into a kind of topsy-turvy turmoil that knocks out all their previous supports and forces them to take on successive roles until they discover their true ones. The latter, as in the Austen novel, takes a sharper, more sophisticated look at how men and women interact and how a breakdown in communication and a failure to express one's true needs and desires can pull lovers apart or make them seek after the wrong person. Like Elizabeth Bennet and Mr. Darcy, the protagonists in a romantic comedy must have their eyes opened to their own capacity for self-protective pride and prejudice.

The Philadelphia Story catapults us immediately into a world where men and women seem incapable of getting along. C. K. Dexter Haven, played to perfection by Cary Grant, storms out of a wealthy home followed by Tracy Samantha Lord, played to equal perfection by Katharine Hepburn. Tracy is about to throw Dexter's golf clubs at him, but instead removes one club and breaks it in half over her knee—a none-to-subtle form of figurative castration. In response, Dexter covers Tracy's face with his hand and pushes her down to the ground. This is not a happy couple. They will clearly need to find a more effective way of communicating with each other!

Or will they? A title card pushes us forward two years, where we learn that rich, spoiled heiress Tracy is about to remarry—not to another suave playboy like Dexter but to a stuffy, rags-to-riches, man-of-the-people industrialist named George Kittredge (John Howard). With the help of her mother and her precocious young sister Dinah (Virginia Weidler), Tracy prepares for a home wedding, but refuses to invite her father because of a compromising, though ultimately innocent flirtation he has had with a singer. Mom wants to forgive Dad and invite him home, but Tracy won't let her do it. As the mother explains to us, "Tracy sets exceptionally high standards for herself, and other people aren't apt to live up to them."

Unbeknownst to the Lord family, the editor of *Spy Magazine* (a cross between *People* and *The Enquirer*) has a scoop on the flirtation, but Dexter, who still loves Tracy and her family, learns of it and cuts a deal with the editor. In return for the flirtation story being suppressed, Dexter agrees to smuggle reporter Macauley (Mike) Connor (James Stewart) and photographer Elizabeth Imbrie (Ruth Hussey) into the house as friends of a relative so that they can get an insider exclusive on the wedding. Tracy hates such invasions of her privacy, but she agrees, setting in motion a sparkling, unforgettable comedy featuring some of the best acting and wittiest dialogue ever put on screen.

Every time I watch the film, I find myself laughing from beginning to end, but I also find myself learning lessons about the sexes, particularly the female sex, that are no longer taught in school. At the core of the film, and at the core of what it has taught me again and again, is a play-within-the-play that I like to call "The Education of Tracy Samantha Lord." At some point in the film, all the characters face off in pairs or triplets or even quartets, and all the exchanges are worth meditating on and chewing over. But it is Tracy's education in what it means to be a full woman and a full human being that has always animated the film for me and caused it to play a key role in my mental, emotional, and even spiritual development.

Growing up in suburbia in a traditional home, I took for granted that men were by nature worse sinners than women. The reason for this was not only the enshrining of motherhood in the American soul or a sense of chivalry vis-à-vis the ladies, but because men's sins are so much more blunt and obvious than those of women. Men's sins, marked as they are by physical or verbal violence, stubborn bluster, cowardly dishonesty, or sheer laziness, are easy to identify and even easier to criticize.

But women are just as fallen as we are. We may flatter them by calling them angels, but they are not so. Just like Adam, Eve was made in God's image but chose the way of disobedience. That is why women possess the same potential for self-sacrifice and selfishness, illumination and self-deception, nobility and depravity as their male counterparts. But their sins, on the whole, tend to be more subtle and easier to cloak. Indeed, their sins often help them to win public praise and social respectability.

Another thing I used to think in my innocence was that hypocrisy and legalism were predominately male sins. I thought that because the chief hypocrites and legalists I knew about were the Pharisees of the gospels, and they were all men. But after some careful people-watching and a few viewings of *The Philadelphia Story*, I came to realize that, just as many men have helped make the sphere of business and warfare ugly through their pride and competition, so many women have helped to make the domestic sphere ugly through their self-righteousness and judgmentalism.

Much is made of how Victorian society never allowed a fallen woman a second chance. That is partly true, but it was more often the social matriarchs than the political patriarchs who prevented the Magdalens of their day from reentering society. A Victorian father *might* allow his son to marry a girl with a checkered past; the mother never!

Please do not read what I have written thus far as an attempt to put down women. On the contrary, until we, men and women alike, come to acknowledge the reality of female sin, we will either hold women up to impossible standards of virtue or we will enable self-destructive hypocrisy by praising them when they are being the most smug, conceited, and critical—by encouraging them, that is, to be as hard and inflexible on the inside as a Barbie doll is on the outside.

Tracy must be put through her education for the very reason that her own mother gives at the start of the film and that I already quoted above: "Tracy sets exceptionally high standards for herself, and other people aren't apt to live up to them." As Dexter warns Tracy in the key line of the film: "you'll never be a first-class human being or a first-class woman until you've learned to have some regard for human frailty."

The trouble with Tracy is not that she is cruel or greedy or licentious or even vain. Her problem is that she does not know how to forgive because she has no empathy or patience with imperfection. Once Dexter realized he was married to a goddess rather than a mortal, a statue rather than a flesh-and-blood woman, he took to drinking. Tracy could have helped him through his addiction, but she did not: not because she thought his drink was sinful in the moral sense, but because she found it dirty and degrading and socially embarrassing. It was a sign of weakness, and she had no tolerance for weakness—either in others or in herself. Rather than support and edify her struggling husband, she looked upon him with what Dexter calls "the withering glance of the goddess."

If only Tracy's foot would slip once in a while, Dexter muses, she might gain the sympathetic warmth she lacks. But she remains stubbornly on her pedestal, distant, aloof, and imperious. At one point Dexter says to Tracy, in the presence of George, that she needs trouble to mature her. When George responds that that is the one thing she won't get from him, the attentive viewer realizes that George is the worst possible husband Tracy could have.

Indeed, shortly after Dexter angers Tracy by labeling her a high priestess in search of devotees, George tells her that, after they are married, he will put her on a pedestal and worship her as a goddess. George means what he says quite sincerely, but Tracy, still smarting from Dexter's words, is able to see, in a moment of illumination, that this is neither what she needs nor ultimately desires. "I don't want to be worshipped," she tells George in a voice that, for the first time in the film, registers self-doubt, "I want to be loved." George assures her that he will love her, but now Tracy and we in the audience know that Tracy's only hope of finding a humble, healthy self-image is if she leaves George and returns to Dexter.

Confused and distraught by her conversations with Dexter and George, Tracy, following the dramatic logic of the flawlessly woven screenplay, runs into her parents kissing on the balcony. Horrified that her mother should stoop so low as to forgive her father and, worse yet, display affection toward him, Tracy interrupts their moment of intimacy and calls her father to account for his hypocrisy. Unfazed, her father turns the tables back on Tracy and accuses her of being a prig and a perennial spinster. He even lays some of the blame for his philandering on Tracy! A man with an adoring daughter who loves him unconditionally does not need to fear growing old, but when he is met instead by disdain and disapproval, he seeks elsewhere for a kind and affirming word.

By this point in the film, Tracy has learned all that she can from the dialogue. Her education, however, will not be complete until she slips and joins the ranks of her fellow imperfect mortals. Her long-awaited faux pas comes in the form of a drunken flirtation and compromising night swim with Mike, who thinks that Tracy, far from being a cold statue, is full of warmth and light. Though the "affair" consists of nothing more than two kisses, George is furious and tells Tracy that he will only forgive her if she swears never to get drunk again. The old Tracy might have agreed, but her education has taught her the importance of losing control once in a while, of going a bit haywire. When she tells George that she cannot make such a promise, he abandons her and the wedding.

Mercifully, Dexter is there to catch her as she falls. Earlier in the film, we in the audience are taught a new word from the world of boating: yare. A boat that is yare, Tracy explains to George, is one that is "easy to handle, quick to the helm, fast, bright." It is what a good boat is like until it develops "dry rot." Near the end of the film, Tracy confesses to Dexter that, as a wife, she was not yare. But Dexter will have none of it. He will not allow Tracy to be overly critical of herself. Throwing caution to the wind, Dexter proposes to her again; he will take the risk of a re-marriage, whether or not she proves to be yare. He never wanted a "perfect" wife to begin with, just a human one.

As Tracy prepares to marry Dexter for the second time, her heart fills with a new-found capacity for love, and she tells her father that she loves him. In return, her father expresses his own love for her and tells her that she looks "like a queen, like a goddess." Tracy, however, has learned her lesson and responds that she feels "like a human, like a human being." No guarantees are offered that Tracy and Dexter will sail off into the sunset, but they have learned a lesson about the need for vulnerability and forgiveness.

Modern critics might balk that Tracy has been domesticated or beaten down, but they would be wrong. Tracy has not so much been tamed as humanized. She has been rendered capable of true intimacy and empathy. She has learned and assimilated the principles that Jesus teaches in the Sermon on the Mount: that we not display our acts of righteousness for all to see, that we not be too quick to judge lest we be judged ourselves, that before we try to take the speck of sawdust out of our brother's eye, we would do well to take the log out of our own (Matthew 6:1, 7:1–2, 7:3–5).

Fun Facts for the Fans

- James Stewart won the best actor Oscar, which is rarely given for a comic role. Many claim he was given a "hold over" Oscar to make up for the fact that he did not win the Oscar the previous year for his magisterial performance in *Mr. Smith Goes to Washington*. Though there is likely much truth to this, Stewart *is* excellent as Mike Connor, balancing bravado, insecurity, and a touch of self-loathing and pulling off his drunk scenes with warmth and vulnerability.
- The film was nominated for best picture, director, actress, and supporting actress (Ruth Hussey); it won for Donald Ogden Stewart's adapted screenplay.
- The film is based on a play by Philip Barry of the same name that was written expressly for Katharine Hepburn, who introduced the role of Tracy on stage.

- *The Philadelphia Story* was remade in 1956 as a Cole Porter musical titled *High Society,* with Grace Kelly (Tracy), Bing Crosby (Dexter), and Frank Sinatra (Mike). Louis Armstrong also appears in the film playing himself. The musical was written directly for the screen and then later reworked for Broadway.
- In the scene where Mike tries to seduce Tracy by telling her she is not a statue but filled with life, Cole Porter's lyrics capture perfectly Tracy's imperious nature. Sinatra sings "I've no proof / When people say you're more or less aloof," and then follows that with "I don't care / If you are called the fair Miss Frigidaire."
- When Tracy asks Mike why he didn't take advantage of her in her drunken state, he tells her she was "a little the worse, or better, for wine, and there are rules about that." That memorable bit of dialogue is repeated in *Postcards from the Edge,* a film based on Carrie (Princess Leia) Fisher's autobiographical novel.
- George Cukor was famous in Hollywood for being a woman's director; he coaxed excellent performances out of such iconic actresses as Katharine Hepburn, Greta Garbo, Norma Shearer, Ingrid Bergman, Judy Holliday, and Judy Garland.

Other Films to Watch

Here is a list of the best romantic comedies that were made between 1934 and 1942, the key years for the genre. These films were slightly less screwball but still offered viewers the instructive fun of watching a mismatched couple battle it out with their wits. But please be warned that the distinction between screwball comedy and romantic comedy is not always a clear one, and many of the movies on this list could easily be interchanged with the list at the end of the previous chapter: *The Awful Truth* (Cary Grant and Irene Dunne are on the road to divorce, but they keep getting thrown back together), *Holiday* (Katharine Hepburn teaches Cary Grant that a life of adventure and spontaneity is more important than a lucrative career), *Love Affair* (Irene Dunne and Charles Boyer seek to escape from their wealthy but meaningless lives; this poignant, sensitive film was brilliantly remade in 1957 as *An Affair to Remember* with Deborah Kerr and Cary Grant), *Midnight* (supreme Cinderella story of American Claudette Colbert choosing between millionaire and taxi driver), *Ninotchka* (Garbo as humorless Russian emissary who falls in love with Paris playboy Melvyn Douglas), *My Favorite Wife* (widower Grant is about to remarry when he discovers his wife Irene Dunne is still alive), *The Talk of the Town* (Jean Arthur must choose between stern judge and handsome revolutionary Cary Grant), and *Woman of the Year* (the first of many films to co-star Spencer Tracy and Katharine Hepburn as two modern career people trying to make their romance work).

Tracy and Hepburn later made four romantic comedies in the spirit of *Woman of the Year*: *Adam's Rib* (husband and wife lawyers), *Pat and Mike* (she's an athlete and he's a trainer), *Desk Set* (she's a librarian and he's a computer programmer), and *Guess Who's Coming to Dinner* (white liberal parents whose daughter marries Sidney Poitier).

If you want more of Cary Grant, here are some additional films not listed above or in the previous chapter that show his range as an actor: *Blonde Venus* (plays second fiddle to sexy Marlene Dietrich), *She Done Him Wrong* (plays second fiddle to sexy Mae West), *Topper* (as a ghost), Gunga Din (grand adventure in India), *Only Angels Have Wings* (tough-as-nails flyer), *Arsenic and Old Lace* (registering three double-takes per minute), *None but the Lonely Heart* (a moving melodrama), *Night and Day* (playing Cole Porter), *The Bachelor and the Bobby Soxer* (highly likeable romantic comedy with teenaged Shirley Temple), *The Bishop's Wife* (as an angel), *Mr. Blandings Builds His Dream House* (a favorite with homeowners), *I Was a Male War Bride* (in drag), *People Will Talk* (a very mature romantic comedy), *Indiscreet* (classy romantic comedy with Ingrid Bergman), *Charade* (excellent spy romance with Audrey Hepburn), and his four films with Hitchcock: *Suspicion, Notorious, To Catch a Thief,* and *North by Northwest.*

And don't miss these great performances by Katharine Hepburn: *Morning Glory* (her first of four Oscars), Little Women (as Jo), *Mary of Scotland* (as Mary, Queen of Scots), *State of the Union* (Capra film with Tracy), *The African Queen* (spinster who reforms drunken Humphrey Bogart), *Summertime* (romance in Italy), *The Lion in Winter* (as Eleanor of Aquitaine), Rooster Cogburn (with John Wayne), *On Golden Pond* (with Henry Fonda).

THE GREATEST OF ALL CAPRA HITS!

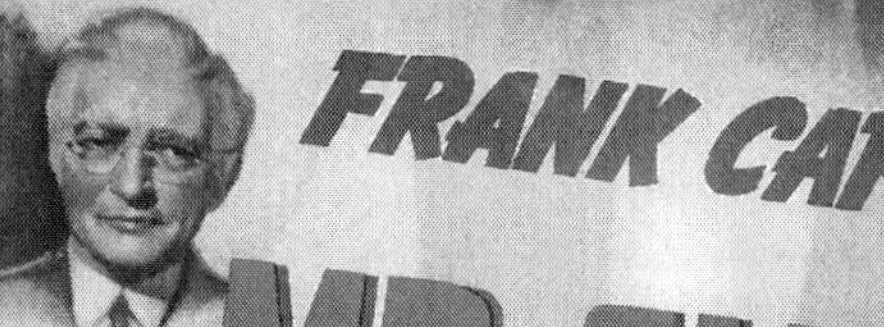

FRANK CAPRA'S

MR. SMITH GOES TO WASHINGTON

Co-Starring

JEAN ARTHUR ★ JAMES STEWART

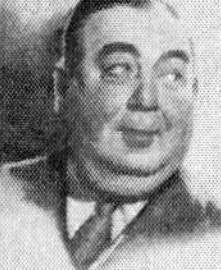

CLAUDE RAINS • EDWARD ARNOLD • GUY KIBBEE • THOMAS MITCHELL • BEULAH BONDI

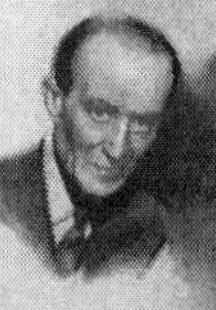

Directed by FRANK CAPRA

Screen play by SIDNEY BUCHMAN

A COLUMBIA PICTURE

COLUMBIA PICTURES

MR. SMITH GOES TO WASHINGTON

(COLUMBIA; 1939; FRANK CAPRA)

When the actor who played Mike Connor teamed up with the director who made *It Happened One Night*, three films were birthed that belong on any list of top 100 films. The first of the three, *You Can't Take It with You*, in which James Stewart plays a supporting role, I will leave for another book. The other two, in which he plays the lead and gives two of the finest performances ever captured on film, I will take up in this chapter and the one that follows. Both of these films have affected me on the deepest possible level, indelibly shaping my image of what it means to be an American and what it means to be a human being. Had Capra only made these two films, I would still consider him a central member of the director's pantheon. I simply cannot imagine living in a world that did not contain *Mr. Smith Goes to Washington* and *It's a Wonderful Life*.

In the former film, Stewart plays Jefferson (Jeff) Smith, a wholesome, patriotic American from Montana—the state is not mentioned by name in the film—who leads the local Boy Rangers troupe (a stand in for the Boy Scouts, which has never allowed its name to be used in movies). When one of the senators from his state suddenly dies, the corrupt political machine run by James Taylor (Edward Arnold) kicks into action to find a replacement who won't rock the boat while Taylor uses the other senator, Joseph Paine (Claude Rains), to push through a graft bill. The honest but naïve Jeff is chosen, and he sets off for Washington under the watchful eye of Paine, who, when he was younger, had partnered with

Jeff's father to fight a losing battle against a corrupt mining syndicate. In the end, Jeff's father was found dead at his desk while Paine, by tying himself to Taylor's apron strings, found his way in to the Senate.

All goes well until Jeff innocently proposes building a boys' camp in his state that poses a danger to Taylor's graft scheme. When Jeff refuses to be warned away by Paine and turns down Taylor's offer to join forces with him and Paine, Taylor unleashes his political machine, causing Jeff to be accused of the very graft he is trying to expose. To defend himself and his cause, Jeff mounts a filibuster, but Taylor prevents Jeff's message from getting out. In the final scene, Jeff faints from exhaustion, but Paine, plagued by conscience and a failed suicide attempt, confesses that Jeff was telling the truth about Taylor, and that he, Paine, is the one who must be expelled from the Senate.

Rarely have I watched a film in which I so fully identified with the hero. Through his dynamic but invisible editing and camera work, Capra allowed me to experience Jeff's journey from light into darkness and back into light as though I were taking it myself. Not only do Capra and Stewart make the physical spaces of Washington, D.C. come alive (the Capitol Building, the Senate, the White House, the Lincoln Memorial); they make the hope and freedom and liberty which dwell within those sacred spaces shimmer and shine.

I said that Capra's editing and camera were invisible, but that is not fully true. He includes a montage sequence that stitches together seamlessly images of Washington, all seen through a billowing flag while patriotic music plays in the background. The montage climaxes at the Lincoln Memorial with a boy reading to his grandpa the immortal words engraved on the monument. A cynical modern viewer will likely dismiss this scene as propaganda, but he will be only half right. Yes, the scene *is* propaganda but of a high and noble kind; it celebrates American virtue and optimism as Virgil's *Aeneid* does the glories of the Roman Empire of Caesar Augustus.

Besides, though Capra, like his young protagonist, has stars in his eyes, those stars do not blind him—as they did not blind Virgil—from the grim reality of fraud, deception, and double dealing. The film offers a searing critique of political corruption in the very heart of America's democracy, a corruption that all but crushes wide-eyed Jeff. The film does not teach us to deny the truth of man's depravity, but to meet that depravity with decency, integrity, and, when necessary, a good swift punch. Innocence need not mean weakness. To the contrary, it provides focus, insight, and the strength to endure.

During his filibuster, Jeff calls on his fellow senators, as he calls on us in the theater, to see the world from a new perspective and in a new light. "Just get up off the ground, that's all I ask. Get up there with that lady that is up on top of this Capitol dome, that lady that stands for liberty. Take a look at this country through her eyes if you really want to see something and you won't just see scenery—you'll see the whole parade of what man's carved out for himself after centuries of fighting and fighting for something better than just jungle law, fighting so's he can stand on his own two feet—free and decent, like he was created—no matter what his race, color, or creed."

Every time I listen to that speech, it brings tears to my eyes, and not just because the speech touches on what is greatest about our country. It makes me weep to think how far the arts have fallen away from their proper role. Art was not meant to reflect the degradation of society, as it has done for much of the last century, but to lift us up to a higher vision and a nobler purpose. To remind us that we all possess intrinsic value and worth, that we are purposeful creatures made to seek justice, love mercy, and walk humbly with our God. There really was a time when Hollywood affirmed such things!

As in any good Hollywood film from the Golden Age, *Mr. Smith* finds a way to mingle its political plot with a love story. That love story, however, far from being gratuitous or irrelevant, plays a central role in Jeff's growth and development and in the timeless lessons that the film teaches us. To support and challenge the idealistic Jeff, Capra matches him up with a cynical, pragmatic secretary named Clarissa Saunders (Jean Arthur) who is well aware of the corrupt practices of Paine and Taylor but has ceased to care. Over the course of the film, Jeff and Saunders will need to work together, both as colleagues and as potential lovers, if they are to stand up against Paine and Taylor.

Rather than mimic each other's strengths, Jeff and Saunders complement each other, with Jeff inspiring Saunders to see the beauties and wonders of the world around her, and Saunders instructing Jeff in how to survive in a world that is just as often ugly and disenchanted. When I first watched the film as a boy, I thought that it was out of step with the true nature of masculinity and femininity. Weren't boys the practical ones and girls the romantic ones? And yet, the more I studied the couples around me, the more I realized that Capra was right. It is the women, and especially the wives and mothers, who are the practical ones, who must keep their husbands and their children grounded in the real world of flesh and blood, diapers and dirty dishes, bus schedules and utility bills. The men, on the other hand, were the dreamers and idealists who had to coax their wives to relax and not take things so seriously. It was all a part of that mysterious, glorious battle of the sexes that Capra had already taught me so much about in *It Happened One Night*.

Men and women don't just need each other to set up house and raise children; they need each other's unique virtues and points-of-view if they are to stay on track and fulfill their appointed tasks. Jeff gently draws Saunders out of the self-protective cynicism she has cloaked herself with and fixes her eyes on life as it should be lived. Later, when Jeff, pressed into a corner by Taylor, loses faith and runs off to hide in a dark corner of the Lincoln Memorial, it is Saunders who finds him and restores the clarity of *his* eyes and heart: "Jeff, listen, remember the day you got here? What you said about Mr. Lincoln? That he was sitting up there, watching, waiting for someone to come along? Well, that was *you*. Someone with a little plain, decent, uncompromising *rightness*, to root out the Taylors, yeah, and really light up that dome for once. This country could use some of that, so could the whole drunken, cockeyed world right now—a *lot* of it!"

There are some who would dismiss such speeches as "Capra corn," but such a dismissal means dismissing humanity as well. We are not products of deterministic forces over which we have no control; but we are also not feathers dancing in the wind without essence or purpose. We are individuals born with unique destinies that we can embrace or reject or pervert. Whichever we choose, our choices *do* make a difference and can have far-ranging consequences for ourselves and those around us. Jeff teaches that lesson to Saunders, who then teaches it back to him.

When Jeff first arrives in Washington, he is a frenzy of hectic energy, running here and there like a chicken with its head cut off. But when he confronts Paine in his office and Paine confesses that he compromised and joined Taylor so that he could serve his state, Jeff becomes stonily and silently motionless. All changes, however, after he gets his pep talk from Saunders and is restored to a vision of who he truly is and of the true nature of the task he must do. During the long filibuster scene, Jeff stands straight and tall, motionless with strength and resolve, while Paine and Taylor rush hectically to and fro in their feverish attempts to silence the now confident and fearless Jeff.

This contrast is even rendered powerfully cinematic in one of my favorite examples of cross (or parallel) cutting. As the Taylor machine marshals its newspapers to print lies about Jeff, the Boy Rangers use a small, makeshift press to print the truth. As Taylor's men distribute their heavy stacks of newspapers via menacing trucks, Jeff's boys use bicycles and scooters and wagons to get their little, four-page tract in to as many hands as possible. More and more rapidly, with greater and greater urgency, Capra cuts back and forth between the two groups, causing the audience to cheer on the cause of these little boys standing tall against an army of Goliaths.

Alas, neither the boys nor Jeff himself prove able to defeat the mighty Taylor, but their brave fight sparks a different kind of change that ushers in the happy ending through an unexpected back door. To understand that change is to uncover the deepest and most eternal truth that lies at the heart of *Mr. Smith*. In order to uncover that truth, however, I will need to play a little game with you, my reader. If you will please extend to me for a moment your trust and your patience, I would like to retell for you the story of *Mr. Smith Goes to Washington* in archetypal terms. That is to say, I will speak of Jeff, Paine, and Taylor as representative types rather than as particular individuals. As I do so, I hope you will notice that, in describing the plot of *Mr. Smith*, I am also describing the plot of a famous film trilogy that I trust you will all be familiar with. Alright, here goes:

Our story concerns a young idealistic man who is on a quest to bring justice to his world. He is the son of a crusading freedom fighter, and he feels impelled to live up to his father's high reputation. On his quest, he meets an older man who knew his father well and who was once an idealist fighting for the same cause—that is, until he compromised and went over to the side of corruption. Though the older man still possesses within him the potential for redemption, his strings are being pulled by an evil leader with no such redeemable qualities. At one point, the evil leader even tries, unsuccessfully, to corrupt the young idealist and bring him over to his side. In the end, despite his courage, our young idealist is overwhelmed by the power of the evil leader, and he and his cause are decisively crushed. All hope seems lost, when something miraculous happens. As the older man watches the purity of the young man being destroyed by evil, his conscience is aroused, and he is converted back to the side of goodness. Though the older man's conversion destroys him, the young man rises up victorious and justice is restored.

Do you see what I have done? In describing the plot of *Mr. Smith,* I have described as well the plot of the original Star Wars trilogy (Episodes 4–6), with Luke Skywalker in the role of Jeff, the Evil Emperor in the role of Taylor, and Darth Vader combining Paine and Smith's father. By pointing out the connection, I do not mean to suggest that George Lucas was consciously imitating *Mr. Smith.* Rather, Lucas's careful study of archetypes in the work of Joseph Campbell led him to create a trilogy that taps the same well of collective secular and spiritual wisdom as Capra's film.

And in the still center of that well, both directors found a mighty and enduring truth that has helped shape my own understanding of good, evil, and the struggle between the two. The dark side, whether it rises up in the enchanted realms of fantasy or the brutal world of realpolitik, is extremely strong and often cannot be defeated in a head-on battle. But there is another way to defeat the darkness, and that is by sacrificing yourself in such a way that you stir up in others the power of goodness, truth, and beauty. Though we cannot, like Christ, die for the sins of others, we can show them the way out of cowardice and despair by the example of our courage and faith.

Had Luke failed to rekindle the spark of goodness left in his father or Jeff failed to awaken in the compromised senator the slumbering knight, both heroes would have been defeated. In matter of fact, they *are* defeated—both end up unconscious before the might of evil—but their indomitable hope and transformative love bounce off of Vader and Paine to deliver the death blow to the seemingly invincible tyrant. Throughout my life I have met, and will continue to meet, foes that cannot be changed, but that need not prevent me from helping to steer and guide those around the foe who yearn to break free from narcissism, resentment, cynicism, and ingratitude.

It may or may not be true, as Jefferson Smith's father liked to say, that the lost causes are the only ones worth fighting for. But it is most certainly true that lost people are always worth fighting for.

Fun Facts for the Fans

- Though nominated for best picture, director, screenplay, music, and art direction, as well as for the performances of Stewart, Raines, and Harry Carey (as the President of the Senate), the film ended up losing out to *Gone with the Wind*. It did, however, win an Oscar for its story.
- Several times in the film, Jeff is compared to Daniel Boone. Had the movie been made a few decades later, he would have been compared to Davy Crockett. Before Disney's TV show made the Alamo warrior a household name, adventurous, outdoorsy types were compared to Boone rather than Crockett.
- *Mr. Smith* follows the same archetypal story arc as Capra's earlier *Mr. Deeds Goes to Town*. Although the male lead is played by Gary Cooper—who would appear again in Capra's *Meet John Doe*—the female lead is played by Jean Arthur, who, as in her role of Saunders, matures from a cynic to a romantic.
- After taking innumerable pictures and measurements of the Senate chamber, Capra returned to Hollywood and rebuilt an exact model in

a Columbia sound stage. This allowed him complete control over the scenes shot in the chamber.

- Although the film was widely popular, the elite D.C. Press corps was horrified. In his autobiography, *The Name Above the Table,* Capra tells how one reporter, in a drunken rage, attacked him for daring to depict D. C. reporters as drunkards!

- Although Joseph Kennedy, Ambassador to Great Britain and father of John F. Kennedy, arrogantly attacked the film as likely to hurt American prestige around the world, Europeans loved the film, particularly the French.

- The hoarseness in Stewart's voice as he approaches the end of his filibuster was produced chemically by swabbing his throat with a mercury solution that irritated his vocal chords. Stewart really *was* struggling to get out each word.

- A few years after making *Mr. Smith,* Capra was commissioned by the army to make a series of seven propaganda films exposing the evils of fascism. The series, titled Why We Fight, makes brilliant use of the Nazi's own propaganda films.

- John Cassavetes, an independent filmmaker who, though he loved Capra, made tough, gritty, depressing movies, had this to say about his unlikely role model: "Sometimes I'm not sure that there's ever been an America. Sometimes I just think it's all been Frank Capra movies."

Other Films to Watch

Best films of Frank Capra: *Lady for a Day* (based on a Damon Runyon tale), *It Happened One Night* (first great Screwball Comedy and Capra's first Oscar for best director), *Mr. Deeds Goes to Town* (country bumpkin gets rich and foils plots of city schemers, Capra's second Oscar), *Lost Horizon* (takes us away to Shangri-La), *You Can't Take it With You* (nutty family builds Shangri-La in a home, Capra's third Oscar), *Meet John Doe* (like Deeds and Smith before him, Doe is a little man who takes on corruption), *Arsenic and Old Lace* (hilarious black comedy from a famous play about two old ladies who kill old men and bury them in the cellar), *It's a Wonderful Life* (best of all Christmas films), and *State of the Union* (excellent populist fare with Spencer Tracey and Katharine Hepburn).

If you enjoy these films, here are some other second-string Capra films that you might enjoy: *The Strong Man* (silent comedy with Harry Langdon), *Ladies of Leisure* (first film with Barbara Stanwyck about cross-class love affair), *Miracle Woman* (Stanwyck as phony evangelist), *Platinum Blonde* (Cinderella Man reporter who marries heiress Jean Harlow), *American Madness* (first great populist film that ends with a run-on-the-bank a la *It's a Wonderful Life*), *The Bitter Tea of General Yen* (cult classic of love affair between Stanwyck and Chinese "gangster"), *Broadway Bill* (breezy romantic comedy about horseracing and breaking from social conformity), *Riding High* (remake of *Broadway Bill* with Bing Crosby), *Here Comes the Groom* (entertaining musical with Crosby and Jane Wyman), *A Hole in the Head* (fun comedy with Frank Sinatra as black-sheep brother), *A Pocketful of Miracles* (his last film, a sentimental remake of *Lady for a Day* with Bette Davis in the lead role). Capra also produced four semi-animated science documentaries for television that build a much-needed bridge between science and religion: *Our Mr. Sun, Strange Case of the Cosmic* Rays, *Hemo the Magnificent* (about the circulatory system), *Unchained Goddess* (about the weather).

British actor Claude Raines, who plays Senator Paine, was one of Hollywood's greatest character actors, though he never won an Academy Award. Here is a list of his most iconic roles: *The Invisible Man* (his voice made him famous; we only see his face in the last thirty seconds), *They Won't Forget* (as an ambitious and unscrupulous Southern lawyer), *The Adventures of Robin Hood* (as the villainous Prince John), *Four Daughters* (as a sentimental father), *Juarez* (as Napoleon III), *The Sea Hawk* (as Don Jose Alvarez de Cordoba), *Here Comes Mr. Jordan* (as a bureaucratic angel), *King's Row* (as a doctor), *Now Voyager* (as a sympathetic psychologist), *Casablanca* (as Louie Renault), *Phantom of the Opera* (as the

Phantom), *Passage to Marseille* (with Humphrey Bogart), *Mr. Skeffington* (as a long-suffering husband), *Caesar and Cleopatra* (as Julius Caesar to Vivien Leigh's Cleopatra), *Angel on My Shoulder* (this time as the devil), *Deception* (as a jealous, egomaniacal composer), *Notorious* (as a sympathetic Hitchcock villain).

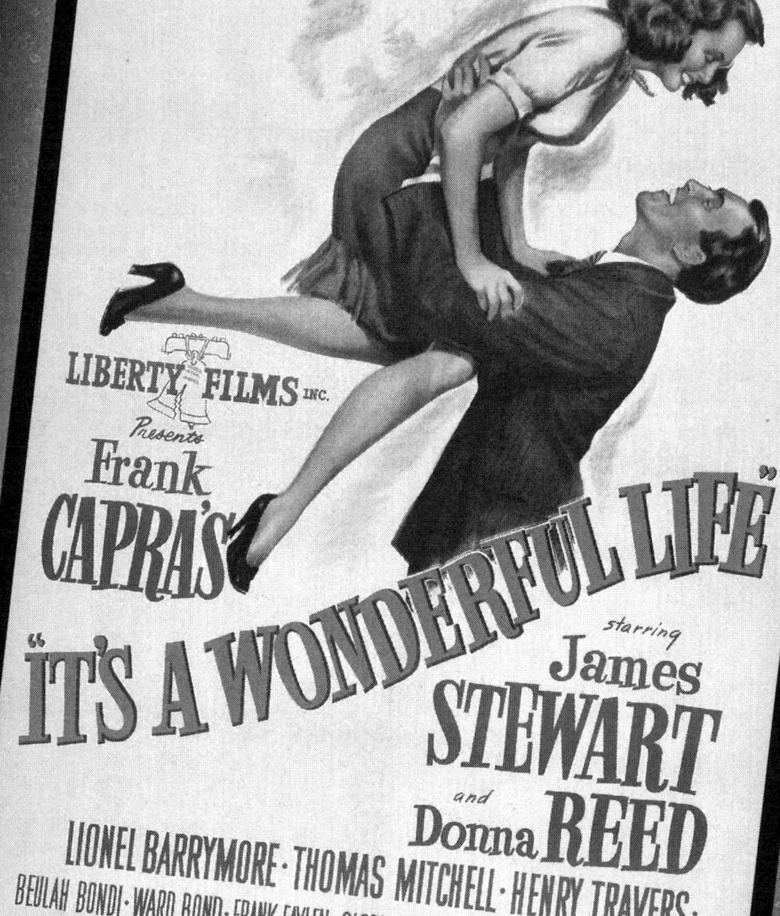
LIBERTY FILMS INC.
Presents
Frank CAPRA'S
"IT'S A WONDERFUL LIFE"
starring
James STEWART
and
Donna REED
LIONEL BARRYMORE · THOMAS MITCHELL · HENRY TRAVERS ·
BEULAH BONDI · WARD BOND · FRANK FAYLEN · GLORIA GRAHAME
PRODUCED AND DIRECTED BY FRANK CAPRA
Screen Play by FRANCES GOODRICH · ALBERT HACKETT · FRANK CAPRA — Additional Scenes by JO SWERLING — Released by RKO Radio Pictures, Inc.

IT'S A WONDERFUL LIFE

(LIBERTY; 1946; FRANK CAPRA)

In Chapter 9 of his autobiography, *The Name Above the Title,* Frank Capra tells of a strange meeting he had with an unnamed, nondescript man who ripped open his vanity and set him on a new path. Before the meeting, Capra prided himself on being a smooth craftsman able to knock out pictures in fast succession; after it, he matured into an artist with a conscience committed to slowing down and making films that would uplift and ennoble his audiences. But what was it that the "faceless man" said that so changed Capra's life and art?

According to Capra, these were the man's prophetic words to him as the voice of Hitler blared behind them on the radio: "Mr. Capra, you're a coward ... an offense to God. You hear that man in there? ... That evil man is desperately trying to poison the world with hate. How many can he talk to? Fifteen million—twenty million? And for how long—twenty minutes? You, sir, you can talk to *hundreds* of millions, for two hours—and in the dark. The talents you have, Mr. Capra, are not your own, *not* self-acquired. God gave you those talents; they are His gifts to you, to use for His purpose. And when you don't *use* the gifts God blessed you with—you are an offense to God—and to humanity. Good day, sir."[1]

When Capra met the faceless man, he was on the brink of the great popular and critical success he would win from *It Happened One Night.* Rather than revel in that success, he put his nose to the grindstone and produced a series of films—*Mr. Deeds Goes to Town, Lost Horizon, You*

1 Frank Capra, *The Name Above the Title* (New York: Da Capo Press, 1997), 176.

Can't Take it With You, Mr. Smith Goes to Washington, Meet John Doe, It's a Wonderful Life, State of the Union—that taught even as they entertained and that held up a Judeo-Christian vision of man as made in God's image but fallen that would counter the totalitarianism of Hitler's Germany and Stalin's Russia. In all of these films, he would enshrine for all time "the rebellious cry of the individual against being trampled to an ort by massiveness—mass production, mass thought, mass education, mass politics, mass wealth, mass conformity."[2]

Like *San Francisco, It's a Wonderful Life* is a movie that supposedly rises or falls on the basis of a gimmick: for the former, that's the great earthquake of 1906; for the latter, it is the protagonist's chance to see what the world would have been like had he never been born. And yet, the two films are so engrossing, so intimately human that they transcend their gimmicks to provide a window into the struggles of real people for whom we come to care intensely. Although the life of George Bailey (James Stewart) is narrated in flashback from a senior angel to a novice angel, every time I watch the film, I quickly forget about the heavenly framing device and throw myself into the frustrated dreams and small triumphs of Capra's reluctant hero.

As a boy growing up in the idyllic town of Bedford Falls, George demonstrates courage and integrity beyond his years. At the age of twelve, he dives into a frozen pond to save his drowning brother, an act of heroism that costs him his hearing in one ear. Later, when the local druggist, Mr. Gower, driven to despair by news of his son's death, accidentally gives George a poisonous prescription to deliver to a child, George prevents him from doing so, earning himself, for his pains, a rap on his bad ear from the drunken, grief-stricken Gower.

George idolizes his father, who, as owner of the Building and Loan company has been waging a losing battle against Mr. Potter (Lionel Barrymore), the town miser who "hates everybody who has anything he can't have." Like a spider, he devours the life blood of Bedford Falls, lining his pockets with money that he neither spends nor enjoys. Potter is a

2 Ibid., 186.

modern-day Ebenezer Scrooge but without the possibility of redemption. When young George overhears Potter calling his father a failure for refusing to foreclose on his clients, George defends his father, calling him the biggest man in town.

Even as a boy, George shares his father's (and Capra's) deep-seated belief in the value of each individual human being. When his father dies, George carries on his crusade against Potter, keeping the Building and Loan alive so that people can purchase and eventually own their own homes rather than live in Potter's squalid apartments. Potter tries to stop him at every turn, ridiculing him for wasting away his potential income and power to serve a lazy rabble that care nothing about him.

But George knows what he believes and is unafraid to let Potter know it: "Just remember this, Mr. Potter, that this rabble you're talking about … they do most of the working and paying and living and dying in this community. Well, is it too much to have them work and pay and live and die in a couple of decent rooms and a bath? Anyway, my father didn't think so. People were human beings to him, but to you, a warped, frustrated old man, they're cattle. Well, in my book he died a much richer man than you'll ever be!"

Up to this point, it might seem that George is a simple hero, a David happy to stand straight and tall against the local Goliath. But he is not. George spends most of the movie trying to *leave* Bedford Falls, to escape from the pressures that have been laid upon him by his family and his community. He sacrifices his chance to go to college so that his younger brother Harry can go—but with the expectation that when he returns, he will take over the Building and Loan. Instead, Harry marries a wealthy city girl and takes a job with her father, leaving George saddled with the Building and Loan. To make matters worse, when George tries to resign, the board tells him that if he does, they will have to close the Building and Loan—for no one but George has the strength and know-how to stand up to Potter.

Does anyone know what George *really* wants to do with his life? Well, George thinks he does. In no uncertain terms, he describes his plans to Mary (Donna Reed), the girl who has loved him since they were children:

"I know what I'm going to do tomorrow and the next day and the next year and the year after that. I'm shaking the dust of this crummy little town off my feet and I'm going to see the world.... and then I'm going to build things. I'm gonna build air fields. I'm gonna build skyscrapers a hundred stories high. I'm gonna build bridges a mile long."

But he won't do any of those things. At least not in the way he imagined.

I think often of the dramatic conversions of Peter and Paul. When Peter left his fishing nets to follow Jesus and Paul forsook his training as a Pharisee to become the first great Christian missionary, both men must have bemoaned the fact that they had clearly wasted the first several decades of their lives. Or had they? Peter would no longer be a fisherman, that is true; but he would be something grander and more splendid: a fisher of men. As for Paul, all those grueling years he had spent studying the Hebrew Scriptures would not be wasted; rather, they would enable him to write much of the New Testament, opening the eyes of the readers of his epistles so that they could see how completely and gloriously Jesus had fulfilled the prophecies Paul had spent his childhood memorizing.

George Bailey never builds a single air field or skyscraper or bridge. What he builds instead is a community. The homes that his carefully guarded, fiercely fought for Building and Loan finances provide a hearth and a refuge for dozens of families who would have otherwise been forced to live in Potter's slums. While his friends are fighting in World War II, George, unable to enlist on account of his deaf dear, stays behind and fights the battle of Bedford Falls. While Potter uses the war to increase his profits, George protects and supports the people of his town so that the veterans will have an intact and healthy community to return to.

I was thirteen years old when Steven Spielberg's *Close Encounters of the Third Kind* hit movie screens everywhere. I remember feeling a thrill when I watched Richard Dreyfuss's character board the spaceship at the end and sail off for an intergalactic adventure. Spielberg clearly felt that way himself when he made the film, but he later changed his mind. In an interview he gave many years later, he confessed that were he to make the movie again, he would not have Drefyuss's married-with-children character leave on the ship. You see, in the interim between the film and the interview, the young, single, hotshot director had acquired a family and learned how important familial and communal connections are to our own lives and the lives of those around us.

In a similar way, had Capra invented the character of George Bailey when he was in his twenties, he might very well have sent him off on adventures around the world. Not so the Capra who had spent the last four years using his filmic gifts to inspire the troops and the civilians back home during World War II and who had had over a decade to meditate on the challenge of the faceless man. Some would call the vision of *It's a Wonderful Life* sentimental; I call it mature. That is why George's marriage does not come at the end of the film but in the middle. It is not enough for George to win a single victory, as Jefferson Smith does in his filibuster. George must wage a life-long battle, not only against Potter, but against his own restlessness, his own frustration, his own capacity for despair.

There are a few dozen key scenes in the history of cinema that if I merely run them through the projection room inside my head will bring tears to my eyes. A number of those come from *It's a Wonderful Life*, in particular the scene where George and Mary speak together on the phone to Sam Wainwright, a mutual friend of theirs who went off to the city to become rich and who wants George to join him in his new business venture. While Mary's mother hopes the soon-to-be-rich Sam will propose to Mary, Mary gazes longingly at George in hopes that he will suddenly understand what *his* mother has been trying to tell him: that Mary is the kind of girl "who will help [him] find the answers."

As the two press their cheeks together so that they can hear from and speak into the same phone, a fierce internal struggle breaks out within George. Sam offers George the chance of a lifetime, the chance to get out from under the Building and Loan, to be free to dream big dreams and do great deeds, but George tunes him out as he feels himself being drawn irresistibly toward Mary. Suddenly, he catches himself and rebels. Dropping the phone and grabbing Mary by the shoulders, he yells at her that he will never get married to anyone, that he wants to do what he wants to do and will not be tied down. But the pull toward Mary is too strong. Unable to finish his tirade, he pulls Mary toward him in an embrace and mumbles her name over and over.

The two marry shortly afterward, and George and Mary prepare to go on a whirlwind honeymoon to all the exotic places George has been longing to visit. But this too will be denied him. Before they can get out of town, they learn that a panic has ensued and that George's Building and Loan customers have made a run on the bank. George rushes back to the bank and does his best to calm his investors, many of whom are prepared to go over to Potter, who tries to use the crisis to crush the Building and Loan. All seems lost when Mary arrives and offers up the $2000 they had planned to spend on their honeymoon to appease their frightened customers. With the help of the money and by appealing to the better angels of his fellow townsmen, George makes it, barely, to the end of the business day and closes his doors. Once again, he has beaten Potter, but at the price of his honeymoon.

Well, almost. Mary, sensitive to her new husband's yearning for adventure, converts their run-down home into the Waldorf Astoria, replete with posters of all the distant lands that George had hoped to visit. They will never see those places in person, but they will live the rich life of the imagination right there in Bedford Falls. And that they do, with occasional ups and downs, until the fateful day arrives when George's faith and courage will be tested to the breaking point.

On the very day that the bank examiner arrives for his annual visit to the Building and Loan, Billy, George's slow-witted uncle, accidentally hands over to Potter the $8000 he was supposed to deposit in the bank to square the books of the Building and Loan. Things quickly spiral out of control, and George is brought face-to-face with his every fear, his every broken and frustrated dream. The trap is sprung, and it closes in on him swiftly and relentlessly.

In his desperation, he even begs Potter to give him a loan, only to have his failure and humiliation thrown back in his face: "Look at you. You used to be so cocky! You were going to go out and conquer the world! You once called me a warped, frustrated old man. What are you but a warped, frustrated young man? A miserable little clerk crawling in here on your hands and knees and begging for help. No securities—no stocks—no bonds—nothing but a miserable little five hundred dollar equity in a life insurance policy. You're worth more dead than alive. Why don't you go to the riff-raff you love so much and ask them to let you have eight thousand dollars? You know why? Because they'd run you out of town on a rail."

As all that he thought was good and firm and stable crashes down around him, the beleaguered, Job-like George sends up a prayer for help—only to be greeted with a punch in the face. That does it for George. Remembering what Potter said about his being worth more dead than alive, he prepares to throw himself from a bridge—only to be stopped by a guardian angel named Clarence (Henry Travers) who, it turns out, is the *real* answer to his prayer. In order to save George from suicide, Clarence throws himself off the bridge knowing that the noble-hearted George will dive into the water to save him.

The plan works, but it cannot save George from the deeper, existential cause of his despair. George vocalizes that cause when he confesses to Clarence that it would have been better for everyone if he had never been born in the first place. It is then that Clarence, with the help of heaven, arranges for George to see what the world would have been like had he not been born. Immediately, the mood, lighting, and cinematic look of the film darkens, becoming more fragmented, angular, loosely framed, and disorienting.

Capra then takes us into a nightmare world that is all the more nightmarish because it is a picture of what post-war America was quickly becoming: a world of smoky bars and seedy dance halls, pawn shops and peep shows, soul-crushing slums and joyless tenement houses, broken families and cast off relatives. And all of it run by Potter, a man with no bodily pleasures of his own who feeds off the lusts of the people he despises, supplying them with sex and alcohol divorced from intimacy and camaraderie. Without George there as the glue to hold together his family and community, Ma Bailey has become a bitter old women, Uncle Billy has landed in an asylum, Mr. Gower is a drunken ex-convict, Mary an old maid, and Harry is dead. And because Harry is dead, because

George was not there to save him from drowning, an army transport full of people that Harry the war hero had saved now lies still and cold beneath the ocean.

"Strange, isn't it? Each man's life touches so many other lives. When he isn't around he leaves an awful hole, doesn't he?" This is the lesson that Clarence tries to teach George as he rushes blindly from one terrifying revelation to the next. We in the audience experience the horror through George's eyes, but with two odd twists that many viewers sense intuitively in their spirit without being aware of it on the conscious, rational level.

First, though we realize exactly what the absence of George has done to Bedford Falls and its inhabitants, George himself does not. All he wants is to be reunited with his family members who no longer recognize who he is. He is unselfconsciously innocent of the good that he has done; his left hand does not know what benevolence and joy and hope his right hand has brought. His good deeds were never done for show, or even to please himself. He did what was right, sacrificing again and again his own dreams and desires for the sake of others.

And that leads to the second twist that is too often overlooked by critics. For a moment, Clarence gives George what he always thought he wanted: complete freedom. In the nightmare sequence, George becomes a fully autonomous individual without ties of any kind. As a nameless stranger, George steps out from under all the social pressures and obligations that have weighed so heavily on him throughout his life. He breathes the air of pure freedom and finds that it is poisonous. Apart from his family, his neighbors, and his community he has no identity; he is unmoored and adrift in a meaningless sea of confusion, a mere sport of chance.

Unlike *Mr. Smith Goes to Washington*, *It's a Wonderful Life* makes no mention of George Washington or Thomas Jefferson or Abraham Lincoln. That is not because Capra has ceased to be a patriot, but because the ideals of our Founding Fathers have become so fully internalized they do not need to be quoted. Well, that and something else. Whether Capra himself was fully conscious of it, *It's a Wonderful Life* exposes one of the dark sides of the Enlightenment. Though secular Enlightenment ideals of liberty helped inspire the founding of our nation, they also gave birth to an image of the individual as radically autonomous, divorced from all past traditions, religious codes, and external authorities.

By looking back to the Judeo-Christian principles from which the Enlightenment acquired its belief in the intrinsic value and worth of each individual, Capra succeeded in ennobling the average man without cutting him off from family, church, and community. Through many years of reading and studying, I have come to understand, intellectually, the importance of this distinction, but I had already absorbed it viscerally many years before through repeated viewings of *It's a Wonderful Life*. Such is the power of film that it can, properly used, allow us to experience life as it should and could be, not through rose-colored glasses—as critics continue to unfairly criticize Capra for doing—but straight on with a hopeful eye that need not avert its gaze from tragedy and despair.

It's a Wonderful Life ends with a sort-of reverse run on the bank, as George's neighbors, friends, and family descend upon his house. All they know is that George is in trouble and needs money; their deeply-instilled sense of community does the rest. In true Capra fashion, the movie concludes with a happy ending, not because it has been tacked on in a contrived way, but because it rises up organically from the plot and characters.

After all, if the Bible is right, then all of human history is leading up to a happy ending: not to Armageddon and the Antichrist, but to the Great Marriage of Christ and the Church with which the Book of Revelation comes to a close.

Fun Facts for the Fans

- Though nominated for best picture, director, actor (Stewart), and editing, *It's a Wonderful Life* lost to William Wyler's film about GI's returning to civilian life: *The Best Years of Our Lives*. The two films are, to my mind, the best melodramas ever made; together they could drain a viewer dry of his tears—with every one of those tears being honestly earned rather than mawkishly manipulated.

- After the war, Capra joined forces with two other top-notch directors, William Wyler and George Stevens, to form Liberty Films as a way of making high-quality pictures free from the compromises of the studio. Ironically, the success of Wyler's *Best Years of Our Lives,* which he made for Sam Goldwyn, ended up hurting the future of Liberty Films, which was essentially taxed out of existence. Capra made *It's a Wonderful Life* and *State of the Union* under the Liberty banner before it was disbanded.

- The husband/wife team of Frances Goodrich and Albert Hackett who wrote the screenplay also wrote the screenplays for *Father of the Bride, Easter Parade, Seven Brides for Seven Brothers, The Thin Man,* and *The Diary of Anne Frank.*

- The screenplay was adapted from a story by Philip Van Doren Stern who originally wrote it as a Christmas card!

- *It's a Wonderful Life* did not do well at the box office; however, because its copyright was not renewed in 1975, it was shown frequently on television, causing it to slowly gain its reputation as the quintessential Christmas movie.

- Although *It's a Wonderful Life* remains firmly on my top five list, it has sadly perpetuated a soft heresy within Christianity—the notion that we become angels when we die. Neither the Bible nor the Church teaches such a thing. Angels and humans are two different creations of God. In heaven, we will continue to be human; indeed, at the Second Coming, we will receive Resurrection Bodies and will continue for all eternity to be fully physical/fully spiritual creatures.

- *It's a Wonderful Life* also had the negative effect of perpetuating the unfair stereotype of librarians as repressed spinsters.

- Donna Reed, who plays the all-American girl-next-door Mary, won her Oscar for playing a prostitute in *From Here to Eternity*!

- The town of Bedford Falls was a huge set; Capra even had live oaks planted to increase the realism.

- During the school dance scene, the floor is retracted to reveal a swimming pool underneath into which George and Mary fall. That was not a special effect but was filmed at an actual high school in Beverly Hills.
- The famous telephone scene in which George finally realizes his love for Mary was shot in one take.

Other Films to Watch

James Stewart is one of the best-loved actors in movie history. Here is a list of some of the other great roles of the star of *Mr. Smith Goes to Washington* and *It's a Wonderful Life: You Can't Take it with You* (his first film with Capra in which he plays the son of a tycoon attracted to the daughter of a goofy family), *Destry Rides Again* (a wonderful Western spoof), *The Philadelphia Story* (for which he won his Academy Award in a comic role), *Call Northside 777* (as a crusading Chicago reporter), *Rope* (as a professor whose dangerous ideas corrupt his students; his first of four Hitchcock films), *Winchester 73* (good Western role), *Broken Arrow* (tries to make peace with the Indians), *Harvey* (as a loveable crank who is friends with a giant rabbit), *The Greatest Show on Earth* (as a clown), *Bend of the River* (another good Western role), *The Glenn Miller Story* (as Miller trying to find his "sound"), *Rear Window* (as a man with a broken leg who thinks he has witnessed a murder; second Hitch film), *The Man Who Knew Too Much* (doctor whose child is kidnapped; third Hitch), *The Spirit of St Louis* (as Charles Lindbergh), *Vertigo* (his fourth Hitch gives him his most nuanced role), *Bell, Book and Candle* (falls in love with a witch), *Anatomy of a Murder* (as a small-town defense attorney), *The Man Who Shot Liberty Valance* (excellent Western with John Wayne), *Shenandoah* (a father of many sons who tries to stay neutral in the Civil War).

Thomas Mitchell was a much beloved Irish character actor on whom one could always count to bring warmth and humanity to a film. He made his best films with John Ford and Frank Capra. Here are just a few of his best roles: *Lost Horizon* (as a tough businessman converted by Shangri-La),

The Hurricane (on a tropical island hit by storm), *Stagecoach* (as a drunken doctor with a good heart; won Academy Award), *Mr. Smith Goes to Washington* (as a drunken Washington reporter who is transformed by Smith's idealism), *The Hunchback of Notre Dame* (as the king of the gypsies), *Gone with the Wind* (as Scarlet O'Hara's father), *Our Town* (fine dramatic role), *The Black Swan* (as a pirate), *It's a Wonderful Life* (as the absent-minded uncle), and many, many others, including his last film, *Pocketful of Miracles,* which was also Capra's last.

Although it is often said that Capra's films are outdated and can't be made in our modern, cynical world, every so often a Capraesque film slips through. Here, in no particular order, are some relatively recent films that I believe capture well the Capra magic: *Dead Poet's Society* (a charismatic teacher in a strict school sets his students' imaginations free), *Field of Dreams* (a man reconnects with his dead father by building a baseball field in the middle of an Iowa cornfield), *Mr. Holland's Opus* (a would-be composer turned high school music teacher changes the lives of his students), *The Milagro Beanfield War* (poor farmers in New Mexico wage war against developers; directed by Robert Redford), *Tucker: The Man and His Dream* (underdog inventor takes on the car companies), *The Terminal* (Tom Hanks is stranded in an airport terminal and converts it into a home; directed by Steven Spielberg), *The Family Man* (career-driven man gets to see what his life would have been like had he married his sweetheart instead of pursuing wealth), *Groundhog Day* (a Scrooge-like man is reformed as he is forced to live the same day over and over), *The Majestic* (blacklisted Hollywood writer loses his memory and becomes part of a small town), *It Could Happen to You* (kindly policeman shares his lottery ticket with a poor waitress), *Dave* (a clever and patriotic reworking of the *Prisoner of Zenda*), *The Hudsucker Proxy* (a Coen brothers movie that manages to parody Capra while also affirming most of his ideals), *Rocky* (underdog boxer gets a shot at the title), *Cinderella Man* (another underdog boxer gets a shot), *Saving Mr. Banks* (the abrasive author of *Mary Poppins* resists Walt Disney's attempts to turn her novel into a film). *Mr. Holland's Opus* best sums up one of the central themes of *It's a Wonderful Life* by quoting this surprisingly profound line from a John Lennon song: "Life is what happens to you while you're busy making other plans."

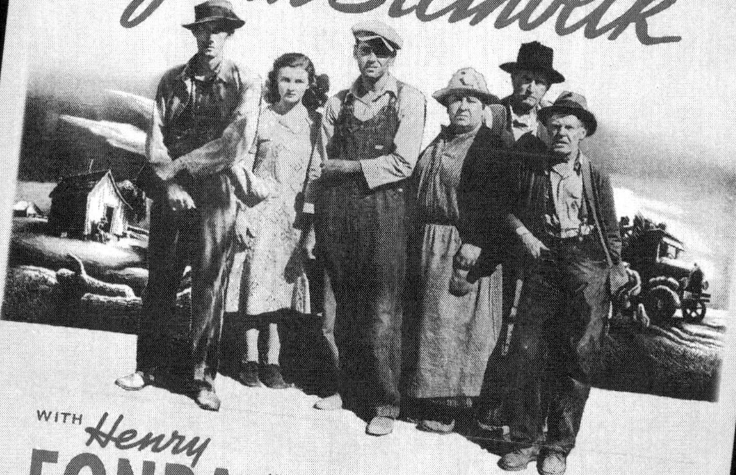
DARRYL F. ZANUCK'S production of
THE GRAPES OF WRATH
BY John Steinbeck
WITH Henry FONDA
AND Jane DARWELL John CARRADINE
Charley GRAPEWIN Dorris BOWDON
Russell SIMPSON - O.Z. WHITEHEAD - John QUALEN - Eddie QUILLAN - Zeffie TILBURY
Directed by JOHN FORD
ASSOCIATE PRODUCER and SCREEN PLAY by NUNNALLY JOHNSON
A 20th CENTURY FOX PICTURE

THE GRAPES OF WRATH

(FOX; 1940; JOHN FORD)

From Frank Capra's *It's a Wonderful Life*, I learned how an American can love his country while yet discerning seeds of darkness deep in her soul. But there is another classic film from the 1940s, this one directed by an Irish-American (John Ford) rather than an Italian-American (Capra), that taught me that lesson in a grimmer, more disturbing, yet just as indelible manner. *The Grapes of Wrath*, based on the acclaimed, but controversial novel by John Steinbeck, took me on an equally harrowing journey, not through the soul of the depressed and suicidal George Bailey, but through the heart of a family who must leave behind all that they know in order to survive and remain intact.

Like no other film before or since, *The Grapes of Wrath* succeeds in combining two things that rarely go together in art: a searing exposé of the natural, political, and economical forces that press down the poor and dispossessed; a celebration of the indomitability of the human spirit and the hardiness of the family unit. Some might argue that Ford's success at achieving this fusion rests on the novel on which it is based, but I would disagree.

For all its virtues, Steinbeck's novel is strongly Marxist and anti-religious in tone and ideology. Not so Ford's film (based on Nunally Johnson's excellent adapted screenplay), which, while remaining essentially faithful to the novel, transforms it from a soft communist tract into a profound and timeless work of what might be called Christian socialism. While never downplaying the sociological forces that all but annihilate the Joad family, the film affirms the freedom, dignity, and integrity of the family itself and each individual member of it.

The novel, brilliant as it is, reads like the work of a statistics- and ideology-driven social scientist; the film, in sharp contrast, is richly humanistic and profoundly spiritual. Both Steinbeck and Ford extend their support for labor unions, but their motivation for doing so couldn't be more different. While Steinbeck's support is systemic and political, calling out for a wholesale restructuring of society, Ford's is temporary and pragmatic, a necessary evil that will pass away once America makes it through her growing pains. Whereas both novel and film are realistic in their depiction of man's inhumanity to man, only the novel is naturalistic—that is, it presses man down so that he becomes part of the natural cycle, a victim of the deterministic Darwinian forces of heredity and environment.

In what follows, I will attempt to gauge the overwhelming and lasting impact that the film has had on me by first considering how Ford uses his camera to bring his vision to life with power and conviction and then analyzing how the film alters the novel in such a way as to be faithful to the heart of the story without tumbling into the anti-humanistic black hole of Marxism. But first, a quick overview of the plot would be helpful.

During the Depression, as the dustbowl ravages the farms and livelihoods of countless subsistence farmers in Oklahoma and Arkansas (the Okies and Arkies), Tom Joad (Henry Fonda) returns home from a jail sentence. No sooner is he reunited with his family than he learns that they are about to set off in their jalopy for California, lured by the promise of jobs as fruit pickers. Ma Joad (Jane Darwell) burns what few trinkets she has and sets off with Pa (Russell Simpson), Grandpa (Charley Grapewin), Grandma, and the kids, along with a former revivalist preacher named Casy (John Carradine) who has lost the Spirit and decides to journey with Tom and his family. Before leaving, Tom meets the dispossessed Muley (John Qualen) who tells him about the tractors that came and flattened his home, and of his inability to find a single villain to put the blame on.

As they drive along Route 66, the Joads lose both grandparents and face prejudice and persecution. In California, they join a worker's camp where they are exploited. Casy, his spiritual fervor revived, helps organize a strike in the camp that drives up salaries to a living wage, but he is killed by strike breakers. Tom, who witnesses the murder, kills the man who killed Casy and is forced to flee the camp with his family. Temporary relief arrives in the form of a clean, well-run government camp, where the exploited Okies and Arkies, their spirits renewed, win a small but splendid victory against their exploiters. In the end, however, the fugitive Tom must set off on his own while Ma, Pa, and the younger kids press on in search of work and hope.

John Ford, the greatest director of westerns in the history of film, was a master of the extreme long shot, pulling his camera back and up to capture huge natural vistas, as if seen from the point of view of a plane or a bird or God himself. *The Grapes of Wrath* is book ended by two such shots. Our first view of the plight of the Joad family is of Tom, a tiny dot walking along an endless road in search of his home; our last is of a line of cars moving across the horizon, the Joad car lost in a sea of vehicles seeking a friendly port in the storm. Throughout the film, these opening and closing images are complemented by panoramic shots of the rolling plains and valleys of Oklahoma and New Mexico, Arizona and California: landscapes that are at once beautiful and lonely, fruitful and barren.

The cumulative effect of these cinematic vistas on my psyche was to conjure up a powerful and disturbing sense of an unseen fate or destiny, a bodiless, impersonal force that whips us frail mortals along like dust on a dry prairie. The Joads seemed so small, so insignificant against those vast landscapes. How could they possible survive? How can any of us survive in a world that seems so cold, distant, and uncaring?

But that is not where Ford left me. Even as the film offers a visual meditation on those crushing forces, it imbues its characters' lives with meaning, purpose, and the will to endure. *The Grapes of Wrath* is epic in its scope, and it centers on a journey-quest, but its heroes are decidedly non-epic. There is no Achilles or Hector, Odysseus or Aeneas among the Joad clan; they are simple, uneducated, mostly passive. They move through a world stripped clean of objects of permanence; the few that Ma has she burns. They have nothing but each other on which to project their fears and hopes and desires.

Yet they matter, and the camera *tells* us they matter by alternating its extreme long shots with intimate close-ups of all the characters. The photography of the human face reaches new heights in the hands of Ford's cameraman, Gregg Toland, to my mind, the greatest cinematographer of the Golden Age—or of any age. Everyone in the film looks "real," as though they had been captured off guard; yet, every close-up is carefully framed and precisely lit. We see their worn, weather-beaten faces caught in the flickering light of a match or a candle or a lantern or the stab of a headlight: sometimes fully illuminated; sometimes half obscured in shadow. Every inch of the face, with all its suffering and passion, is brought out by the camera. The intensely human faces balance the impersonal vistas, asserting their existence and their worth. The landscapes are part of God's creation, but only those tired yet resilient faces were made in the image of God.

Ford's camera is as sensitive as it is merciless: sensitive for it caresses the Joads and their companions, documenting every detail of their lives; merciless for it does not let them hide—before it they are naked. The camera cannot solve or answer their plight—it points out no simple villain for us to blame—but it stays with them, accompanies them on their journey, imploring us to affirm them and their simple desire for survival. Though Ford seeks to show rather than to judge, he uses lighting, editing, and framing to explore the souls of his protagonists. He is as concerned with psychological truths as he is with socio-economic ones. That is because his concern is not merely with Depression America but with all people at all times who have suffered and been displaced—as, for example, his fellow Irishmen were by exploitative English landlords.

In the beginning of the film, Casy tells Tom that he has lost the Spirit; near the end, just before he is killed, as he explains to Tom in a lamp-lit tent his vision for the strike and the justice it will bring, we suddenly realize that he has gotten it back. But our realization of Casy's re-inspiriting does not come to us via the dialogue. It is the strange, spiritual light that Ford casts on Casy's ecstatic face that conveys this information. Tom confirms this to Ma as he prepares to leave his family by referring to Casy as a "lantern" who helped him, finally, to see things clearly. Yes, Casy is cruelly and unjustly murdered but not before the inherent nobility within him shines out. He does not die, the camera assures us, as a nameless, faceless statistic but as a martyr, a Christ figure who achieves enlightenment and the confirmation of his calling before he is struck down—only to rise again in the renewed spirit of Tom.

Casy is Casy, set in a particular time and place, but he is also an every man who has suffered into wisdom and found light and glory at the end of his journey. The same is true for Muley, though he, sadly, never achieves Casy's moment of clarity. Still, Ford uses all the resources of his camera to tell Muley's story as if he were one of the warriors in the Trojan War. When Muley recounts his troubles to Tom, he calls himself an old graveyard ghost, and that is how the camera presents him, a man dodging in and out of the shadows, vainly trying to reassemble the life that has been stolen from him.

Muley fears that people will think he is "touched" (crazy), but the camera tells us that he is merely confused and forlorn, his mind and memory fragmented by the ordeal through which he has suffered. Three times the camera moves back and forth from Muley's face telling the story to the incident itself; since it happened, time has lost its natural rhythm, stranding Muley in a physical and temporal no-man's-land. As Muley speaks, his voice wavering, of the tractors that bulldozed his home, we see a powerful montage of unstoppable machines crisscrossing the screen, cold, remote, and aloof. When the tractor actually topples his house, the camera shifts to focus on the shadows of Muley and his family. That is all they are now; the substance of their lives has gone. The camera dissolves back once more to Muley telling his story, but in such a way that, for a moment, the fading image of the tractor seems to roll over the storytelling graveyard ghost.

And then there is the scene of Ma Joad burning her few belongings before setting out to California—a scene with all the timeless power of Aeneas fleeing the burning ruins of Troy with his son, his household gods, and a ragged band of survivors. In this moment, Ma Joad is everyone's Ma, every mother who has ever dreamed of a better life for her family. She holds a pair of earrings up to her ears and turns to look at herself in a stained, dusty mirror, her reflection caught for a moment by a camera that refuses to glamorize or sentimentalize her, yet still renders her as human and as noble as any biblical matriarch.

I am aware that I am starting to sound like a movie critic obsessed with the technical minutiae of filmmaking, but that is only because Ford uses those techniques to engrave his characters and their all-too-human plight on the mind's eye of his viewers. Ford will not let us *not* pay heed to Tom and Casy and Muley and Ma. We must extend to them our attention and our compassion. We must not be like the gas station attendants who, as the Joads ride off to cross the desert, say to each other: "Them Okies ain't got no sense and no feelings. They ain't human. No human being could live the way they do. A human being couldn't stand to be so miserable."

Ford and Toland humanize and ennoble Steinbeck's characters, but they are only able to do so because of a series of subtle changes that Ford and Johnson make to the novel. The novel employs a unique narrative technique that Steinbeck also uses in *East of Eden*: that of interweaving long plot-driven chapters with shorter, more objective inter-chapters written in a realistic, reportage style. While following, with a few later changes, the basic progression of the plot chapters, the film transfers some of the information contained in the inter-chapters from the realm of the objective to that of the subjective.

The scene I described earlier when Muley tells his tragic story is just so lifted and transformed from Chapter 5 of the novel. In this inter-chapter, Steinbeck tells, in general terms, of the fate of the Okie farmers as they are evicted, a displacement that he describes clinically with no-name farmers as the victims. By offering a single example in which Muley, whom we know and care about, is driven off his land, the film personalizes the human tragedy involved. And the same goes for the moving scene when Ma burns her belongings, a detail that appears in an inter-chapter but with no connection to the Joads.

But the most memorable transfer is taken from Chapter 15, a scene that is easy to skip over in the novel, concerning as it does a no-name family of travelers and written in a dispassionate style, but which, once experienced in the film, can never be forgotten. Pa Joad, in need of some bread, asks the waitress at a truck stop diner if she can sell him ten cents worth of bread. When she answers, with annoyance and scorn, that they sell sandwiches, not bread, the cook gruffly tells her to give him a loaf. As the Joads prepare to leave, the two youngest gaze longingly at two peppermint sticks. When Pa asks if the sticks are penny candy, the waitress hesitates, and then says, "no, they're two-for-a-penny candy." When the Joads leave, two truck drivers ridicule the waitress, telling her that she knows well and good that the sticks are nickel-a-piece candy. A few seconds later, the truckers leave themselves, placing two half dollars on the counter. The waitress tries to give them change, but they scowl at her and say, "what's it to you." As they drive off, the waitress holds the two half dollars to her breast and exclaims, lovingly, "truck drivers."

Well, that's my blow-by-blow description of the episode, but it must be watched to be appreciated. To watch the scene played out is to be drawn into the power of charity as it passes, sulkily and unsentimentally, from cook to waitress to truck drivers. Even Capra would have been hard pressed to create such a scene in which goodness peeks out in the most unlikely of places and among the most unlikely of people. The actual scene is Steinbeck's, but the film transforms it into something magical, universal, and indelible.

Aside from integrating and personalizing material from the interchapters, the film also alters elements of the plot in such a way as to increase the centrality of the Joads and their family bonds. In the novel, the returning Tom meets Pa first and then Pa takes him inside to see the family and be reunited with Ma. In the film, we see and meet the family at breakfast before Tom walks in, and Tom is noticed first by Ma. The changes are subtle, but they strengthen the film's focus on the unity of the Joad family and their joy at the return of the "prodigal" Tom, as well as emphasizing the intimate, but unsentimental, bond of mother and son that makes the film more accessible to a wider audience.

Perhaps the biggest change from novel to film, however, is that the film leaves out the Wilsons, a husband and wife with whom the Joads join up on their way to California. The film, which embraces a Christian socialist rather than Marxist worldview, champions a Judeo-Christian/ American ideal in which the Joad family face their hardships alone, relying on each other and their faith, while yet being willing to accept, with humility and gratitude, the help that is extended to them. Steinbeck, in sharp contrast, has the Joads and Wilsons join together to form a new type of community, one that transcends the family but is not linked to religion. To flesh out his communist vision, Steinbeck includes two interchapters that are significantly left out of the film. In the first, he discusses, in Marxist terminology, the rise of a collective consciousness among the dispossessed Okies and Arkies. In the second, he introduces the reader to small vagrant communities that have set up their own laws and codes that include the punishment of ostracism for those who break them. Needless to say, their laws and codes are divorced from all traditional notions of church or family or state.

The film's toning down of the more radical aspects of the novel is perhaps best displayed in the slight changes that are made to Casy's character. While retaining Casy's embrace of a one-soul idea reminiscent of Ralph Waldo Emerson, the film does not have Casy abandon Christian doctrine as forcefully and heretically as he does in the novel. Rather the film gives Casy a spiritual arc in which his revelation that he has been called to serve poor migrant workers through political action comes near the end of the film, rather than toward the beginning as in the novel. The dramatic spacing out of Casy's revelation makes his story less about the birth of an anti-creedal revolutionary and more about a mystic who has lost and regained the Spirit.

Finally, in order to end on a more optimistic and affirming note, Ford and Johnson move the novel's hopeful scene in the government camp to almost the end of the film, placing it *after* Tom kills Casy's killer, rather than before. It then drops the dark and despairing chapters with which the novel closes—chapters in which the Joads hook up with yet another family to form another Marxist commune, only to have their renewed hopes destroyed by sociological and natural forces, climaxing with their daughter delivering a stillborn child and then offering her breast to feed an old dying man. Instead, the film ends with two personal-familial exchanges—one between mother and son, the other between husband and wife—that are mostly lifted from the novel, but that have greater resonance in the film and that incarnate powerfully the ability of the human spirit to rise above the forces that would obliterate it.

I said above that no movie since *The Grapes of Wrath* has achieved its balance of outrage against social-political-economic exploitation with a Christian-humanist faith in the sanctity of the family and the innate and unique dignity of each individual; but that is not fully true. The television miniseries Roots, which aired in 1977, did for the horrors of slavery what Ford did for the inhumane mistreatment of the Okies and Arkies.

The American screen, whether big or small, could use more such works of art that have the courage to expose and criticize our excesses while yet affirming the basic decency of our country and its people. *The Grapes of Wrath* and Roots helped remove some needed blinders from my eyes, but without thereby blinding me to the goodness that still resonates in the heart of America.

Fun Facts for the Fans

- *The Grapes of Wrath* won Oscars for best director (the second of Ford's four Oscars) and supporting actress (Darwell). It was nominated for best picture, actor (Fonda), script, and editing.
- Fonda, whose portrayal of Tom Joad ranks among the twenty best performances in cinema history, lost to James Stewart in *The Philadelphia Story*, which Oscar was likely given to Stewart because he failed to win it for *Mr. Smith* the previous year. Fonda would win his Oscar forty-one years later for *On Golden Pond*.
- Fonda desperately wanted the role of Tom Joad, but producer Zanuck, who knew that Fonda was the only actor who could do it, pretended that he wanted Tyrone Power. By this ploy, Zanuck got Fonda to sign an eight-picture deal to get a role he intended to give him anyway! Steinbeck praised Fonda's performance.

- John Carradine, whose portrayal of Casy is nothing short of brilliant, is the father of David Carradine, who played Kung Fu on television.
- When she was in her 80s, Jane Darwell (Ma Joad) played the role of the Little Old Bird Woman in *Mary Poppins*.
- Gregg Toland, the greatest of Hollywood's black-and-white photographers was responsible for the look of such classics as *Les Misérables* (1935), *Dead End, Intermezzo, Wuthering Heights* (1939), *The Grapes of Wrath, The Westerner, Citizen Kane, The Little Foxes, The Best Years of Our Lives,* and *Enchantment*.
- In addition to *The Grapes of Wrath* screenwriter Nunnally Johnson wrote many literate, mature scripts. They include *The House of Rothschild, The Prisoner of Shark Island, Jesse James, Tobacco Road, Roxie Hart* (on which the musical *Chicago* is based), *The Woman in the Window, The Mudlark, The Desert Fox, My Cousin Rachel, The Man in the Gray Flannel Suit,* and *Three Faces of Eve*.
- Some of the cars seen heading to California were actual families making the trek. Ford paid them $5 each to appear in the film.
- Producer Darryl F. Zanuck, who was also the mogul of Twentieth Century Fox, sent spies to see if the migrant camps were as bad as Steinbeck had described them. His spies reported back that they were even worse than described!
- Zanuck was unique among Hollywood moguls in his willingness to make serious message films. While he was at Warner Brothers, he oversaw such tough realistic pictures as *Little Caesar* (based on Al Capone), *Public Enemy* (about another gangster), and *I Am a Fugitive from a Chain Gang* (calling for prison reform).
- Though he was the only major mogul who was not Jewish, Zanuck produced *Gentleman's Agreement*, the first Hollywood movie to take on anti-Semitism.

- After John Ford left the set, Zanuck himself directed the up-beat closing scene, which he asked Johnson to write, where Ma and Pa Joad talk about the people. When Ford later saw the scene, he approved of it.
- Steinbeck received death threats, and his novel was banned in many states and in many counties of California, including Salinas County, the author's home town. The Association of Farmers of California was so outraged by the movie that they called for a boycott of *all* Twentieth Century Fox films!

Other Films to Watch

Although John Ford was a tough, taciturn man who never expressed any artistic pretensions, he directed some of the finest, most literate films to come out of Hollywood. Here are some of his best: *The Informer* (highly expressionistic film about the Irish troubles; won his first Oscar), *Prisoner of Shark Island* (about doctor who treated John Wilkes Booth and was unfairly condemned), *The Hurricane* (early disaster film), *Stagecoach* (*the* archetypal western), *Young Mr. Lincoln* (with Henry Fonda in the title role), *Drums Along the Mohawk* (set in colonial America; with Fonda), *The Grapes of Wrath* (second Oscar), *Tobacco Road* (plays like a humorous *Grapes of Wrath*), *How Green was My Valley* (a Welsh mining town is brought to life; third Oscar), *My Darling Clementine* (Gun Fight at OK Corral, with Fonda as Wyatt Earp), *The Fugitive* (based on a Graham Greene novel, with Fonda as a priest on the run), *Fort Apache, She Wore a Yellow Ribbon,* and *Rio Grande* (his famed Cavalry trilogy; all with John Wayne), *The Quiet Man* (in Ireland with John Wayne; fourth Oscar), *Mogambo* (adventure in Africa), *Mister Roberts* (shipboard comedy with Fonda and James Cagney), *The Searchers* (his most mature Western, with an excellent performance from Wayne), *The Last Hurrah* (Spencer Tracey plays an old political boss fighting his last campaign), *The Man Who Shot Liberty Valance* (about how legends rise up in the West).

Henry Fonda became something of an American institution, bringing a quiet dignity to his roles. In addition to his films with John Ford listed above, Fonda starred in *Jezebel* (as a Southern gentleman), *Jesse James* (as Frank James), *The Lady Eve* (a comic role in a Preston Sturges farce), *The Ox Bow Incident* (he tries unsuccessfully to stop a lynching), *The Wrong Man* (heavy-handed Hitchcock thriller with falsely-accused Fonda), *War and Peace* (miscast as Pierre, but film is worthwhile), *Twelve Angry Men* (as a conscientious juror who tries to convince the other eleven to look again at the evidence), *Spencer's Mountain* (as a widower who raises a large family; inspiration for *The Waltons*), *The Best Man* (as ex-President being courted by political candidates), *Fail-Safe* (as US President trying to stop a nuclear Armageddon), *Once Upon a Time in the West* (cast against type as a ruthless killer), *On Golden Pond* (plays alongside Katharine Hepburn and his real-life, long-estranged daughter, Jane).

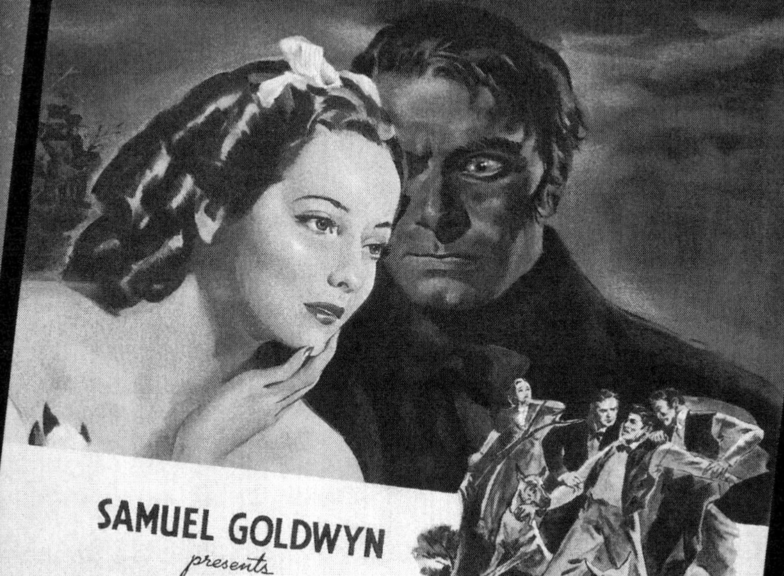
I am torn with Desire... tortured by hate!
SAMUEL GOLDWYN
presents
WUTHERING HEIGHTS
MERLE OBERON · co-starring LAURENCE OLIVIER · DAVID NIVEN
with FLORA ROBSON · DONALD CRISP · GERALDINE FITZGERALD · Released thru UNITED ARTISTS
Directed by WILLIAM WYLER

WUTHERING HEIGHTS

(GOLDWYN; 1939; WILLIAM WYLER)

Like *The Grapes of Wrath*, William Wyler's 1939 film of *Wuthering Heights* is fairly faithful to its source novel—well, at least the first half. Whereas Emily Brontë's novel is multi-generational, extending to the children of its star-crossed lovers, the film puts its full focus on the intense, but doomed passion of Cathy and Heathcliff. And what a focus! I've seen at least five-hundred romantic movies in my life, but no film has ever captured so precisely the power of passion to bring both blissful joy and utter desolation. And no other film has presented me, simultaneously, with a solid ethical warning against the dangers of unchecked passion and an invitation to throw off the falsely pious chains of society in pursuit of a higher kind of love that shatters all barriers.

While retaining all the key gothic elements of Brontë's dark and brooding novel, Ben Hecht and Charles MacArthur's excellent script tightens, simplifies, and unifies the tragic love affair. As Capra does in *Mr. Smith Goes to Washington* and Ford does in *The Grapes of Wrath*, Wyler succeeds in telling a universal, archetypal tale in a very concrete and particular setting. The moors, Penistone Crag, and the stately-but-forbidding façade of Wuthering Heights itself engrave themselves on the viewer's eye as firmly and as viscerally as the Senate chamber and the Lincoln Memorial in *Mr. Smith* or the barren, wind-swept plains in *The Grapes of Wrath*. And yet, the journeys, or, better, pilgrimages, that Jeff Smith, Tom Joad, and Cathy and Heathcliff go on transcend time and place.

I appreciate and enjoy Brontë's *Wuthering Heights* and Steinbeck's *The Grapes of Wrath,* but if I were forced to give up either the novels or the films, I would sacrifice the former to keep the latter. I know that is a strange and disturbing thing for an English professor to say, but the films have spoken to me and changed me in ways the novels could not do on their own. In the case of *Wuthering Heights,* the film, by alchemically condensing and purifying the plot down to its essentials, allowed me to absorb into my being the white hot passion that drives and deludes and destroys Cathy and Heathcliff.

As Golden Age Hollywood was so adept at doing, *Wuthering Heights* is told in the form of a lengthy flashback with dramatic book ends on either side. The opening scene is unforgettable, as a stranger (Lockwood), lost and alone on the cold and inhospitable moors, finds himself at the door of the colder, more inhospitable Wuthering Heights. With Lockwood as our eyes into this intriguing but ominous world, the camera invites us into a large sitting room utterly devoid of life. There are people in it, to be sure, but they are like figures made of wax. A pair of dogs rushes, barking, at the terrified Lockwood, but they are called off by a human voice more ferocious than the dogs. The voice comes from the aged Heathcliff (Laurence Olivier), his rigid immobility a striking contrast to the ferocity of his barked commands.

I was immediately hooked. Like Lockwood, I was both repelled by and drawn to Heathcliff, eager to unlock the mystery of this noble yet tormented man and his funereal home, which seemed to sag under the burden of a secret curse. As it turned out, neither Lockwood nor I had to wait long for some answers. In the middle of the night, the film's rich, orchestral score rises up in the darkness, and the camera peers at the sleeping Lockwood from the footboard of his bed. Then, as the music swells, the camera pushes *through* the footboard, as though it were crossing a threshold between two worlds. Ghostly cries emanate from the window and wake Lockwood from his sleep. Lured by the sound, he throws open the casement and sticks out his hand, only to feel a cold, clammy hand touch his. He yells for Heathcliff, who questions him gruffly until Lockwood tells him that the wraith that touched him identified itself as Cathy.

The moment Heathcliff hears the name Cathy, his former immobility gives way to hectic motion. He is now a spring of fervent energy that cannot be contained. He rushes out impulsively into the snow, leaving the door open behind him. Heathcliff gone, Ellen (Flora Robson), Cathy's old governess, sits down with Lockwood and explains to him that Cathy is dead. The logical, empirical Lockwood is taken aback. He does not, he insists, "believe in phantoms sobbing through the night" or "that life comes back once it's died and calls again to the living." "Maybe if I told you her story," Ellen responds gently, "you'd change your mind about the dead coming back. Maybe you'd know, as I do, that there is a force that brings them back if their hearts were wild enough in life."

And so begins the tale, sweeping us back to a happier time when Wuthering Heights was filled with warmth and joy. On a fateful day, the father of the sweet but tomboyish Cathy Earnshaw and her boorish brother Hindley returns from the city with a dark little urchin that he has adopted and given the name of Heathcliff. Though the selfish, bullying Hindley hates his new brother and torments him, Cathy and Heathcliff become fast friends, living out a romantic life of the imagination on the moors and calling Penistone crag their castle. When the father dies, Hindley, against his father's wishes, disinherits and demotes Heathcliff to a stable boy, forcing Cathy and Heathcliff to meet in secret.

As they grow, Heathcliff remains ever loyal to Cathy (Merle Oberon), enduring the cruelty of Hindley just to be near her. Cathy, on the other hand, swings back and forth between her passionate love for the moody, unkempt Heathcliff and her vain attraction to the beautiful but superficial world of the Grange, where she meets the aristocratic Edgar Linton (David Niven) and his pretty sister Isabella (Geraldine Fitzgerald). One moment she dismisses Heathcliff as a dirty stable boy that she is ashamed to be seen with; the next moment she dresses herself in rags and stands lovingly beside him beneath Penistone crag. "Heathcliff," she begs, "make the world stop right here; make everything stand still. Make the moors never change, and you and I never change." To which Heathcliff responds: "The moors and I will never change. Don't you, Cathy."

At this point, those familiar with the novel might think that I am being unfair to Cathy. After all, in Brontë's telling, the lovers are equally to blame for the wreck that they make of their own lives and the lives of those around them. Not so in the film, where Cathy is portrayed as more of a social climber obsessed with gaining material things, while Heathcliff is rendered less violent and evil with clearer motivations for the revenge he exacts. Why the changes? Because the film, despite its British cast, is decidedly American. That is to say, the script takes the side of the underdog Heathcliff and his refusal to kowtow to aristocratic airs and graces. Though this change makes the film less complex than the novel, it does make it more focused and less diffuse.

In the novel, the passion of Cathy and Heathcliff is simply too intense, twisted, and self-destructive to survive. In the film, we feel that their passion could be realized and even be healthy were it not thwarted again and again by the phoniness and hypocrisy of "polite" society, by Cathy's vanity and willfulness, and by the ill luck and tragic timing that hinder and obstruct their every chance at happiness. When I say that the timing is tragic, I mean that in the literal-literary sense. As in the best of the Greek tragedies, dramatic irony—in which we in the audience know things of which the protagonists are ignorant—leads to catastrophe. We cry out to Cathy and Heathcliff to warn them of the terrible mistakes they are about to make, but they cannot hear us. All we can do is watch powerlessly as they are pulled apart: he by his impatience and refusal to conform; she by her desire for a vain, empty world that she knows cannot satisfy her.

Wyler engraved this central dichotomy in my mind through concrete images of searing clarity. I said earlier that when the older Heathcliff runs out in the snow, he leaves the door open. This image reappears frequently, a visual metaphor for his impulsiveness, his tendency to begin things without finishing them and to flout all established norms and conventions. Again and again, we see Heathcliff appear out of nowhere in places he does not belong, poorly dressed and with the surly manners of a stable boy, yet demanding full acceptance by his social betters. This is a fault in him, but one that, the film suggests, could be moderated if only Cathy would be faithful to her true and better nature and stand by his side against the world.

But Cathy will not stay true to herself or to Heathcliff. She yearns for the high society of the Grange, a detailed set that Wyler always shows us through a window or reflected in a mirror. The Grange offers Cathy a world of beauty, but it is a mediated, artificial, choreographed world that lacks the directness and spontaneity of the moors. Nevertheless, when Heathcliff, thinking Cathy despises him, runs away to America in hopes of making a fortune that will satisfy her materialism, Cathy denies her passion for Heathcliff and marries the handsome but weak Edgar Linton.

The scene in which bad timing and tragic misunderstanding cause Heathcliff to flee is the key episode around which the entire film pivots. In the scene, Cathy confesses her feelings, good and bad, for Heathcliff to Ellen, while Heathcliff, unbeknown to Cathy but known to Ellen and us, eavesdrops from an adjoining room. As Heathcliff listens in the dark, Cathy tells Ellen that Heathcliff gets worse every day and that it would degrade her to marry him. Sadly, it is after hearing this that Heathcliff steals away into the night, his exit made known to us and Ellen, but not Cathy, by a flickering of the candles.

The tragedy of it all is that right after he leaves, Cathy's demeanor changes, and she shares what is truly on her heart. She knows that she does not belong among what Ellen calls "the Linton angels." She is only herself when she is with Heathcliff. Here are her heartbreaking words, made all the more so by the fact that Heathcliff just misses hearing them: "I don't think I belong in heaven, Ellen. I dreamt once I was there. I dreamt I went to heaven and that heaven didn't seem to be my home and I broke my heart with weeping to come back to earth, and the angels were so angry they flung me out in the middle of the heath on top of Wuthering Heights, and I woke up sobbing with joy. That's it, Ellen, I have no more business marrying Edgar Linton than I have of being in heaven ... everything [Heathcliff has] suffered, I've suffered; the little happiness I've known, he's known. He's more myself than I am. Whatever our souls are made of, his and mine are the same—and Linton's is as different as frost from fire. My one thought in life is Heathcliff. Ellen, I *am* Heathcliff. Oh,

Ellen, if everything in the world died and Heathcliff remained, life would still be full for me."

Both Cathy and Heathcliff are lost souls, wandering on the lonely moors of the world. They belong together; they are soul mates in the fullest sense of that overused phrase. They don't really belong anywhere *but* with each other. When Heathcliff, now rich from his mysterious dealings in America, returns to the Grange, Cathy praises him for looking so grand, exclaiming how much better things now are for him. "They used to be better," Heathcliff replies, his voice tinged with melancholy and regret. "Don't pretend," counters the seemingly self-assured Mrs. Linton, "life hasn't improved for you." "Life has ended for me," says Heathcliff, and then turns on Cathy for her coldness and self-deception: "How can you stand here beside me and pretend not to remember, not to know that my heart is breaking for you, that your face is the wonderful light burning in all this darkness."

Cathy knows in her heart that Heathcliff speaks the truth, but she holds up her sham marriage to Linton as a shield to protect her from that truth. "No, Heathcliff, I forbid it," she says with petulant desperation in her voice, "I'm not the Cathy you knew. I'm another man's wife and he loves me." Heathcliff's ardent response embodies the fullness of their all-consuming passion: "If he loved you with all the power of his soul for an entire lifetime, he couldn't love you as much as I do in a single day." That's one of the great lines in film, made even greater by the fact that Olivier, my choice for best actor of all time, delivers it in a single breath. Said by a lesser actor or in a less perfect script, the line might descend into melodrama. Here it stands as a statement of fact, a fact that Cathy wants to deny, but which she cannot deny without killing her soul.

And which Heathcliff also cannot deny—though he foolishly and cruelly tries to punish Cathy and fill the emptiness in his heart by marrying the poor innocent Isabella. Isabella is wise enough to see that Cathy enjoys dangling Heathcliff on a string, but foolish enough to think that she can make Heathcliff happy, can make him forget Cathy and give his love to her. For a brief period, it seems that Isabella might succeed, that she might be the medicine needed to bring respite to Heathcliff's angst-ridden soul. When she visits Heathcliff on the pretence that her horse is lame, Heathcliff sees through her ruse and reaches out to her with romantic words that melt her tender heart: "My dear, your horse is not lame, and it never was. You came to see me because you are lonely, because it *is* lonely sitting like an outsider in so happy a house as your brother's. Lonely riding on the moors with no one at your side. You won't be lonely anymore."

Perhaps, just perhaps Isabella and Heathcliff can find a shelter from their mutual loneliness in each other's arms. Empowered by what he thinks is his love for Isabella, Heathcliff even gains the courage to confront Cathy directly on what their love could be like: "If you ever looked at me once with what I know is in you, I would be your slave. Oh, Cathy, if your heart were only stronger than your dull fear of your God and the world, I would live silent and contented in your shadow. But no, you must destroy us both with that weakness you call virtue. You must keep me tormented with that cruelty you think so pious. You've been smug and pleased with my vile love of you. Haven't you? Well, after today, you can think of me as something more than Cathy's foolish and despairing lover. You can think of me as Isabella's husband. And be glad for *my* happiness, as I was for yours."

One of the things I love about the Golden Age of Hollywood is that its best films, though secular on the surface, often touch on great spiritual truths. Neither the novel nor the film of *Wuthering Heights* can properly be identified as a Christian work of art; yet, the film demonstrates great Christian insight in its exposing and skewering of false piety. It does not exactly promote a Christian vision for life, but it does reveal that the smug, negative virtues promoted at the Grange are miles away from that glorious life to the full to which Christ calls his followers (John 10:10). Cathy cannot find that life with Linton, but then neither can Heathcliff find it with Isabella. "Why isn't there the smell of heather in your hair?" Heathcliff asks Isabella in a poignant line that echoes with grief and regret. Isabella cannot fill the void in Heathcliff's tormented psyche.

As Cathy lies on her deathbed, Heathcliff explains to her, and to us, the real cause of their failed and broken love: "Oh Cathy, I never broke your heart; you broke it. Cathy, Cathy, you loved me. What right to throw love away for the poor fancy thing you felt for [Linton], for a handful of worldliness. Misery and death and all the evils that God and man could have hammered down could not have parted us. You did that alone. You wandered off like a greedy, wanton child to break your heart and mine." Cathy's sin is not passion but worldliness. She is like the seed in Jesus' Parable of the Sower that falls among the thorns; it begins well, but its potential fruitfulness is choked out by the "cares of this world, and the deceitfulness of riches, and the lusts of other things entering in" (Mark 4:19). The real problem with worldliness, both for Jesus and for the film, is not that it makes us too happy but that it crushes our happiness, not that it provokes desires that are too strong but desires that are too weak to satisfy the cravings of the human heart.

After Cathy dies, Heathcliff is left profoundly empty and alone. His knowledge of this impels him to cry out a forlorn, ultimately demonic prayer for her departed soul which is really a curse that he lays upon his own stranded soul: "I'll pray one prayer ... I'll repeat till my tongue stiffens. Catherine Earnshaw, may you not rest while I live on. I killed you. Haunt me then! Haunt your murderer! I know that ghosts have wandered on the earth. Be with me always—take any form—drive me mad! Only do not leave me in this dark alone where I cannot find you. I cannot live without my life! I cannot die without my soul!" Like Cain, Heathcliff will live on, but he will forever bear a mark that will separate him from his fellow man—and from himself. He will live as an outcast, cut off from fellowship, but he prefers this self-exile to a world utterly devoid of her ghost.

Or, as Ellen explains to Lockwood after sharing with him, and us, the full story, not Cathy's ghost, but her "love, stronger than time itself, still sobbing for its unlived days and uneaten bread." Heathcliff, who has been out in the cold searching for Cathy while we have warmed ourselves by the fire, never returns. His body is discovered on the moors, frozen to death beneath Penistone crag. But this is Hollywood in her prime, and so our final image is not of Heathcliff's dead body or of the slowly-decaying Wuthering Heights, but of a pair of ghosts, clasped arm and arm, making their way to the castle that stands, in their eternal imagination, atop Penistone crag.

Each time I re-watch *Wuthering Heights,* I am shocked anew by the bad choices of Cathy and Heathcliff, and yet, at the same time, I feel that neither of them could have acted differently. An internal destiny seems to drive them forward to their doom. As I listen to Ellen tell her tale again, I am overwhelmed by the same emotions I feel when I read many of the stories in the Old Testament—a sense of sadness and despair for what we make of ourselves and our world, a longing to turn back the clock and make the *right* decision this time. And yet, mingled with that emotion, comes a tragic enlightenment—what Aristotle called a catharsis—that this is the way that it must be, that this is the condition of our lives on this broken, melancholy earth.

And with that wrestling comes another wrestling. On the one hand, I feel grateful to Cathy and Heathcliff for braving the extremes of passion on my behalf, so that I won't have to; the very waters that drown them point me back to the shore of stability, societal norms, and sanity. On the other hand, they beckon me, just a little, to test those waters, to not be afraid of life and passion, to know that the petty laws and games of society are not enough, are but so many masks that we hide behind.

I think the collective experience of the fifth-century BC Athenians who watched the tragedies of Aeschylus, Sophocles, and Euripides is not so far removed from my own experience watching *Wuthering Heights,* especially with a group of college students who have signed up for my film class. There is the same feeling of awe and wonder in the face of necessity, the same communal weeping at the predicament of man. Though modern films, shot as they are on location rather than in sound stages, are more realistic in the narrow, literal sense of the word, *Wuthering Heights,* like Oedipus or Antigone, is more believable because we do not even think to question it. All three pull us into their artistic world, seducing and compelling us by their archetypal power and mythopoeic force.

When we leave the theater, we don't question whether what we just saw was true. It *is* true. That is because, rather than try to pose as life, as most modern films do, it constructs for itself its own unique microcosm.

Far from a mere copy of life, it is life remade, recast in a new form to operate by means of universal laws that transcend any one time or place. Aristotle would say it was a plot rather than a story, something with a beginning, a middle, and an end that moves forward in accordance with necessity and probability to its appointed telos, its purposeful end.

Wuthering Height has been for me something far greater and more lasting than an entertaining melodrama. It is life lived at its most intense, with a pair of doomed lovers that I cannot save but who nevertheless haunt my dreams as Cathy's ghost haunts the murderer who is also the best and deepest part of herself.

Fun Facts for the Fans

- *Wuthering Heights* was nominated for best picture, director, screenplay, actor (Olivier), supporting actress (Fitzgerald), music, and art direction, but up against *Gone with the Wind*, it only won for Gregg Toland's moody photography.
- *Wuthering Heights* was produced by an independent producer named Samuel Goldwyn who financed all of his pictures out of his own pocket. Although he only worked briefly at MGM, he contributed the "G" to Metro-Goldwyn-Mayer.
- After William Wyler closed up production on *Wuthering Heights* and Olivier and Oberon had left the set, Goldwyn himself shot the ghostly finale with stand-ins for Olivier and Oberon. He was able to do this since we only see the backs of the ghosts. Wyler was opposed, but I think Goldwyn made the right call!
- The screenplay was co-written by Ben Hecht, a critic and newspaperman who was lured to Hollywood by large paychecks for little work. In addition to bringing wit to the comedies and dramas of the Golden Age (especially *Nothing Sacred*), he wrote the screenplays for two Hitchcock pictures: *Spellbound* and *Notorious*.

- In the months following the release of the film, hospitals reported that as many as one-third of newborn girls were named Cathy.
- Though Olivier and Oberon convey intense passion on the screen, they were both deeply in love at the time with their soon-to-be spouses: Vivien Leigh (famous for playing Scarlett O'Hara) and Alexander Korda (one of England's greatest movie producers). Interestingly, both Oberon and Leigh were born in India.
- It was Wyler who took the Shakespearean stage actor Olivier and taught him how to act for the screen; Olivier won his Oscar for portraying Hamlet.
- Edgar Linton is played by David Niven, but he is so young, some of his fans might not recognize him. His most defining role would be in *Around the World in Eighty Days*, where he played Phileas Fogg.

Other Films to Watch

Best films of Laurence Olivier: *Fire over England* (in Elizabethan England with Vivien Leigh), *The Divorce of Lady X* (sparkling romantic comedy with Merle Oberon), *Rebecca* (see next chapter), *Pride and Prejudice* (as Mr. Darcy), *Lady Hamilton* (as Admiral Nelson having affair with Vivien Leigh), *Henry V, Hamlet, Richard III, Othello* (in the title roles), *Carrie* (from Theodore Dreiser's depressing novel, *Sister Carrie*), *The Prince and the Showgirl* (with Marilyn Monroe), *Spartacus* (as Crassus), *The Entertainer* (as an old vaudeville star), *Khartoum* (as a charismatic African Muslim holy man and general), *Sleuth* (a clever, two-man whodunit with Michael Caine), *Marathon Man* (as a Nazi), *The Seven Percent Solution* (as the evil Moriarty), *Jesus of Nazareth* (as Nicodemus; TV miniseries), *The Boys from Brazil* (as a Nazi-hunter), *Dracula* (as Van Helsing), *Clash of the Titans* (as Zeus), *Brideshead Revisited* (as Lord Marchmain; TV miniseries).

Best films of William Wyler: **Dodsworth* (from the acclaimed novel), **Dead End* (social realism with Humphrey Bogart), *Jezebel* (Bette Davis version of *Gone with the Wind*), *The Letter* (from Somerset Maugham), **The Westerner* (about Judge Roy Bean), **The Little Foxes* (from a great play about a conniving Southern family), *Mrs. Miniver* (British civilians in World War II, won first Oscar), **The Best Years of our Lives* (vets come home, second Oscar), *The Heiress* (from the Henry James novel), *Detective Story* (modern Greek tragedy with Kirk Douglas), *Carrie* (from a Theodore Drieser novel), *Roman Holiday* (beautiful romantic comedy), *The Desperate Hours* (tense film about killer holed up in middle-class home), *The Friendly Persuasion* (about the Quakers), *The Big Country* (excellent Western), *Ben-Hur* (greatest of all epics; third Oscar), *The Collector* (excellent film but very depressing), *How to Steal a Million* (entertaining caper film), *Funny Girl* (musical biopic of Fanny Brice, played by Barbra Streisand).

In addition to producing the Wyler films listed above with a *, Goldwyn was responsible for such entertaining family films as *The Kid from Spain* and *Roman Scandals* (both with Eddie Cantor), *The Hurricane* (tropical disaster), *Stella Dallas* (famous weeper with Barbara Stanwyck), *The Adventures of Marco Polo* (with Gary Cooper), *Ball of Fire* (screwball comedy), *The Pride of the Yankees* (Cooper as Lou Gehrig), *The Kid from Brooklyn* and *The Secret Life of Walter Mitty* (both with Danny Kaye), *The Bishop's Wife* (angel helps bishop), *Enchantment* (a house tells its story), *Hans Christian Anderson* (with Danny Kaye), *Guys and Dolls* (in which Marlon Brando sings quite well!).

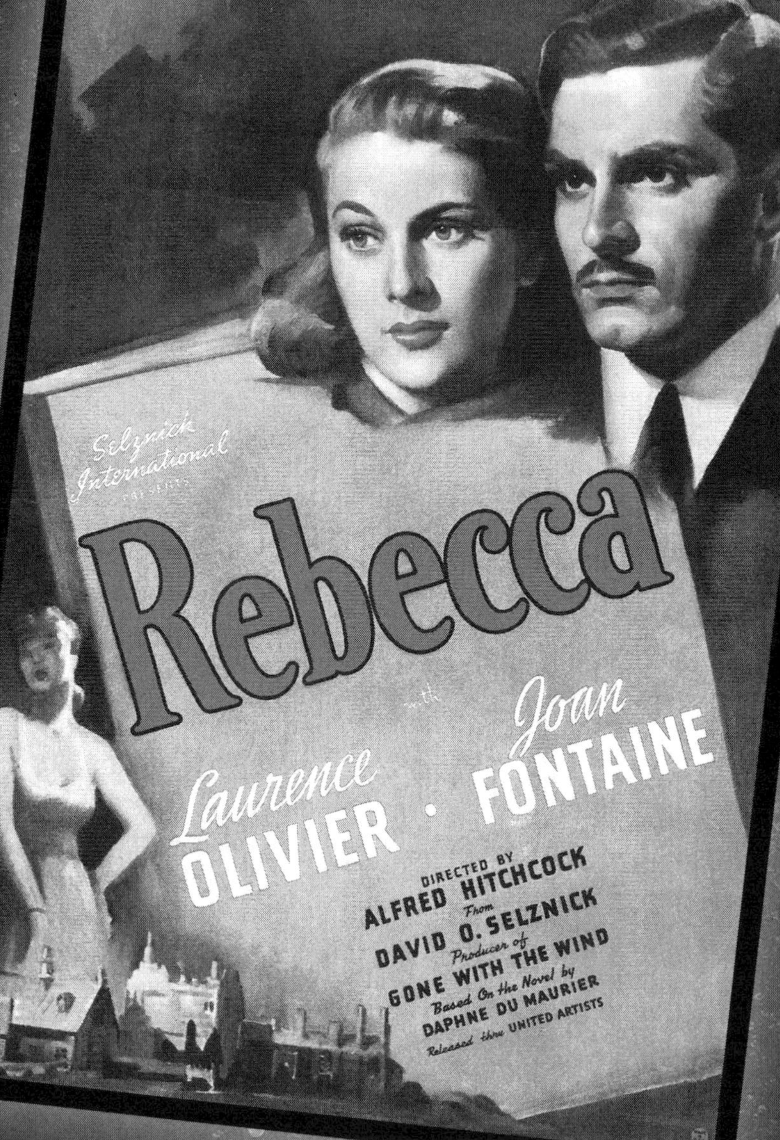
Selznick International presents
Rebecca
with
Laurence OLIVIER
Joan FONTAINE
DIRECTED BY ALFRED HITCHCOCK
From DAVID O. SELZNICK
Producer of GONE WITH THE WIND
Based On the Novel by DAPHNE DU MAURIER
Released thru UNITED ARTISTS

REBECCA

(SELZNICK; 1940; ALFRED HITCHCOCK)

One year after *Wuthering Heights,* Laurence Olivier returned to the screen in another gothic romance, this time based on Daphne du Maurier's 1938 novel *Rebecca.* Just as the former film embodies the dual gifts of its meddling independent producer (Samuel Goldwyn) and headstrong director (William Wyler), so the latter embodies the dual gifts of its even more meddling independent producer (David O. Selznick) and even more headstrong director (Alfred Hitchcock). Hitchcock would henceforth make it his practice to base his films on second-rate novels, in great part because Selznick forced him to stay extremely faithful to du Maurier's beloved novel. Though I feel a stronger allegiance to Hitch than to Selznick, in the case of *Rebecca,* I think Selznick got it right.

Thanks to the serendipitous combination of Hitchcock's cinematic genius and Selznick's ability to smoothly and effectively transfer literary novels to the screen, the film version of *Rebecca* manages to encapsulate, in just over two hours, every virtue, passion, and nuance of a complex, psychological, four-hundred page novel. Indeed, though I am a fan of the novel, I would, as in the previous two chapters, be willing to sacrifice it for the film for the simple reason that the movie captures all that is best about the novel and then adds its own overwhelming visual power. Every time I watch the film, and I never get tired of doing so, whether alone or with my students, my entire being is drawn in to its melodramatic world of heightened but literate passion and intrigue.

Whereas Olivier's moody Heathcliff lives and moves in the borders of society, his equally moody Max de Winter must survive, physically, emotionally, and spiritually, in the midst of an aristocratic, high society world from which he has become disconnected. Indeed, he is also disconnected from us as viewers, for the story is told, not from his vantage point, but from that of Joan Fontaine, who plays the nameless girl whom Max takes as his second wife, one year after the death of Rebecca in a drowning accident.

The novel is told in the form of a flashback from the first person point-of-view of the second Mrs. de Winter. The film begins the same, with a haunting voice-over narration from Fontaine. Once we enter the narrative, however, we completely forget, as we do not when we read the novel, that we are watching a flashback and experience it as though it were happening in the present. Still, despite the camera's ability to move where it will, we "see" everything from the perspective of the shy, frightened Fontaine. Her opening narration, like most of the dialogue in Robert E. Sherwood and Joan Harrison's brilliant screenplay, is lifted word-for-word from the novel and then edited down, always selecting those phrases and sentences that are most vivid, concrete, and memorable.

Here are the strange, supple, poetic words that invite us into the film: "Last night I dreamt I went to Manderley again. It seemed to me I stood by the iron gate leading to the drive, and for a while I could not enter for the way was barred to me. Then, like all dreamers, I was possessed of a sudden with supernatural powers and passed like a spirit through the barrier before me. The drive wound away in front of me, twisting and turning as it had always done.

"But as I advanced, I was aware that a change had come upon it. Nature had come into her own again, and little by little had encroached upon the drive with long, tenacious fingers. On and on wound the poor thread that had once been our drive, and finally there was Manderley. Manderley, secretive and silent. Time could not mar the perfect symmetry of those walls. Moonlight can play odd tricks upon the fancy, and suddenly, it seemed to me that light came from the windows. And then a cloud came upon the moon and hovered an instant like a dark hand before a face. The illusion went with it. I looked upon a desolate shell with no whisper of the past about its staring walls."

I quote the opening narration in full, for it sets the mood so perfectly, conveying the unique, elegiac atmosphere of memory and regret that hangs, brooding, over the film and that seeps into the subconscious of the viewer, prodding and troubling him long after the film ends. But the words alone do not have that effect. As the words hover in the air, Hitchcock provides us with a long, graceful, almost hypnotic tracking shot that moves, like a phantom, through the iron gates and along a winding path. The viewer feels, quite literally, as though he were traveling down the grooves of memory into a primal place punctuated by eerie trees and foliage seen through the mist. Suddenly the camera turns and we see the mansion of Manderlay. It hits us with the force of a revelation, as it will later when Fontaine is taken there in Max's car.

For a moment, Manderley is held in a long shot, as though frozen in time. Then Hitchcock's fluid camera begins to move again, climbing over trees toward a lit window. We in the audience feel as if we are dreaming ourselves, wanting, like the narrator, to find life in this dim, shadowy ruin. But we realize, as she does, that no one can really go back to the past. And so we nod our heads as she finishes her narration: "We can never go back to Manderley again. That much is certain. But sometimes, in my dreams, I do go back to the strange days of my life which began for me in the South of France."

As she speaks the last sentence, the camera cuts to a raging sea and changes its direction. Thus far, the camera has moved horizontally along the ground. Now, it moves vertically, from the shore line up a steep cliff, causing the reader to hold his breath. At the very top, on the edge of the dizzying cliff, the camera discovers Max, and cuts to a close-up of his anguished face. Fontaine appears behind him, and the camera cuts back and forth between their faces, telling us without words that Max is contemplating suicide and that Fontaine realizes this but is at first too frightened to speak. Film technique just doesn't get better than this, though here the camera work and editing do not exist as ends in themselves. Rather, they prepare the viewer for a journey that will take them into the past even as it tries to break from its deadly grip.

It will be some time before we see Manderley again, with its dark secrets and its forbidding grandeur. The opening sequences of the film take place in sunny Monte Carlo where the viewer is treated to a warm romantic comedy with a fairy tale ending. Fontaine (identified in the novel as twenty-one years old) is in Monte as a traveling companion to the wealthy but vulgar Mrs. Van Hopper when she meets the handsome, dashing, very rich Max (who is forty two). The audience cannot help but fall in love with the clumsy, self-effacing Fontaine and to cheer on Max as he defends her from the pompous Hopper. Like her, we are drawn to Max, even as we are confused and a bit frightened by his dark and inexplicable mood swings. For a moment, it seems Fontaine will return to America with Hopper, but Max proposes in the nick of time, managing, quite deliciously, to humiliate Hopper in the process. Our Cinderella will be rescued by the prince from her ugly stepmother and will be swept off to live in his castle.

Well, not exactly. Hitchcock manages to make the huge cavernous Manderley feel like a suffocating prison, or, yet again, like a labyrinth from which Fontaine cannot escape. Worse yet, we and Fontaine discover together that this elegant prison is run by an even uglier, more sinister stepmother than Mrs. Van Hopper: the skeletal Mrs. Danvers who used to be the first Mrs. de Winter's personal maid and who runs the house as if she were the mistress, holding it in stasis as a sort of mausoleum to the dead Rebecca.

In case we miss the connection between Hopper and Danvers, Hitch clarifies it for us through a subtle use of the camera. After announcing to Hopper that he is about to marry Fontaine, Max runs off, leaving her with Hopper, as he will do again and again with Danvers. The moment Max is gone, Hopper turns on Fontaine, telling her that she doesn't have it in her to be the lady of a great house. Then, she scans her eyes up and down Fontaine's slender frame and exclaims with bemused contempt: "Hmm! Mrs. de Winter!" Both Hopper and the camera "check out" Fontaine and find her wanting. She will never be able to pull this off.

Shortly thereafter, Fontaine is introduced to the house staff of Manderley, with Danvers standing erect and rigid at the center. Fontaine, shaking nervously, approaches Danvers. She wants to look calm and self-assured, but instead, she clumsily drops her glove on the floor. Without relaxing the rigidity of her spine, Danvers bends over to pick up the glove. As she rises to give it back to Fontaine, both she and the camera scan

Fontaine's slender frame from the bottom of her feet to the top of her head. Danvers does not say what she is thinking—"ha, you little fool, you will be no match for me"—but we know she it thinking it because of the direct parallel to the previous scene with Hopper.

This first exchange between Fontaine and Danvers is taken from the novel, but Hitch adds one detail that intensifies Fontaine's humiliation. As Max and Fontaine approach Manderley in a convertible, it begins to rain. By the time they enter the house, Fontaine is soaked to the skin, looking more like a wet puppy than the new Mrs. de Winter and the mistress of Manderley. This added humiliation makes the film work even better, for it gives us great sympathy and empathy for Fontaine, who is so obviously out of her league. We want her to succeed, to defeat Danvers and draw Max out of his angst and depression. But how can she: how can she resist both Danvers and the ghost of Rebecca, whose presence haunts every inch of the house? And how can she help Max forget the first wife he adored so passionately and find strength in her?

There have been other films that have worked through a similar dynamic, but none of them have so skillfully conveyed the gothic power of a dead past to haunt the living—a dynamic made all the more unique and compelling by the fact that the haunting of Rebecca is not physical, but emotional, spiritual, and psychological. As a stand in for Rebecca, Danvers shadows Fontaine wherever she goes. We rarely see her enter a room; she just appears as if out of a nightmare. The light, jittery Fontaine will think she is alone in a room, only to turn and find the immobile Danvers at her elbow.

When she is not being shadowed by Danvers, Fontaine is left alone and isolated. Hitch conveys this isolation most effectively in a purely cinematic episode. The scene begins with an extreme close-up of a dinner napkin bearing the initials "R de W" on it. Then, in one slow, graceful movement, the camera pulls back and spirals around to reveal a formal dining room table with Max at one end and Fontaine at the other. From there it cuts to an exterior long shot of Manderley. There is no dialogue in this brief scene, but none is needed, for the camera tells us all we need to know: Manderley is a cold, lonely place, elegant and grand, but bereft of warmth and intimacy. The love between Max and Fontaine cannot thrive in such a stately tomb. If they stay, their love will be strangled.

At one point, Max and Fontaine quarrel, with Max wondering if he was not being selfish when he brought Fontaine to Manderley. He knows he is difficult to live with and that Fontaine should have married someone her own age. Fontaine insists their marriage is a success and that they are terribly happy, but she knows it isn't true. The dialogue for this scene is lifted directly out of the novel, but Hitch frames it in a different way. Just before they quarrel, they are watching home videos of their honeymoon—a honeymoon that is skipped over in both the novel and film. The brief joy they had between leaving Monte and arriving in Manderley is nothing now but flickering images on a screen, a ghost of happiness that cannot stand up against the stronger ghost of Rebecca.

As she slowly gains more confidence, Fontaine decides that the best way to purge Rebecca's ghost is to throw a grand ball and dress herself in a gown that will rekindle Max's love for her and help him to forget the past. She asks advice of Danvers who shows her an old family portrait on the wall. The figure in the portrait wears a stunning gown that Danvers says she has heard Max speak of with admiration. Fontaine immediately sets out to have an exact replica of the gown made. She is filled with energy and excitement, and we in the audience experience it with her. We so much want her to impress the moody Max and prove to be the heroine we know she has the potential to be.

Finally, the evening arrives. As Max waits, his back turned, at the foot of the grand staircase, Fontaine floats down in her Cinderella gown. We hold our breaths, hoping, along with Fontaine, that Max will be overjoyed when he sees her. Finally, the past will be overcome and forgotten, and our two lovers will live happily every after. In the final seconds before Max turns to see her, we notice shocked looks on the faces of the people beside him. One even exclaims under his breath, "Rebecca." Then Max turns. His face lights up for a moment and then is overcome by anguish and rage. He screams at her to take off the dress, which, we later learn, had been the very dress that Rebecca had worn on the night of her fatal boating accident.

Distraught, confused, and burning with humiliation, Fontaine runs upstairs and enters the room that once belonged to Rebecca. She will take on the ghost face-to-face. Instead, she is met by Danvers who, in one of the most grotesque, psychologically-disturbing scenes in movie history, gives her a "tour" of Rebecca's room. She invites Fontaine to sit down by the vanity while she mimics her evening ritual with Rebecca, moving a brush up and down behind Fontaine's head as if she were brushing Rebecca's hair. The usually stiff Danvers then bends down to open Rebecca's lingerie drawers. She invites Fontaine to caress Rebecca's silken underwear and nightgown, asking her if she has ever seen anything more beautiful and delicate. Fontaine cannot help but do as she is bid. Danvers is clearly mad, consumed by her homoerotic passion for Rebecca, but Fontaine is unable to break from her spell. The past is too strong.

Danvers leads her to the window and whispers in her ear that it would be so much easier for her and everyone else if she ended her life with a simple jump. "Why don't you?" Danvers repeats again and again, as if she were the fork-tongued serpent in Eden. Another second and Fontaine will succumb to the repressed terror that haunts the room and breathes through the skeletal lips of Danvers. But she is saved by the sound of canon fire that wakes her from the trance into which Danvers has lulled her. She runs down the stairs and out of the house to a cottage by the sea that belonged to Rebecca. There she meets Max who finally tells her the full, ugly truth.

I still remember vividly the first time I watched *Rebecca* in college. Since I had not yet read the novel, Max's words left me shocked and breathless. And yet, such is the power of the film, that I re-experience that same breathless shock each time I re-watch it. We, like Fontaine, have believed that Max had loved Rebecca with all of his heart and that her death had left him incapable of loving another woman. But we have been deceived. Max did not love Rebecca; he hated her.

Though Rebecca had beauty, brains, and breeding, Max explains, "she was incapable of love or tenderness or decency." Only four days after marrying the naïve, love-struck Max, as they stand together by the edge of the cliff in Monte Carlo where Fontaine met him, she reveals to him all the details of her vile and venial nature. Then she proceeds to make a deal with him. If he remains married to her, she will be, on the outside, the perfect wife and mistress of Manderley, will convince everyone that they are the ideal couple. Max, not wanting to soil his family's name with divorce, accepts this deal with the devil, but, from that day forward, he never knows a moment's peace or happiness. While all of high society thinks that Max is the luckiest man in the world, he suffers silently in a hell of his own making.

Finally, after several years of torment, Max decides to confront Rebecca and her lover in the cottage where she usually holds her adulterous trysts. He expects she will be with her lover, but she is alone, a pale look on her otherwise beautiful face. Slowly, dispassionately, she confesses to Max that she is going to have a child, a child that is not his but that she will raise as his child. She will be a perfect mother to the boy, just as she has been a perfect wife to Max. And when Max dies, the bastard will inherit all his wealth and prestige. What a marvelous joke it will be, she laughs, and then asks Max, her voice thick with scorn, why he doesn't kill her right now. Surely he wants to. In a fit of passion, Max loses his head and pushes Rebecca away from him. She falls and hits her head, killed instantly by the blow. Max, in a panic, takes her body and puts it in the cabin of her sailboat. Then he opens the water cocks and sets the boat adrift, knowing that it will be dragged under the sea with Rebecca's body in tow.

As Max tells his story in voice over, Hitch replays the full incident visually, but as if the camera were Max. That means we do not see Max, but we also do not see Rebecca. We only see the cottage with its physical objects, climaxing with the fishing tackle on to which Rebecca has her fatal fall. We are inside Max's mind as he replays the incident—as he has, in fact, replayed the incident again and again for the last year. The scene is as dreamy, unreal, and inescapable as the opening tracking shot that guides us to the ruins of Manderley. The past cannot be killed; it is too strong. It plays itself out ad infinitum in a traumatic repetition compulsion in the theater of Max's mind.

Max had escaped justice because, by coincidence, another drowned boat had been discovered with the body of an unnamed, unclaimed girl (like Fontaine!) whom Max had falsely identified as that of Rebecca. But now, this very evening, Rebecca's boat has resurfaced, and Max will have to face the police he had eluded a year earlier. Rebecca, it seems has won. He has found temporary happiness with Fontaine, but Rebecca's dead fingers have reached out of their watery grave to drag him back down.

After this point, the film, admittedly, gets bogged down in plot, as an inquest is held and Max is almost blackmailed by Rebecca's lover, Favell (George Sanders). In the end, however, it is discovered that Rebecca was not pregnant but was dying of cancer, a fact unknown to everyone, including Favell and Danvers. In light of this new information the court decides that Rebecca's death was a suicide and that Max is innocent, though the audience realizes that Rebecca had purposely angered Max in hopes that he would kill her, thus ending her pain and destroying Max at one blow.

Despite the plot-heavy ending, Hitch keeps us interested by what he does with Fontaine, who, once she learns the truth from Max, gains strength and confidence. Her clothing even becomes darker and "smarter," and she wisely warns Max that he must not lose his temper at the inquest. Indeed, when Max *does* start getting agitated at the judge's questions, she fakes a fainting fit to prevent him from incriminating himself. Our shy and nervous girl has grown up, and she will fight tooth and nail to defend her husband.

This is a good thing, but it is also sad. As Max says to her with dejection in his voice: "Ah, it's gone forever, that funny, young, lost look I loved. It won't ever come back. I killed that when I told you about Rebecca. It's gone. In a few hours, you've grown so much older." How sad that, even if we defeat the past, it always takes its toll. Max and Fontaine have escaped from Rebecca, but they will bear the scars forever.

In the final scene, Max drives back to Manderley, fearing for Fontaine's safety. As he turns toward the house, he sees what he thinks is the Northern Lights. But it is not. It is Manderley on fire, set ablaze by Danvers, who refuses to allow Max and Fontaine to be the happy master and mistress of what she considers Rebecca's property. Though Fontaine escapes from the blaze, the house is consumed, together with Danvers, a fit metaphor for the twisted passion of Rebecca.

The final image that Hitch leaves us with is of a burning pillowcase on top of Rebecca's bed that bears the initial R. As the fire moves toward the center of the case, obliterating the R, we sense that the ghost of Rebecca has finally been exorcised: "all passion spent," to quote the last line of Milton's *Samson Agonistes*.

Still, the gothic element of the story will not allow for a conventional happy ending, though the film is less dark than the novel. The novel, that never lets us forget its flashback structure, makes it clear that, after the burning of Manderley, Max and Fontaine have lived a nomadic life all over Europe, unable to find a new home or any real stability. The film leaves this out, allowing us to harbor some hope for our couple. And yet, the viewer senses, even as Max and Fontaine embrace, that we cannot simply shrug off the darkness around us. Max and Fontaine have matured, but they must dwell now outside the Garden in that vale of tears that lies to the east of Eden.

Fun Facts for the Fans

- Though nominated for best script, direction, music, actress (Fontaine), actor (Olivier), supporting actress (Anderson), art design, and editing, *Rebecca* only took away two: for best picture and photography.
- The Oscar for best picture went to Selznick the producer, not Hitchcock the director. Regrettably, Hitch would never win a non-honorary Oscar of his own.
- Before becoming, like Goldwyn, an independent producer, Selznick was put in charge of his own film unit at MGM. This was partly granted because he married Louis B. Mayer's daughter, whom he later divorced to marry the actress Jennifer Jones. At MGM, he was teased with the phrase: the son-in-law also rises.
- Selznick's brother Myron essentially invented the role of the Hollywood agent, causing great strife to the studios, which were thereby forced to pay their stars higher salaries. Interestingly, Myron Selznick was Hitch's agent!

- Hitchcock, who had a love-hate relationship with Selznick, found ways to parody his old boss in two of his later pictures. In *Rear Window*, the villain played by Raymond Burr looks like a double of Selznick. In *North by Northwest*, Cary Grant says the O in his name, Roger O. Thornhill, means nothing, but gives him the initials ROT; Selznick added the O to his own name to lend it more gravitas.
- Hitch makes his signature cameo appearance near the end of the film outside of a telephone booth. He is a bit hard to spot.
- Although *Rebecca* is very faithful to the novel, the film did make one major change to satisfy the censorship board. In the movie, Max's killing of Rebecca is accidental; in the novel, Max, purposely prodded on by Rebecca, shoots her dead! The fact that the bullet does not hit any bones and therefore leaves no trace allows for the same resolution in the novel and the film.
- Joan Fontaine was the sister of Olivia de Havilland, who would be nominated for *Gone with the Wind* and go on to win best actress Oscars for *To Each His Own* and *The Heiress*. Though Fontaine did not win the Oscar for *Rebecca*, she was awarded the Oscar the following year for her performance in Hitch's *Suspicion*.
- Fontaine, who was born in Britain but grew up in America, excelled at the archetype of the shy English rose, which she played to perfection in *Jane Eyre*.
- In 1939, Hitchcock directed an atmospheric, well-cast, but rather stilted version of du Maurier's novel *Jamaica Inn*. Good films were also made of her novels *Frenchman's Creek* (with Joan Fontaine) and *My Cousin Rachel* (with Olivia de Havilland and a young Richard Burton in his first American movie). Hitchcock's *The Birds* was based on one of du Maurier's short stories.
- Daphne du Maurier was the granddaughter of George du Maurier, whose novel *Trilby* introduced the character of Svengali, a maestro

who exerts a mesmeric power over his pupil. Danvers plays Svengali to Fontaine's nervous character.

- Dame Judith Anderson, like Sir Laurence Olivier, would go on to be knighted; she would later play a Vulcan in *Star Trek III: The Search for Spock*!
- George Sanders who plays Rebecca's oily lover Favell, was one of Hollywood's best character actors. He made a career playing sophisticated but cynical bad guys—including winning an Oscar for *All About Eve* and voicing Shere Kahn in Disney's *Jungle Book*—though he also played the James-Bond-like Saint on TV.
- Sanders committed suicide at age 65, leaving this note: "Dear world, I am leaving you because I am bored. I am leaving you with your own worries. Good luck."
- Nigel Bruce, who plays Max's brother-in-law, is best known for playing Dr. Watson to Basil Rathbone's Sherlock Holmes.

Other Films to Watch

Hitchcock's best British films are *The Lodger* (silent movie about Jack the Ripper), *Blackmail* (first English sound picture), *The Man Who Knew Too Much* (spies kidnap a child), *The Thirty-Nine Steps* (innocent hero on the run ends up handcuffed to heroine), and *The Lady Vanishes* (all filmed on a train). His best American films, after *Rebecca,* include *Foreign Correspondent* (encourages America to enter World War II), *Suspicion* (Fontaine thinks her husband Grant is trying to kill her), *Saboteur* (ends with man falling off Statue of Liberty), *Shadow of a Doubt* (beloved uncle may be killer), *Lifeboat* (all filmed in a tiny lifeboat), *Spellbound* (plays with Freudian psychoanalysis and includes a dream sequence by Salvador Dali), *Notorious* (mature love story between spies), *Rope* (experimental film shot in long takes with no editing), *Strangers on a Train* (two men swap murders), *Dial M for Murder* (with lovely Grace Kelly), *Rear Window* (man with broken leg witnesses a crime), *To Catch a Thief*

(Grant as ex-cat burglar), *The Trouble with Harry* (black comedy with an ever-moving corpse), *The Man Who Knew Too Much* (remake of British film), *Vertigo* (the most artistic, personal film to come out of the studio system), *North by Northwest* (breezy spy caper with Grant atop Mount Rushmore), *Psycho* (with a killing in a shower that caused viewers to take baths instead), *The Birds* (apocalyptic tale of birds gone amok), and *Marnie* (psychologically-disturbed heroine).

In addition to *Rebecca,* Selznick produced fine film versions of Dickens's *David Copperfield* and *A Tale of Two Cities,* Twain' s *The Adventures of Tom Sawyer,* Tolstoy's *Anna Karenina* (well, just the central love affair), Frances Hodgson Burnett's *Little Lord Fauntleroy,* and Margaret Mitchell's *Gone with the Wind.* His last film, an adaptation of Hemingway's *A Farewell to Arms* proved, sadly, to be unsuccessful. In addition to these adaptations, Selznick produced a series of highly literate, splendidly acted films; they include *Dinner at Eight, A Star is Born, The Prisoner of Zenda, Nothing Sacred, Intermezzo, Since You Went Away, Spellbound, Duel in the Sun,* and *Portrait of Jennie.*

FRANK CAPRA'S GREATEST PRODUCTION

RONALD COLMAN AND A NOTABLE CAST

LOST HORIZON

with
JANE WYATT
JOHN HOWARD • MARGO
THOMAS MITCHELL • EDWARD EVERETT HORTON
ISABEL JEWELL • H.B.WARNER • SAM JAFFE

FROM THE NOVEL BY JAMES HILTON
SCREEN PLAY BY ROBERT RISKIN
A COLUMBIA PICTURE

LOST HORIZON

(COLUMBIA; 1937; FRANK CAPRA)

Though I had seen *Mr. Smith Goes to Washington, It's a Wonderful Life,* and *It Happened One Night* many times before I graduated college, I did not see Capra's *Lost Horizon* until my graduate years. I saw it at a party on a small television, and, despite the fact that most of the folks at the party seemed only casually entertained, I found myself deeply moved and utterly captivated, catapulted into a world of wonder and awe I had never thought existed. It was as if the party and the room itself had disappeared, and I was living in and through the film. Now the odd thing was that, when I was a teenager, I had seen on television a flat, tedious musical remake of *Lost Horizon* (1973) with truly awful songs. Still, despite its many weaknesses, I had retained a dim recognition of being intrigued by its premise. That dim recognition returned as I watched the original Capra film, helping me to scale the heights to the hidden utopia of Shangri-La.

The film is based on James Hilton's bestselling 1933 novel in which four people crash land in the inaccessible mountains of Tibet, only to be rescued/kidnapped and taken to an unknown lamasery called Shangri-La. There, in the temperate valley of the Blue Moon, shielded on four sides from the elements by embracing mountains, they encounter a gentler form of life far from the madness and strife of the outside world. Diet, climate, and a meditative life free from anxiety have gifted the inhabitants of Shangri-La with healthy and extremely long lives. The lamasery is overseen by a High Lama who is actually a priest, Father Perrault, who stumbled his way into the valley over two hundred years earlier. Since that time, the High Lama has shaped Shangri-La, not only into a community of peace and brotherhood, but a repository for all that is good, true, and beautiful in the history of mankind—but he is in need of a successor.

Lost Horizon is a short novel, barely half the size of *Rebecca*, yet Capra and his long-time writer Robert Riskin transform it into a screen epic like no other. Though most of the epics I had seen revolved around the history of a turbulent time—the rise of the Roman Empire or the Crusades, the American Civil War or the Russian Revolution, World War I or World War II—*Lost Horizon* took me outside of history to a place that offered an alternative to the violent march of armies and nations and ideologies. It was a fantasy, but one grounded in man's potential for goodness that drew me back to the lost Garden of Eden, even as it urged me forward to the promised New Jerusalem. Indeed, it set off a yearning within me for another kind of life, for a higher mode of being that always seems to lie just out of reach. The novel *does* inspire some of that yearning, but Capra-Riskin's success at simultaneously Americanizing and universalizing Hilton's vision makes it more appealing and, on the emotional-spiritual level, more achievable.

For me, the appeal of the film, its ability to tap directly my archetypal desires for an earthy paradise, begins immediately with a series of titles that appear on the screen in the form of pages in a grand book: "In these days of wars and rumors of wars, haven't you ever dreamed of a place where there was peace and security, where living was not a struggle but a lasting delight? Of course you have. So has every man since Time began. Always the same dream. Sometimes he calls it Utopia, sometimes the Fountain of Youth, sometimes merely 'that little chicken farm.' One man had such a dream and saw it come true. He was Robert Conway, England's 'Man of the East'—soldier, diplomat, public hero."

From that beguiling opening that always lulls me into a state of hopeful peace and contentment, Capra cuts, quickly and arrestingly, to a scene of danger, desperation, and madness. We are in Baskul, China in the midst of a revolution. It is the night of March 10, 1935, and Conway (Ronald Colman) "has been sent to evacuate ninety white people before they are butchered" by the natives. The images that follow are violent and chaotic and drive from the viewer's mind all thoughts of utopia. This is the real world where death and destruction reign, and it is only the resourcefulness and decisive action of Conway that saves the lives of those under his care—particularly the four other people who end up on his plane.

Along with Conway, we meet his younger brother George (John Howard), Henry Barnard (Thomas Mitchell), a swindler and speculator on the run, Gloria Stone (Isabel Jewel), a bitter, down-on-her-luck prostitute who is dying of tuberculosis, and Alexander P. ("Lovey") Lovett (Edward Everett Horton), a timid, excitable geologist added to the film for comic relief. When their pilot takes them in the wrong direction, they realize they have, for unknown reasons, been kidnapped. Eventually, the pilot tries to take them over the highest mountains of Tibet, but ends up crash landing the plane and dying in the process. In the harrowing, almost documentary-like scenes that follow, our five heroes struggle through a barren, nightmarish landscape of ice and snow, which, together with the riot scene in Baskul, prepares us for a stunning contrast when we enter Shangri-La.

And to make that contrast, that transition from a world of despair to a world of hope, even more stunning, Capra gives us a visual image that has been burned into my mind more indelibly than almost any other image in the history of film. To mark the threshold between the wasteland where nothing can live and the utopia where life can be lived as it was meant to be lived Capra places a simple wooden post. When I first saw Conway stand by that post and look backward and forward, from the nightmare that had passed to the dream that beckoned, I felt as if I had stumbled on to the gateway that leads to paradise. I knew then that the kingdom of God is not so much "up there," as it is alongside us, ever ready to break in. It's just around the corner, if only we can find that corner and the post that marks its turning.

In all my book reading and movie watching, only one other work has triggered so powerfully my deep yearning to locate that post and look around that corner, *The Lord of the Rings*. In the closing chapter of Tolkien's epic fantasy, as he prepares to go on his final journey into the West, Bilbo composes this poem:

Still round the corner there may wait

A new road or a secret gate;
And though I oft have passed them by,
A time will come at last when I
Shall take the hidden paths that run
West of the Moon, East of the Sun.[3]

The moment I read that poem, I committed it to memory, just as I did the image of the wooden post in *Lost Horizon*. Both speak of the nexus point between worlds that dreamers like Conway, Bilbo, and myself are always looking for. In fact, in the film, George refers to his brother as "the man who always wanted to see what was on the other side of the hill."

While staying faithful to the core of the novel, Capra makes a series of subtle changes that draws out this aspect of Conway in more tangible and accessible ways. First of all, though Conway's character is almost identical in the novel and the film, Capra makes him into a more famous, sought-after diplomat who is about to be appointed as foreign secretary. Even as he remains in Shangri-La, we are told, "a British cruiser [is] waiting at Shanghai, smoke pouring out of its funnels, tugging at its moorings, waiting to take [him] back to London." The choice that Conway must make between returning to his career in the "real" world and living out his dream in Shangri-La, between staying in the paradise regained that he has found and risking the dangerous trek back to "civilization," is thus magnified many times.

That choice lies at the core of the film, and perhaps of the human psyche. I know that I, at least, have felt that wrestling within. As in the novel, the film renders that choice more concrete by setting Conway's idealism against George's pragmatism. From the moment he gets there, George wants to leave and to take his brother with him. George lacks eyes to see the beauties and wonders of Shangri-La and faith to believe in the health and longevity of those who live there. He thinks Conway has been deceived and has lost his mind, brainwashed by a gigantic confidence trick

3 J. R. R. Tolkien, *The Lord of the Rings* (New York: Houghton Mifflin, 1994), 1005.

orchestrated by the High Lama. George simply will not allow himself to share in the life and joy and peace of Shangri-La.

This struggle between George and Conway is lifted directly from the novel, but with a difference. In the novel, George is not Conway's brother but a young officer named Captain Charles Mallinson, H. M. Vice-Consul. By changing Mallinson into Conway's brother, Capra and Riskin make the struggle more personal and familial, calling up not only the sibling strife between Cain and Abel, but, more importantly, one of the most difficult sayings of Christ: "If any man come to me, and hate not his father, and mother, and wife, and children, and brethren, and sisters, yea, and his own life also, he cannot be my disciple" (Luke 14: 26). Christ does not mean that we should literally hate our father, mother, brother, and sister, but that our love for him must be so great that it takes priority even over familial claims.

What Conway finds in Shangri-La is the purpose toward which his whole life has been leading him, a purpose that transcends family ties and his diplomatic career. He only meets twice with the High Lama (Sam Jaffe), but he is transformed by those meetings, his eyes lifted to a higher vision of what life should and could be like. It is not just the peace and serenity of Shangri-La that draws Conway, but the fact that his life there would be filled with a purpose more vital and fulfilling than anything he could accomplish as foreign secretary. As the High Lama explains to him, the world has gone mad, a "scurrying mass of bewildered humanity crashing headlong against each other, propelled by an orgy of greed and brutality."

In the face of this madness, the High Lama, impelled by a vision of the doom to come, vowed "to gather together all the things of beauty and culture that I could and preserve them here against the doom toward which the world is rushing. ... For when that day comes, the world must begin to look for a new life. And it is our hope that they may find it here. For here we shall be with their books and their music and a way of life based on one simple rule: Be Kind. When that day comes, it is our hope that the brotherly love of Shangri-La will spread throughout the world. Yes, my son, when the strong have devoured each other, the Christian ethic may at last be fulfilled, and the meek shall inherit the earth."

With the exception of that Capraesque bit about the simple rule of being kind, this speech is lifted word-for-word out of the novel, as are the dying words of the High Lama, in which he commissions Conway to inherit his vision and mission: "I am placing in your hands the future and destiny of Shangri-La. . . . You, my son, will live through the storm. You will preserve the fragrance of our history, and add to it a touch of your own mind.

"Beyond that, my vision weakens. But I see in the great distance a new world starting in the ruins—stirring clumsily—but in hopefulness, seeking its vast and legendary treasures. And they will all be here, my son, hidden behind the mountains in the Valley of the Blue Moon, preserved as if by a miracle."

I truly believe that part of my passion for being an English professor, for lecturing for our Great Books Honors College, for writing books like this one, and for giving public lectures can be traced back to the High Lama's commission. I yearn, like Conway, to play a role in the preservation of all that is good and true and beautiful. Though I am fairly hopeful we will not blow ourselves up, I do fear that western culture is heading toward a new dark age that will cut us off from our Greco-Roman, Judeo-Christian past. I can think of no greater purpose than helping to hold back that dark age while also making provision for its arrival. And how wonderful to think that in preserving the tradition I so love, I might be given the opportunity to add to it something of myself!

For the Conway of the novel, the High Lama's commission is enough in itself, but not for the Conway of the film. Capra's greatest addition to the novel, an addition that brought the story alive for me, was to give Conway a love interest. Now, if truth be told, Hollywood has ruined many a good novel by inserting an unnecessary love interest, but that is not the case with *Lost Horizon*. In the screenplay, but not in the novel, both the High Lama and an added female character named Sondra, who was rescued as a baby and raised in Shangri-La, have read carefully a number of books by Conway, in one of which he wrote, "There are moments in every man's life when he glimpses the eternal."

Although, in the novel, Conway crashes in Tibet by accident and only then comes to the attention of the High Lama, in the film, the High

Lama and Sondra have *arranged* to have Conway brought there—Sondra because she is in love with him and knows he will be happy in Shangri-La; the High Lama because he has come to believe, from reading his books, that Conway is the right man to succeed him. Sondra functions in the film as far more than a love interest. She, it soon becomes clear, is the only person who really understands him. Though she has never met him in person, she has discerned from reading his books what no one else in England has: that he is empty, that he has not accomplished what he wanted, that he is, in reality, "a little boy whistling in the dark."

We expect at first, as does Conway himself, that he will be furious at Sondra for having arranged to kidnap him and bring him to Shangri-La against his will. But that is the blessed strangeness of it all. He feels perfectly at home in the valley of the Blue Moon. "I can't quite explain it," he tells Sondra, "but everything is somehow familiar. The very air that I breathe. The lamasery, with its feet rooted in the good earth of this fertile valley, while its head explores the eternal. All the beautiful things I see, these cherry blossoms, you—all somehow familiar."

Although Conway does feel at home in the novel, Capra and Riskin give him as well an overwhelming sense of déjà vu, a sense that he has been here before, that he has, in some real sense, always been a citizen of Shangri-La. He has made it to the end of a life-long quest that he did not realize he was on. If George is his doppelganger, his dark other who draws him away from the light he so desires, then Sondra is his soul mate, his other half, who completes him by revealing to him his true home and purpose.

In what I consider the single most beautiful bit of wooing in film history, Conway conjures up a lovely metaphor to explain to Sondra the exact nature of the relationship between them: "You know, when we were on that plane, I was fascinated by the way its shadow followed it. That silly shadow racing along over mountains and valleys, covering ten times the distance of the plane. It was always there to greet us with outstretched arms when we landed. And I've been thinking that somehow you're that plane, and I'm that silly shadow. That all my life I've been rushing up and down hills, leaping rivers, crashing over obstacles, never dreaming that one day that beautiful thing in flight would land on this earth and into my arms." To hear Ronald Colman deliver this speech in his golden voice and inimical phrasing is to glimpse the essence of love, of the mystical way in which a man and a woman can complement and complete one another.

Sondra and Shangri-La are two parts of the same whole, together filling the void in Conway's life and redirecting him toward his true purpose. In the novel, there is no Sondra, only the commissioning of the High Lama. In keeping with the Buddhist philosophy of Tibet, the novel promotes an ideal of passionlessness. In fact, in a line that does not appear in the film, Conway is told that the "mere presence of human passions is an unwelcome and, at [the High Lama's] age, an almost unendurable unpleasantness."[4] Whereas the film puts its emphasis on the absence of strife, the novel preaches that "the exhaustion of the passions is the beginning of wisdom."[5] Such a philosophy will not do for an American audience, but I also do not think it will do as a final answer to the yearning of the soul for purpose, joy, and intimacy. In the novel, if Conway is to be the new High Lama, he must, it seems, live a celibate, ascetic life separate from human passion. In the film, it is clear that Conway can carry on the role of the High Lama while being happily married to Sondra and having children of his own.

And what the film does for Conway, it does for the rest of the characters and for Shangri-La itself. In the hands of Capra and Riskin, the valley of the Blue Moon becomes what it is not in the novel: an appealing village bustling with boisterous life and laughing children. In both novel and film, Barnard abandons his lust to mine the gold of Shangri-La and chooses to stay; but only in the film does he come up with a scheme to bless the whole village with modern plumbing. Meditation is a good thing in its place, but it must be combined with a good American work ethic if life is to thrive.

As for Gloria, she is an added character whom Capra substitutes for the female traveler in the novel: a tough, no-nonsense missionary named

4 James Hilton, *Lost Horizon* (New York: Pocket Books, 1939), 128.

5 Ibid, 130.

Roberta Brinklaw. Though Roberta changes and grows, her change cannot compare to the wonderful metamorphosis in Gloria, who is healed physically, emotionally, and spiritually by Shangri-La. By the end of the film, we know that Gloria will marry Barnard and that the two, like Sondra and Conway, will complement and redeem each other. Capra is not merely imposing a Hollywood happy ending on the novel; he is affirming Shangri-La as a place where life and love and fruition are both possible and desirable.

Just as he does in *Mr. Smith Goes to Washington* and *It's a Wonderful Life*, Capra shows in *Lost Horizon* that people can change, that they can abandon greed and cynicism for goodness and faith. But he also shows, in all three pictures, that there are some people who refuse to change, who refuse to open their eyes to the goodness around them. In *Lost Horizon*, George is that character. He not only denies the magic of Shangri-La; he is fully prepared to fly over it and bomb it to smithereens. By means of his counsel of despair, George temporarily robs Conway of his faith in and love for Shangri-La, convincing him to leave his beloved utopia and brave the snowy passes of Tibet.

But have no fear. Conway returns, though he must suffer greatly for his decision to leave, must go through an ordeal to test the purity of his resolve. The final image of the film is not of Conway and Sondra reunited in an embrace, but of a lone figure, small against the snow-capped mountains, catching a glimpse of that sought-for wooden post that marks the gateway to Shangri-La. Conway's face, though mostly covered by a weather-beaten scarf, lights up with ecstasy and rapture. As silent as it is visionary, that timeless image lingers in the mind, a visual complement to the last spoken words in the film, words that do not appear in the novel.

Rather than show us the heroic efforts that Conway makes to fight his way back to Shangri-La, his story is told to us by a British Lord, who describes Conway's almost superhuman efforts to fight his way back to the valley of the Blue Moon to his fellow aristocrats at the Embassy Club. As he ends his tale, he lifts his glass and says: "Gentlemen, I give you a toast. Here is my hope that Robert Conway will find his Shangri-La! Here is my hope that we all find *our* Shangri-La."

I love that ending, with its promise that we can, to borrow a line from *Paradise Lost,* find a paradise within us happier far. More than that, it makes me think of a verse from the epistles of Paul: "Therefore if any man be in Christ, he is a new creature: old things are passed away; behold, all things are become new" (2 Corinthians 5:17). The change that Christ effects in the believer is, at first, only internal, but, when he returns, that newness will spread to all of creation, bringing about a new heaven and a new earth. Capra's Shangri-La offered me a glimpse of that coming glory, a glimpse that is quite invisible to the Georges of the world, but that is as clear as crystal to all those who, like Conway, yearn to see what is on the other side of the hill.

Fun Facts for the Fans

- The film won an Oscar for best art direction and nominations for picture, music, and supporting actor H. B. Warner, who plays Chang, the High Lama's assistant.
- H. B. Warner appeared in many of Capra's pictures, most memorably as Mr. Gower in *It's a Wonderful Life,* the druggist whom the young George Bailey prevents from accidentally poisoning a child. Warner was best known, however, for playing Christ in the silent version of *King of Kings.*
- The film originally began with a ten-minute framing device taken from the novel. When audiences felt that the framing device slowed down the picture, Capra made the difficult but wise decision to, as he put it, "burn the first two reels." Sadly, no copies of those first two reels exist.
- Once America entered World War II, the pacifist message of *Lost Horizon* caused it to lose much of it reputation with fans and critics.
- Over the years, the original running time was edited down drastically, and some of the edited footage was lost. Thankfully, a full version of

Lost Horizon was later pieced together, though seven minutes of the restored version consist of an audio track illustrated by stills from the movie. Though this technique makes the film seem a bit static, I think it intensifies the timeless, frozen nature of Shangri-La.

- Jane Wyatt, who plays the lovely, innocent Sondra, would later play the mother in *Father Knows Best* and Spock's mother in an episode of *Star Trek*.
- Capra made this film, and all his films before it, at Columbia, one of the Poverty Row studios that could not match the budgets of MGM and Paramount. Still, Capra was able to convince Columbia's dictatorial mogul Harry Cohn to let him spend two million dollars on the film, a price tag equal to the cost of twenty other Columbia pictures combined. The film helped make Columbia an "A" studio.
- The breathtaking scenes where Conway and his party make their way through the snow and ice of Tibet were all filmed in a large ice house.
- The role of the High Lama was played by thirty-eight-year-old Sam Jaffe.
- Capra followed up *Lost Horizon* with *You Can't Take it with You*, a film which may best be described as "Shangri-La in a frame house": a utopian ideal lived out by a wacky, free-spirited "family" in the middle of New York City.
- James Hilton wrote several other novels that were made into fine films, in particular *Knight without Armour*, *Goodbye Mr. Chips*, and *Random Harvest*.
- James Agee, one of the great movie critics of his day, made the following quip about the film: "The best film I've seen for ages, but will somebody please tell me how they got the grand piano along a footpath on which only one person can walk at a time with rope and pickaxe and with a sheer drop of 3000 feet or so?"

Other Films to Watch

Ronald Colman, one of my favorite actors, was the embodiment of sophisticated, gentlemanly charm. His best roles include: a foreign legionnaire in the silent *Beau Geste,* an amateur adventurer in *Bulldog Drummond,* a cat burglar in *Raffles,* Sinclair Lewis's self-sacrificing doctor in *Arrowsmith,* an ethical lawyer who has an affair in *Cynara,* a British imperialist in *Clive of India,* Sidney Carton in *A Tale of Two Cities,* a commoner who impersonates a nobleman in *The Prisoner of Zenda,* Francois Villon in *If I Were King,* a judge in *The Talk of the Town,* an amnesiac in *Random Harvest,* a loveable *Arabian Nights* rogue in *Kismet,* an old fashioned father in *The Late George Apley,* and an actor playing Othello in *A Double Life* (a stilted film, but it gave him his Oscar).

In addition to the films discussed in this book, the Golden Age of Hollywood produced these fine adaptations: Dickens's *David Copperfield* (34) and *A Tale of Two Cities* (35), Hemingway's *A Farewell to Arms* (32) and *For Whom the Bell Tolls* (43), Faulkner's *Intruder in the Dust* (49), Steinbeck's *Of Mice and Men* (39), Hugo's *Les Misérables* (35) and *The Hunchback of Notre Dame* (39), Dumas' *Three Musketeers* (48), Remarque's *All Quiet on the Western Front* (30), Alcott's *Little Women* (33 and 49), Lewis's *Dodsworth* (36), Buck's *The Good Earth* (37), Kipling's *Captains Courageous* (37), Mitchell's *Gone With the Wind* (39), Austen's *Pride and Prejudice* (40), Brontë's *Jane Eyre* (43), Wells's *The Invisible Man* (33), and Warren's *All The King's Men* (49).

A STORY AS
EXPLOSIVE
AS HIS
BLAZING
AUTOMATICS!

HUMPHREY
BOGART
MARY
ASTOR

THE
Maltese
Falcon

by
DASHIELL
HAMMETT
Author of
THE THIN MAN

GLADYS
GEORGE · PETER
LORRE · BARTON
MacLANE · LEE
PATRICK · SYDNEY
GREENSTREET

Directed by
JOHN HUSTON · Presented by
WARNER BROS.

THE MALTESE FALCON

(WB; 1941; JOHN HUSTON)

The sound of gunshots in the night; faces silhouetted on the wall by neon lights streaming through the blinds of a seedy motel room. At the bar, an icy blond fixes a drink; in the back room, a pair of thugs caress their revolvers. And everywhere, smoke and shadows and shattered glass. This is the world of film noir ("black film") into which I was ushered by John Huston's brilliant film adaptation of Dashiell Hammett's *The Maltese Falcon* (1930). The novel had been effectively filmed twice before—in 1931 and again as *Satan Met a Lady* in 1936—but Huston's version soared above both to establish a key Hollywood style that predominated in the decade after World War II.

Film noir marked a serendipitous convergence of three streams: the first visual, the second social, and the third literary. The visual style came from the silent films of the post-World War I German Expressionist movement (*The Cabinet of Dr. Caligari, The Golem, Nosferatu, Metropolis*) and the Universal horror films of the early 1930s (*Frankenstein, Dracula, The Mummy, The Invisible Man*). The social attitude came from the gangster films of the Depression, most of them made at Warner Brothers (*Little Caesar, Scarface, Public Enemy, You Only Live Once, The Roaring Twenties*). The literary plots, characters, and dialogue came from the "hard-boiled" school of detective fiction: Dashiell Hammett (who created Sam Spade), Raymond Chandler (who created Philip Marlowe), and James M. Cain (author of *Double Indemnity* and *The Postman Always Rings Twice*).

Expressionism in the arts or film, not to be confused with Impressionism, defines a style that is highly subjective and that makes no attempt at realism. The expressionist wrenches out of his own private psyche a self-enclosed microcosm that does not exist anywhere in the "real world." The originals for his work come not from the natural or human world around him but, Kafka-like, from his own angst-ridden guilts and fears. He scoops out the dark, hidden figures of his subconscious and flings them on to the canvas or the screen. The result is a sinister, nightmarish world of contorted shapes that crawl or limp or slither their way across dimly-lit streets, sharp angles that destabilize, disorient, and even violate the landscapes, and fragile glass-like surfaces that threaten to shatter at the slightest touch. The small amount of light that does exist does not comfort or warm or protect: it stabs, imprisons, exposes, and accuses. The few straight lines that run across the screen offer no escape, but turn back on themselves in labyrinthine fashion. The mood is one of entrapment and paranoia, as if, to quote the famous trick-ending of *Caligari*, all reality were but the projection of the ravings of a madman.

If the expressionist films of the 1920s embodied the influence of Sigmund Freud, then the gangster films of the 1930s, inspired by the Great Depression and the cynicism, disillusionment, and mistrust of authority that were its fruits, embodied the legacy of Charles Darwin. These tough, unsentimental films present a Darwinian world of survival of the fittest where nothing, not money, reputation, career, friendship, or even the family unit, is stable, and where arbitrary forces seem in control of a universe that is essentially tragic. The heroes of these films are really anti-heroes, social outcasts who either refuse to conform to society's rules or who have tried to conform but been frustrated one too many times by a series of fatalistic catastrophes beyond their control.

Noir was born when these artistic heirs of Freud and Darwin collided with the novels of Hammett, Chandler, and Cain. These cold, hard-hitting detection stories were of a far different order from the works of Arthur Conan Doyle and Agatha Christie. The Sam Spade-Philip Marlowe private eye is not a ratiocinative detective like Sherlock Holmes or Hercule Poirot, who solves the crime using logic and deduction.

Rather, the "hard-boiled" detective solves the mystery "on his feet" by physically and emotionally entering into the morally ambiguous realm of the criminal: a sort of Dantean descent into the underworld. He is a marginalized, anti-establishment figure—half cowboy, half vigilante—who distrusts authority and treats the police less as an ally to be confided in than as an additional enemy to be eluded. Rather than getting clearer as they go along, the cases they pursue become less and less certain as they become and more and more morally ambiguous. What they uncover is not a single, master villain like Dr. Moriarty, but a corrupt society where justice has little meaning and no clear definition.

But enough of this abstract, academic talk! Noir is a visual and visceral medium that needs to be felt in the nerves and along the veins. That is certainly how I experienced it when I first saw *The Maltese Falcon*. I invite you to take that journey with me, a journey into darkness that yet finds some light in the end.

The movie begins with an extreme long, establishing shot of San Francisco, a shot that turns out to be ironic, since the rest of the movie is claustrophobic and tightly framed, punctuated by low ceilings, angular shadows, and blinds to block out the sun. There is no escape from this world, no opportunity to step back and get a wider perspective. Nearly all the shots are interior ones; the few times the camera ventures outside, it is into a bleak, lifeless terrain of asphalt and neon. I was getting a glimpse of the underbelly of society, of a world I found both frightening and compelling.

The first thing the camera showed me was the glass door to the offices of private investigators Sam Spade (Humphrey Bogart) and Miles Archer (Jerome Cowan). I saw the names Spade and Archer engraved into the glass, but those names were shown to me in backward reflection. This tough urban world, it seemed, was also a fragile, topsy-turvy one, one lacking in rational order and moral clarity that could shatter at any moment. The next shock came when Spade's secretary Effie (Lee Patrick) tells him that a woman is waiting to see him. "You'll want to see her," she says, "She's a knockout." Tough gal that Effie; she's slick and pretty, but she talks and thinks like one of the guys.

And then I saw the knockout, Brigid O'Shaughnessy (Mary Astor), the icy blond femme fatale who would change her name twice before the end of the film. She walked right up to the camera, allowing us to look her full in the face, but there was something shifty about her eyes. She told her story to Spade in a fast, clipped manner, always focusing on money. Spade kept his cool throughout, but the foolish, gawky Archer let himself fall for O'Shaughnessy's sexy legs. One felt that she was sending them off on a wild goose chase, but it was hard not to be fooled by her, hard not to *want* to be fooled.

The scene ended with an ominous shot of Spade and Archer's desks spread apart, separated by a reflection from the glass door of their names. Then, cut! I was in a dark alley looking at an extreme close-up of a gun. The gun fires into Archer's belly, and his body rolls down the hill in rough, jagged fashion. Then, cut again to a telephone ringing in the night. While the camera remains focused on the phone, we hear Spade's voice off screen getting the news of Archer's death. And then one more cut to the crime scene: a desolate noir landscape that looks like the Valley of Ashes from *The Great Gatsby* or the Wasteland, devoid of water and vegetation, that T. S. Eliot describes in his epic poem.

Spade confers with Tom the policeman (Ward Bond), and gives his reading of how the body fell. He speaks in an emotionless monotone, as if he were describing the death of a dog rather than of his partner. "Terrible, getting it like that," Tom says to Spade, "Miles had his faults just like any of us, but I guess he had his good points too." "I guess so," Spade responds, his voice empty of sentiment. A few minutes later, we see Spade with Iva (Gladys George), Archer's widow. They've clearly been having an affair, but it is even clearer that Spade does not love her. To the contrary, he looks at her with disgust and disdain when she suggests Spade killed Archer. The opening sequence ends with Spade having Spade and Archer removed from the door and replaced with Samuel Spade. This is a temporary world indeed!

What was I supposed to make of this Sam Spade character? He was certainly being presented as the hero, or at least the protagonist, but why then was he so dark and cold-hearted. Is he a villain in disguise, a corrupt private eye trying to cash in? Perhaps he is just cocky, out of his league but unwilling to admit it. "You worry me, Sam," Effie tells him early on in the film, "You always think you know what you're doing. But you're too slick for your own good."

He seemed to be living out the male fantasy. Every time he returned to his office or his apartment—we never see any homes in this transient world—there was that cool, mysterious blonde waiting for him. The cat-and-mouse banter that fell from their lips was priceless. She reclines on the couch and sighs, plays to perfection the weak, helpless female. But he sees through it. In fact, they both see through each other. They know they are being manipulated by the other, but they play the game anyway, accept the illusion, believe the lie.

"You must trust me, Mr. Spade," she says, her voice fluttering, "Oh, I'm so alone and afraid! I've got nobody to help me if you won't help me. Be generous, Mr. Spade. You're brave. You're strong. You can spare some of that courage and strength, surely. Help me, Mr. Spade! I need help so badly." I wanted to believe her damsel in distress pose, to accept her as a vulnerable lady in need of protection, but Spade is not fooled: "You won't need much of anybody's help. You're good. It's chiefly your eyes, I think, and that throb you get in your voice when you say things like, 'Be generous, Mr. Spade.'" For her part, she accepts his rebuke, but then bends it back to her advantage: "I deserve that. But, oh, the lie was in the way I said it and not at all in what I said."

And then there was the gallery of rogues to complement the dangerous female. *The Maltese Falcon* introduced me to three bad guys who were as twisted as they were oddly likeable. There was the fastidious, effeminate Joel Cairo (Peter Lorre) who smelled of gardenia and was particularly good at whining. In contrast, there was the loquacious Kasper Gutman (Sydney Greenstreet), the affable fat man who put his arm around you and gave you drinks while plotting your demise. And poor Wilmer (Elisha Cook Jr.), the petulant young hit man-bodyguard (Hammett calls him a gunsel) whom Spade humiliates by giving him the slip and stealing his guns. They make quite an unholy trio, linked by lies, avarice, and a subtext of barely suppressed homoerotic passion. The three are ready to sell each other out at any moment, and Gutman, though he looks upon Wilmer as a son, is quite ready to sacrifice him to achieve his prize, the jewel-encrusted Falcon.

In his interactions with Cairo and Gutman, as in his endless banter with Miss O'Shaughnessy, the subject inevitably comes back to money. Spade is no man of leisure, no amateur consulting detective; he's a working stiff who needs to make money if he wants to eat and keep a roof over his head. When Miss O'Shaughnessy runs out of money with which she can secure Spade's loyalty and trust, she is quite willing to give herself in exchange. In the dark world into which Spade descends, everything is a commodity, everything is for sale. At the same time, nothing is secure, nothing is for certain. The only real claim one can make on something is the claim of possession. At one point, Spade, fooled and drugged by Gutman, loses consciousness itself.

The deeper Spade descends, the deeper and more entangling the lies become. At one point he calls Miss O'Shaughnessy a liar, only to have her respond that she's always been a liar. "Well don't brag about it," says Spade with a smile, then adds, "Was there any truth in that story." "Not very much," she admits, then adds in a melodramatic flourish: "I'm so tired of lying and making up lies. Not knowing what's a lie and what's the truth." I doubt that she can tell the difference anymore.

Gutman, on the other hand, prefers people who shoot straight, telling him up front what they're after, rather than hiding behind pretences to love or justice or fair play: "I distrust a close-mouthed man. He generally picks the wrong time to talk and says the wrong things. Talking's something you can't do judiciously, unless you keep in practice. Now, sir, we'll talk if you like. I'll tell you right out, I'm a man who likes talking to a man who likes to talk ... I do like a man who tells you right out he's looking out for himself. Aren't we all? I don't trust a man who says he's not."

How does one navigate a world like this? Spade tries his best, but his hunches are as often wrong as they are right. As in so many of the noir films that would follow in the wake of *The Maltese Falcon*, things get less clear the deeper one digs, ever preventing the private eye from getting to the center. And yet, in a way, *The Maltese Falcon* is different, for it *does* have a center, or at least it seems to. At the center of the film lies the oldest archetype of them all, the archetype of the quest—not the quest for the Holy Grail but for the legendary Maltese Falcon.

Even before we meet Spade and his noir world, we see these words projected on the screen: "In 1539 the Knight Templars of Malta paid tribute to Charles V of Spain by sending him a Golden Falcon encrusted from beak to claw with rarest jewels—but pirates seized the galley carrying this priceless token and the fate of the Maltese Falcon remains a mystery to this day." After that tantalizing teaser, we hear nothing at all about the Falcon until halfway into the film, when Gutman recounts for Spade the strange history and genealogy of the black bird and his lifelong quest to secure it for himself.

The finding of the Falcon promises to explain everything, atoning somehow for all the wrongs done in its name and awarding all the characters with their heart's desire. But it is a false lure, as false as the love between Spade and O'Shaughnessy or the friendship between Cairo and Gutman. When Gutman takes his knife to the Falcon, hoping to scrape off its black enamel coating and reveal the jewels beneath, he discovers that it is a fake, a phony. Seventeen years of searching has led him to this, to a worthless lead statue. But how can it be otherwise. The noir world is inherently unstable; it affords nothing on which one can count or lean or rely.

Or does it? After Wilmer, refusing to be the fall guy, runs off, and Cairo and Gutman, undaunted, leave to continue their quest, purchasing Spade's silence with a thousand dollar bill, the final, dramatic showdown between Spade and O'Shaughnessy begins. What will our anti-hero do now? He knows the police are closing in and that he needs a fall guy to take the wrap for the murder of Miles Archer. But what can he do? Wilmer has disappeared, and he is the chief suspect for his partner's death. Taking on a tone of fear and urgency, Spade pushes O'Shaughnessy to admit what he already has figured out: that she, in fact, is the one who killed Archer.

For a second, we, like O'Shaughnessy, think that Spade will cover for her and get her off the hook. But no, he intends to turn her over to the police. He won't play the sap for her as so many men before him have done; she is going to take the fall! She begs him in the name of their supposed love, but Spade will not budge. She doesn't understand. Can Archer really have meant that much to him? Slowly, thoughtfully, Spade tries to explain to her, and to us, why he must turn her over.

"Listen," he says, "this won't do any good. You'll never understand me, but I'll try once, and then give it up. When a man's partner is killed, he's supposed to do something about it. It doesn't make any difference what you thought of him. He was your partner and you're supposed to do something about it. Then it happens we're in the detective business. Well, when one of your organization gets killed, it's bad business to let the killer get away with it—bad all around—bad for every detective everywhere.... I've no earthly reason to think I can trust you, and if I did this and got away with it, you'd have something on me you could use whenever you wanted to. Since I've go something on you, I couldn't be sure you wouldn't decide to put a hole in me some day. All those are on one side. Maybe some of them are unimportant. I won't argue about that. But look at the sheer number of them. What have we got on the other side? All we've got is that maybe you love me and maybe I love you."

O'Shaughnessy protests that he knows full well whether or not he loves her, to which he sardonically replies, "Maybe I do. I'll have some rotten nights after I've sent you over, but that'll pass. If all I've said doesn't mean anything to you, forget it and we'll make it just this. I won't because all of me wants to—regardless of consequences—and because you've counted on that with me, the same you counted on that with the others." "Look at me and tell me the truth," she pleads in a last-ditch effort to sway him, "Would you have done this to me if the Falcon had been real, and you had been paid your money?" "Don't be so sure I'm as crooked as I'm supposed to be," he replies, "That reputation might be good business, bringing in high-priced jobs and making it easier to deal with the enemy. But a lot of money would have been at least one more item on your side of the scales."

There it was, the light at the end of the dark tunnel, the center I was looking for. Even the cold, cynical, calculating Sam Spade lives by a code. For all his distrust of authority, he knows that rules exist, rules that somehow transcend the laws of survival and acquisition. Yes, like a good utilitarian, he balances the pros and the cons, but he is clearly motivated by more than simple pragmatism. He has a sense of himself as a masked crusader, as someone fighting an enemy, a hidden enemy that can't be faced or even seen in safe, well-lit, morally-respectable places. He may be trapped in a morally ambiguous world, but he has not ceased in his quest for justice.

The real mystery at the center of *The Maltese Falcon* is Sam Spade himself. He is an enigma, but then all of us are: a mixture of goodness and depravity, of altruism and egoism, of the angel and the beast. In the final scene, Spade turns in O'Shaughnessy, but he also turns over the thousand dollars with which he was supposed to be bribed. That is not to say that Spade, like Richard Blaine at the end of *Casablanca,* becomes a clear-cut hero and patriot. He is still a denizen of the noir underworld, compromised by the darkness into which he has descended, but he does retain his ability to choose.

In the closing image of the film, O'Shaughnessy is placed behind the bars of an elevator. As the elevator sinks down, Spade walks down the stairs that wrap around the elevator shaft. Both are descending into the darkness below, but Spade, at least, is in control of his movements. Better yet, he has come to understand the true nature of desire. When Spade hands the lead Falcon to Tom, Tom says, "It's heavy. What is it?" Spade's response has become one of Hollywood's most iconic lines: "The, uh, stuff that dreams are made of."

Huston's screenplay for *The Maltese Falcon* follows the novel with remarkable accuracy and precision. Indeed, every single line of dialogue in the film is taken word-for-word out of Hammett's novel. Every line, that is, except the last one. In that famous last line, Huston not only comments on the insubstantiality of our dreams and desires, but on the ephemeral nature of film itself. Dreams are entrancing, but they promise more than they can deliver; something else is needed to give life its stability and its meaning. One doesn't go to a noir picture to find out what that something else is, but such films can, and often do, show us what happens when that something is absent.

At least I have found it to be so in my frequent visits to noir alley.

Fun Facts for the Fans

- *The Maltese Falcon* was nominated for best picture, script, and supporting actor (Greenstreet); this marked the sixty-one-year-old Greenstreet's first film role.
- *The Maltese Falcon* gave John Huston, a successful screenwriter (*Jezebel, High Sierra,* and *Sergeant York,* among others), his first chance to direct. He would go on to write the screenplays for roughly half of the films he directed.
- John Huston was the son of Walter Huston, an excellent character actor who would win a best supporting Oscar for his performance in *The Treasure of the Sierra Madre,* for which film John Huston also won an Oscar for best director.
- John Huston's daughter, Anjelica Huston, would also win a best supporting Oscar for performing in a film directed by her father, 1984's *Prizzi's Honor*.
- Walter Huston has a cameo in *The Maltese Falcon;* he plays the dying Captain Jacobi, who brings the Falcon to Sam's office before succumbing to his wounds.
- After playing the second lead in dozens of films, Humphrey Bogart gained attention by playing the lead in *High Sierra,* star power by playing the lead in *The Maltese Falcon,* and eternal fame by playing the lead in *Casablanca*.
- Dashiell Hammett's *The Thin Man* and *The Glass Key* were also filmed.
- Peter Lorre and Sidney Greenstreet would be re-teamed in *Casablanca, Passage to Marseilles, The Mask of Dimitrios,* and *The Three Strangers*.
- In 1982, German director Wim Wenders released an English-language film titled *Hammett,* in which Dashiell Hammett is a character; it stars Elisha Cook Jr.

Other Films to Watch

Although *The Maltese Falcon* is generally considered the first film noir, World War II's call for more optimistic, patriotic films put the genre on temporary hold. It picked up again with 1944's *Double Indemnity*—a much darker, more cynical film than *Falcon* that introduced the voice over narration as a convention of the genre—and carried on for over a decade.

Humphrey Bogart became strongly identified with the film noir genre, particularly in the four films he made with his wife Lauren Bacall: *To Have and Have Not* (based on a lesser Hemingway novel), *The Big Sleep* (with Bogey as Philip Marlowe), *Dark Passage* (the first third of which is shot with a first-person camera) and *Key Largo* (in which Bogey kills the last of the gangsters). Alan Ladd made three good, but somewhat stilted noir films: *This Gun for Hire* (from a Graham Greene novel), *The Glass Key* (Hammett), and *The Blue Dahlia* (written by Chandler).

Other classic noirs include: *Farewell my Lovely* (with crooner Dick Powell changing his image to play Philip Marlowe), *Laura* (classy detective tale with much humor), *The Mask of Dimitrios* (in seedy Istanbul with a great rogues' gallery) *The Killers* (an expansion of a Hemingway short story), *The Postman Always Rings Twice* (steamy love triangle), *The Strange Love of Martha Ivers* (featuring Kirk Douglas in a wimpy role), *The Lady in the Lake* (experimental noir shot totally in first-person), *Out of the Past* (moody love triangle), *Kiss of Death* (mobster rats on gang), *White Heat* (James Cagney as mother-fixated gangster) *DOA* (victim tells tale in flashback as he dies from poison); *Big Heat* (a particularly sadistic noir), *Kiss Me Deadly* (noir deconstructed that ends with atomic explosion), *Touch of Evil* (Orson Welles beefs up what should have been a B picture).

But noir is as much a genre as it is a visual style, and there are many noir films that, though they move outside the realm of the"hard-boiled" school, maintain the moody, low-key photography and expressionistic landscapes of noir: *Casablanca, Mildred Pierce* (woman's picture from Cain novel), *Crossfire* (about anti-Semitism), *The Asphalt Jungle* (first of the criminal caper film), and *Sunset Boulevard* (cynical look at Hollywood), as well as such later noir Sci-Fi films as *Alien, Blade Runner,* and *Dark City.*

Here is a list of John Huston's best films, with a * by those that star Bogie: **The Maltese Falcon,* **Across the Pacific* (good World War II tale), **The Treasure of the Sierra Madre* (classic film about greed), **Key Largo, The Asphalt Jungle* (caper film that could have used Bogie), *The Red Badge of Courage* (from the novel), **The African Queen* (Bogie won Oscar), *Moulin Rogue* (powerful biopic of Toulouse-Lautrec; his first film shot in color), **Beat the Devil* (a cult classic that is so bad it is good), *Moby Dick* (featuring a script by Ray Bradbury!), *The Misfits* (final performances of Marilyn Monroe and Clark Gable; script by Arthur Miller, who wanted to give his wife a good dramatic role), *Freud* (an unlikely film, but a good one), *The Night of the Iguana* (from a Tennessee Williams play), *The Bible* (in which he plays Noah!), *The Man Who Would Be King* (wonderful adventure from a Kipling story), *Wise Blood* (powerful but disturbing film from a Flannery O'Connor novel), *Prizzi's Honor* (black comedy about the mafia), *The Dead* (his last film, a literal adaptation of a James Joyce story).

EVERYBODY'S TALKING ABOUT IT!

It's Terrific!

ORSON
WELLES

CITIZEN
KANE

The Mercury Actors

JOSEPH COTTEN
DOROTHY COMINGORE
EVERETT SLOANE
RAY COLLINS
GEORGE COULOURIS
AGNES MOOREHEAD
PAUL STEWART
RUTH WARRICK
ERSKINE SANFORD
WILLIAM ALLAND

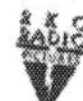

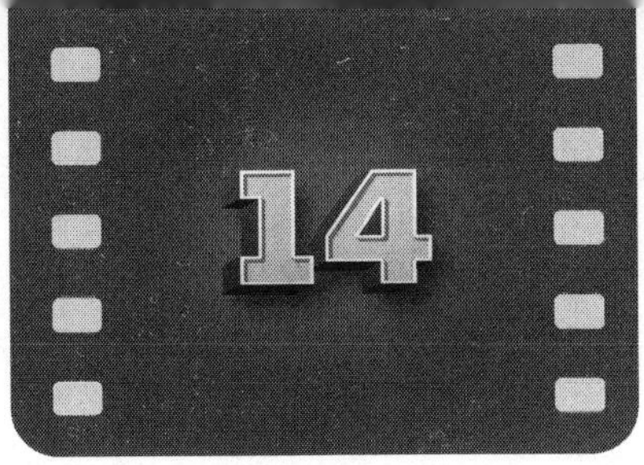

CITIZEN KANE

(RKO; 1941; ORSON WELLES)

In the same year that John Huston essentially invented the hard-boiled film noir genre, Orson Welles left radio and the New York stage to bring a noir look to Hollywood. *Citizen Kane* would be his first film, and it continues to be hailed as one of, if not *the*, greatest American film. I believe that that assessment is both true and just, especially if the word "American" is emphasized. *Citizen Kane* represents American art at its best and most essential, for it fuses perfectly the artistic and the accessible, the high-brow and the low-brow, the technical and the humanistic.

America has produced some very fine literature, classical music, and visual arts, but we cannot compete with England in the first category or Germany in the second or France in the third. But there are two areas where America reigns supreme in her contribution to world culture: in her films, particularly those from the Golden Age, and in her popular songs from the same period, written by such giants as the Gershwins, Cole Porter, Irving Berlin, Rodgers and Hart, Jerome Kern, Harry Warren, and Johnny Mercer.

Both in our classic films and our Tin Pan Alley/Broadway standards, we have shown the world that a kind of beauty could be created that would speak to the whole person, that would engage the mind without losing the heart, that would draw out laughter and tears without being overly sentimental, that would balance realism with optimism, despair with hope, loss with love. At their best, our films and songs tell stories that simultaneously entertain and teach, that compel their audience to enter in to a carefully-crafted world where things do not happen haphazardly and without purpose, but, Aristotle-like, in accordance with necessity and probability. In telling those stories, our screenwriters and directors, lyricists and composers make use of a whole battery of cinematic and musical techniques, but those techniques are always there to serve the story, not vice versa.

When Welles, that celebrated twenty-five-year-old child prodigy, arrived in Los Angeles, RKO allowed him a kind of freedom that very few directors had ever been offered by Hollywood's assembly-line studio system. He was given complete creative control to make a film as he saw fit with his own handpicked cast and crew. As a result, *Citizen Kane,* more than any other film from the Golden Age, bears witness to the sheer joy of filmmaking. Upon seeing all the wonderful gadgets at his disposal, Welles exclaimed with glee, "This is the biggest electric train a boy ever had."

Though he remained throughout the central guiding mind behind the film, Welles, perhaps extending the courtesy that RKO had extended to him, allowed his cast and crew unprecedented creative input, fostering on his set a collaborative spirit of excitement and experimentation. Much has been made of the wrath of William Randolph Hearst, who punished Welles, both directly and through his minions, for patterning Kane on his own life and career. That wrath was real—even prompting Louis B. Mayer of MGM to offer to pay RKO a tidy sum to destroy the negative of the film—and it haunted Welles throughout the rest of his career. But Hearst was not the only cause of Welles's woes.

Welles was done in as much by Hearst as by petty industry envy. The denizens of Hollywood resented Welles, labeling him a spoiled brat and nicknaming him Little Orson Annie. They called him a tyrant, despite his collaborative approach, and a spendthrift, despite the fact that he always brought his films in under budget (*Kane* only cost about $700,000), and had a knack for getting expensive-looking results from relatively small outlays of cash. They were jealous, too, of his drive and his vision, of his willingness to break the rules to get the exact effect he was after.

That drive and vision are evident from the opening scene to the closing credits, imbuing the whole film with a rare kind of energy and exuberance. *Kane* seemed to reinvent movie making, liberating it while also paying homage to all that had come before. *Kane* allows us, today as much as in 1941, to see things afresh—to realize that rooms have ceilings, to remember that the camera knows no boundaries of time or space, to understand how interior spaces, whether they be cavernous or claustrophobic, cluttered or tomb-like, can convey mood and character. And it allows us to *hear* things afresh as well: that groups of people do not speak one at a time but in overlapping dialogue, that voices have a different quality when spoken in different kinds of spaces, that discontinuous sounds and images can comment on each other in surprising ways. Welles, who was a very good amateur magician, loved to show off his cinematic skills while never allowing them to overwhelm the telling of the story.

The opening sequence, a veritable tour de force of camera movement and editing, is our ticket into the strange yet recognizable world of *Citizen Kane*. We begin with a close-up of a sign on a fence that reads "No Trespassing." But the camera ignores the warning, tracking up the fence and then dissolving its way into a huge enclosed area with an imposing mansion in the distance. The mansion seems small, but we are drawn to it, for one of the upper windows is lit from within. Silently, the camera moves and edits from one corner of the grounds to another, revealing monumental, but decaying structures punctuated by gardens and zoos. Our eye takes in each set piece in turn, but without ever losing its focus on that mysterious lit window in the mansion that looms in the distance. We and the camera are twin voyeurs, desperate to make sense of this sprawling exterior space while also longing to peek into that lit window.

By slow stages, we move closer to the mansion, then up to the lit window. For a second, everything freezes, and then, with bated breath, we move through the window and into the room. There we see an old, old man holding a snow globe in his hand. An extreme close-up shows us his lips as he speaks a single word: "Rosebud." Then the globe falls from his hands, bounces down the steps, and shatters. Through the shattered glass, we see a distorted image of a nurse rushing in, but the patient is gone. A slow, somber dissolve shows his body being covered as the sun fades through the window.

A second later, we are shaken out of our slumber by a roaring sound and a succession of grainy images being run through a camera. For the next ten minutes we are treated to a March of Time newsreel recounting the life of Charles Foster Kane, whose death we have just witnessed. The newsreel is entertaining, but it is meant, in great part, to be a parody of itself, with its twisted syntax, its arch posing, and its verbal and cinematic clichés. It tells us everything we want to know about Kane the public figure, but it offers no insight into the man himself. Who was this rich, reclusive tycoon whose newspapers drove history as much as they recorded it? What were his dreams and desires? What motivated him to do the things he did?

As the newsreel ends, we find ourselves in a projection booth with a number of men who debate the merits of what we just saw. What has it really taught us about Kane? Can we say that we know this man who has left so great a mark on America? No, the documentary is missing an angle, a skeleton key that can unlock the inner heart, soul, and mind of Charles Foster Kane. After some debate, they decide that Kane's dying word surely contains that sought-for key. Find out what Rosebud means, and all the other pieces will fall into place, revealing the true portrait of Kane.

The search begins with an interview with Kane's second wife, a night club singer named Susan Alexander (Dorothy Comingore). To aid us in the search, the camera crawls along the ground toward the dome-shaped roof of Susan's Las Vegas night club. It then soars up and over a sign to reach that dome, whereupon it descends *through* it to reveal the drunken Susan within. The camera has taken us there, has almost brutally invaded her privacy, but it cannot force Susan to divulge her secrets. She is not ready to speak of the husband she loved, then hated, then walked out on. We have already hit a snag in our search for Rosebud, a false lure. We are not ready for the intimacy, and intensity, that Susan will bring to her version of Charles Foster Kane. We must back up and start with a less personal, more objective source.

As it turns out that impersonal, objective source is long dead, but that does not stop our intrepid reporter Thompson (William Alland). He descends into the tomb-like vault that houses the unpublished diary of

Walter Parks Thatcher (George Colouris), the banker who became guardian of the young Kane when a gold mine was discovered on his mother's property. Though Thatcher raised Kane, there is no love or affection between the two. Thompson begins to read the diary, and we are transported to an idyllic wintry scene, lit more brightly than any other in the film, where we watch a young boy playing with his sled. As Kane amuses himself in the snow, his mother (Agnes Moorehead) and father meet inside with Thatcher, signing over to him the guardianship of their son.

The scene is a moving one, but it is rendered much more so by Toland's wide-angle lens, that allows us to see, with equal clarity, the adults coldly settling Kane's future while, through the window behind them, Kane plays guilelessly in the snow. Welles uses this deep-focus photography several more times in *Citizen Kane* to establish important character and plot relationships, but never so powerfully as here. We catch Kane in his last moment of innocence. Though he will go on to be one of the richest men in America, this moment represents a loss of Eden and of the mother he adores.

For all its camera tricks and special effects, what stays with me the most each time I watch *Citizen Kane* is this elegiac mood of loss. When Kane meets his second wife on a street corner, he is on his way to visit the warehouse where all the things that belonged to his mother are stored. He hopes, perhaps, that this sentimental journey to the past will heal his nostalgic longings; instead, he turns to Susan as a vehicle to help restore the childhood that was taken from him. As so many of the characters tell us, Kane is a man in search of love; the only problem is that he has no love of his own to give.

Unable to discover any clues to the identity of Rosebud in Thatcher's diary, Thompson turns first to Kane's closest, most loyal business partner Mr. Bernstein (Everett Sloane) and then to his best friend Jedediah Leland (Joseph Cotten), with whom he later parted company. From Bernstein, we learn how Kane took a hole in the wall newspaper and, by means of some flamboyant yellow journalism, turned it into a publishing empire. In sharp contrast to Bernstein's hero-worship, Jedediah introduces Thompson to the dark side of Kane, to his betrayal of his liberal principles, to his failed first marriage to the niece of the President, and to his pathetic attempts to turn his second wife into an opera singer.

On the simplest level, *Citizen Kane* feeds America's unhealthy desire to see rich people depicted as unhappy and unfulfilled. But it goes far deeper than that to explore how we all possess an inner impulse to self-destruction. As Kane ages, shedding his youthful ideals and becoming increasingly manipulative, the light around him darkens, and he slows from a bundle of kinetic energy to a heavy, static figure. This stiffening of the dreams of youth is intensified by Welles's decision to shoot the ageing Kane from lower and lower angles. By the end, he seems a dark, towering figure who might topple over on top of us at any minute. Kane may continue to think of himself as a crusader against the establishment, but he turns out to be his own worst enemy.

Having learned all he can from Bernstein and Jedediah, Thompson returns to Susan, who is finally ready to share her own memories of Kane. Failing in his attempt to make Susan into an opera singer, Kane withdraws from society and builds her the huge mansion of Xanadu that we saw in ruins in the opening sequence. There he promises to give her happiness, but she only ends up lonely, frustrated, and cut off from the world. Out of boredom, she turns to jigsaw puzzles, but they cannot protect her from the strangling presence of Kane. In the end, she walks out on him.

Having been drawn, through Susan's personal testimony, into the dark recesses of Kane's private life, Thompson and the film pull back, seeking their final assessment of Charles Foster Kane from his cold, impassive butler. From the butler's point of view, we witness the rage that explodes from Kane after Susan leaves him. In one of the most painful and disturbing scenes from the Golden Age, the viewer watches in horror as Kane tears apart Susan's room, the jerky madness of his movements contrasting sharply with his bulky, almost immobile frame. All the frustrations, regrets, and empty dreams of a misspent life are concentrated into the stiff, bear-like sweeps of his arms as he smashes her furniture, pushes over her lamps, and tears down the books from her shelves.

Then, his face expressionless, he lumbers through a crowd of shocked, silent servants and enters a narrow hall with full length mirrors on either side. The effect of the double mirror is to present us with a dozen different Kanes stretching on and on to infinity, each offering, like the five separate testimonies we have heard from Thatcher, Bernstein, Jedediah, Susan, and the butler, a fragment of the true Kane. Can such a man ever be fully known and understood? Can any of us?

In the final scene, Thompson and his men wend their way through the hundreds, if not thousands, of crates that litter the marble floors of Xanadu, each filled with expensive statues and rare objects from around the globe: the "loot of the world" as the newsreel calls it. They have been commissioned to photograph as much of the junk as they can, but they are clearly overwhelmed by the magnitude of Kane's fashionable hoarding. Among the bric-a-brac, they even find boxes filled with Susan's jigsaw puzzles.

Hoping to find the clue that will make sense of Xanadu and its untapped and mostly un-enjoyed treasures, they ask Thompson what he has learned from his research and his interviews about the elusive Rosebud. But he cannot answer their question. All he can do is take up one of Susan's jigsaw puzzles and reflect on the mystery he has been unable to solve: "Mr. Kane was a man who got everything he wanted, and then lost it. Maybe Rosebud was something he couldn't get, or something he lost. Anyway, I don't think it would have explained everything. I don't think any word can describe a man's life. No, I guess Rosebud is just a piece in a jigsaw puzzle—a missing piece."

With that the reporters and photographers make their way out, but the camera remains. Just as it tracked its way silently across the grounds of Xanadu in the opening sequence, so now it hovers silently over the seemingly endless crates. Thompson has given up, but the camera, and through it, us, is still searching for an answer. As it moves deeper into the basement of Xanadu, we realize there is some activity going on. Men are grabbing some of the junk from the piles and burning it in a furnace. Someone seizes a sled, the very sled that little Charlie Kane was playing with in the snow, and throws it on the fire. In the earlier scene, a pile of snow had prevented us from reading the lettering on the sled; now we see the sled has a name engraved on it, and that that name is Rosebud.

Only we and the camera witness the burning away of the letters; only we see the smoke from the fireplace rise up the chimney and spew itself out across the sky over Xanadu. The camera knows this, for as it pulls itself back over the gate of Xanadu, it tracks down to show us once again the "No Trespassing" sign that it showed us in the beginning. Rosebud will remain our secret. The rest is silence.

In later life, Welles came to speak derisively of Rosebud as "dollar-book Freud," but I think he was wrong. No matter how often I watch *Citizen Kane*, I am deeply moved by that final scene, experiencing it as the proper climax to the film. Rosebud is more than cheap sentiment, more than psychobabble. It was with that sled the young Kane tried to push Thatcher away from him, and, with him, the new world that Thatcher would usher him in to. For his first Christmas, Thatcher gives Kane a fancier, more expensive sled, but it cannot take the place of the mother and the idyllic life that was taken from him.

Rosebud is a symbol in the best sense of the term: a wordless image that points to something we can no longer access, a dim memory we reach for but cannot grasp. Our memories are the most intimate part of us; whether they comfort or plague, bring hope or regret, they determine much of that intricate web of consciousness that makes us us.

Fun Facts for the Fans

- *Citizen Kane* was nominated for best picture, director, actor (Welles), music, photography, art direction, and editing, but William Randolph Hearst and his cronies made sure that it only won for the script, which was co-written by Welles and Herman J. Mankiewicz. This proved to be the only Oscar that Welles ever won, though it was meant by the Academy as a tribute to Mankiewicz.

- So great was the Hearst-inspired ire against Welles that, at the Academy Awards ceremony, many booed *Citizen Kane* each time it was nominated for an award.

- It is ironic that Welles took all the flack for the film's parody of Hearst, since Mankiewicz was a personal friend of Hearst and his long-time mistress Marion Davies, and used his first-hand knowledge of the two in crafting the script.
- Critics continue to dispute how much of the script credit belongs to Mankiewicz and how much to Welles.
- Mankiewicz was a New York playwright and critic who, like Ben Hecht, was lured to Hollywood by the promise of high pay and much free time for drinking and gambling. He and Hecht helped give 1930s Hollywood its satirical edge.
- Mankiewicz's younger brother, Joseph Mankiewicz, won back-to-back Oscars for script and direction for *A Letter to Three Wives* and *All About Eve*. His grandson, Ben Mankiewicz, is the Prime Time Host for Turner Classic Movies.
- In 1938, the twenty-two-year-old Welles made it on the cover of Time for his original and quite terrifying radio play version of H. G. Wells's *The War of the Worlds*. The broadcast was so realistic, several people committed suicide in fear. Welles would also gain fame for voicing the Shadow on the radio.
- The notoriety over his *War of the Worlds* broadcast, together with his success at the Mercury Theater in New York City won Welles his ticket to Hollywood.
- When he came, he brought most of his acting troupe with him, including Joseph Cotten, who would become a staple Hollywood actor, and Agnes Moorehead, who is best known for playing Samantha's mother Endora in *Bewitched*.
- Welles watched John Ford's *Stagecoach* again and again to learn how to direct.
- In addition to working with Gregg Toland, the Golden Age's greatest black and white photographer, Welles hired two young men who

would have long, famous careers: composer Bernard Herrmann, who would go on to compose the scores for Hitchcock's *Vertigo, North by Northwest,* and *Psycho,* and editor Robert Wise, who would win directing Oscars for *West Side Story* and *The Sound of Music.*

- *Rebecca* (1940) and *Citizen Kane* (1941), two films that take us on a dark, gothic journey in search of the hidden truth behind their dead titular character, both end with the image of an "R" being consumed in a fire.

Other Films to Watch

It is significant that *Citizen Kane* came out the same year as *The Maltese Falcon,* for it is no exaggeration to say that all of Welles's films have a noir look: After *Kane,* he made another masterpiece, *The Magnificent Ambersons,* based on a Booth Tarkington novel about a family struggling to transition into the modern world. After that, his films, though shot through with touches of genius, often suffered from various flaws in production, since Welles had to make them in bits and pieces as the money came in. Still, it is well worth seeing *The Stranger,* a low-budget but stylish Nazi-hunt, *The Lady from Shanghai,* a confusing but memorable tale of cross and double-cross with Rita Hayworth as the femme fatale, *The Trial,* a moody, paranoid filming of Kafka's novel, *Touch of Evil,* a great noir B picture, and, especially, his three Shakespeare films: *Macbeth, Othello,* and *Chimes at Midnight* (which conflates several plays and focuses on Falstaff).

Welles was an accomplished screen actor. In addition to acting in *Kane, The Stranger* (as the undercover Nazi), *The Lady from Shanghai* (as an adventurer), *Touch of Evil* (as a corrupt sheriff), and as Macbeth, Othello, and Falstaff, he gave great performances in such films as *Journey into Fear* (as a Turkish colonel), *Jane Eyre* (as Rochester), *Black Magic* (as Cagliostro the magician), *Prince of Foxes* (as Cesare Borgia), *The Third Man* (as a Machiavellian villain), *The Black Rose* (as a Mongol), *Moby Dick* (as the preacher), *The Long Hot Summer* (as a tough Southern patriarch),

Compulsion (as a lawyer fighting against the death penalty), and *A Man for All Seasons* (as Cardinal Wolsey).

Though Joseph Cotten tends not to make it on the list of screen immortals, he gave fine performances in *Citizen Kane, The Magnificent Andersons, Journey into Fear, Shadow of a Doubt, Gaslight, Since You Went Away, Love Letters, I'll Be Seeing You, Duel in the Sun, The Farmer's Daughter, Portrait of Jennie, The Third Man,* and *Niagara.*

METRO-GOLDWYN-MAYER'S TECHNICOLOR TRIUMPH!

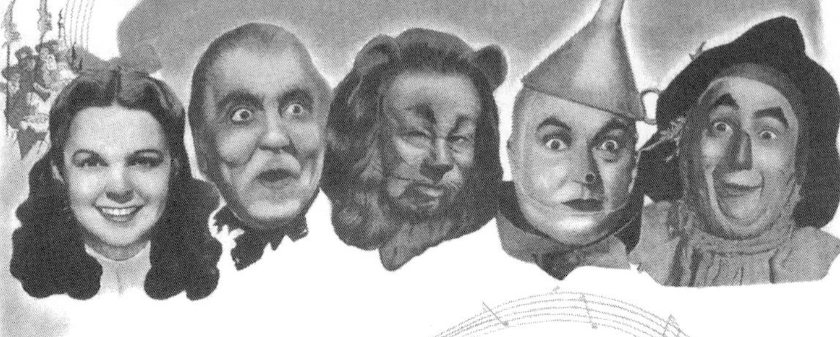

WE'RE OFF TO SEE THE WIZARD..

THE WONDERFUL..

WIZARD OF OZ

WITH

Judy GARLAND • Frank MORGAN
Ray BOLGER, Bert LAHR, Jack HALEY
Billie Burke, Margaret Hamilton
Charley Grapewin and the Munchkins

Directed by Victor Fleming

Produced by Mervyn Le Roy

FOR GENERAL EXHIBITION

BIGGEST SENSATION SINCE "SNOW WHITE"

Songs..
"Over the Rainbow,"
"If I only had a Brain,"
"We're off to see the Wizard,"
"The Merry Old Land of Oz,"
"Ding Dong,"
"If I were King of the Forest"

A Metro-Goldwyn-Mayer PICTURE

THE WIZARD OF OZ

(MGM; 1939; VICTOR FLEMING)

It may seem quite a leap to move directly from a chapter on *Citizen Kane* into one on *The Wizard of Oz,* and yet, there is some sense to the transition. Despite the obvious differences in mood, look, plot, character development, and theme, the two films share a deep-seated Americanism. Both films work in tandem with the American dream, even if it is sacrificed in the former film and maintained in the latter. More to the point, both films work within Hollywood's understanding of the American dream.

I'm not being facetious here. Good arguments can be made, and have been made, that what we call the American dream is an invention of the Eastern European Jewish immigrants, and their children, who built the Hollywood studio system. As long as I'm allowed to add to that group the Sicilian-American Frank Capra and the Irish-American John Ford, then I very much agree with the theory.

Although the first film producers were a WASP-ish band led by Thomas Edison, most of them saw film as a scientific novelty, a plaything with no serious pretensions to art. They were quite happy to confine themselves to making endless shorts to be shown in nickelodeons. At first, this group, known as the Trust, dominated film production, for they controlled the patents on the cameras and held a monopoly on the raw film stock. But their power would eventually be wrested from them by an aggressive, resourceful group of Jewish immigrants (Carl Laemmle, Adolph Zukor, Samuel Goldwyn, Louis B. Mayer, Jack Warner, Harry Cohn, and, a bit later, Irving Thalberg and David Selznick) who would go on to become the absolute monarchs (or moguls) of the movie studios.

Nearly all of these moguls began their lives as poor, dispossessed outsiders who worked their way up in blue-collar entrepreneurial trades: junk-men, furriers, glove salesmen, etc. From there, they purchased theaters and nickelodeons, at first showing only short films but then upgrading to longer, more prestigious films when they discovered two important things about the industry: the customer pays his money *before* seeing the product; in exchange for his money he takes *nothing* away. Soon, they realized that the real money came not from exhibiting the films but from owning the rights to and distributing them to other theaters. From there, it was just one more step before they started producing the films themselves.

And that's when they began to bump heads with the Trust, mostly for financial reasons, but also for artistic/cultural reasons. The Jews who would create Hollywood had a different vision both of film and of themselves as filmmakers. Edison's WASPs were middle-class insiders; to them filmmaking was nothing more than a lucrative game. To the Jewish outsiders, who desperately wanted to be assimilated into American culture and accepted as full-fledged citizens, the movies meant much more. Film, they hoped, would bring them respectability. They would transform it into an art worthy of respect, an art that would embody values that they not only believed in themselves but that they felt were central to the greatness of America.

These values that make up the American Dream include: 1) that hard work, including and especially manual labor, has dignity and is rewarded; 2) that morality too is rewarded, especially virginity in women and honesty in men, and is necessary for a stable society; 3) that the family is central and sacred: fatherhood is wise and just and is to be obeyed; motherhood is pure and selfless and is to be worshipped; 4) that freedom means our ability to practice our skills, to enact our dreams, and to worship our God without discrimination or persecution; 5) that true aristocracy is found in character and not in blood or property; 6) that America is to be defined not by her cynical literati but by the values of her people: both the middle-class and the lower class who struggle to be middle.

In addition to defining the American Dream, even as they tried to live it out themselves, the Jews brought with them an intimate understanding of and identification with the mostly blue-collar patrons that bought the vast majority of movie tickets. Thus, although the Jewish immigrants fought hard to enter the ranks of the rich and powerful, they never lost their natural sympathy for the underdog. Likewise, though many did respect high culture, they understood and felt the immense power and beauty of such popular, common-man art forms as folktales, gypsy dances, and ballads. They knew how to move an audience and make it feel; they were themselves passionate men with strong emotions and volatile temperaments.

Though filmmaking began as an East-coast enterprise, the Jews eventually made it a West-coast phenomenon by moving out, one-by-one, to California. Although their financial centers remained in New York, they all established their studios in southern California. They had at least three good reasons for doing so. First, California lay outside the long-arm of the Trust, keeping the moguls safe from lawsuits. Second, in sunny and diverse California, films could not only be shot year round but benefit from a plethora of distinct natural locales: oceans, deserts, hills, etc. Third, in the vast, empty spaces of Los Angeles, free from an established WASP elite, the moguls could re-make themselves into anything they wanted.

For Louis B. Mayer, MGM was the merry, magical land of Oz. There, in his capacious sound stages, he could dream any dream he wanted and then share that dream with millions of people across America. Indeed, though all of the studios and all of their moguls were responsible for producing and exporting some facet of the American dream, it was MGM and Mayer that offered that dream in its purest form. In the four chapters that follow, I will consider four great musicals that capture elements of that dream as they were refracted through the studio styles of MGM, Warner Brothers, Paramount, and RKO. In this chapter, however, I want to focus specifically on what *The Wizard of Oz*, and Louis B. Mayer, taught me about freedom, innocence, and the life of the imagination.

The Wizard of Oz, the screen informs us, is dedicated to the "young in heart," and, as such, it captures the youthful fervor of America with the same joy and enthusiasm as *The Adventures of Tom Sawyer* and *The Adventures of Huckleberry Finn*. How American that the protagonist of the film should be a young girl from a Kansas farm who goes on an adventure that opens her eyes to the wonders of the world around her. And how American that *The Wizard of Oz*, despite its fantasy setting, is essentially a road picture, even if the Road she goes down is made of yellow bricks!

American writers from Twain to Melville, London to Thoreau, Hemingway to Fitzgerald, Steinbeck to Kerouac preferred to learn their craft and gather their subject matter on their feet in the great outdoors rather than in dusty old libraries filled with books. Like Tom and Huck, Dorothy Gale (Judy Garland), learns, grows, and matures through an active encounter with nature and through a journey that takes her very far out of her comfort zone.

In the opening scenes of the film, shot in sepia, we discover Dorothy in a flat, denuded landscape. In this colorless, shapeless world, there is simply no place for her imagination to inhere, nothing to provoke in her feelings of wonder or beauty or awe. All that her world has to offer are the dark fears and anxieties of childhood, as she and her dog Toto are chased by the terrifying Miss Gulch (Margaret Hamilton), who threatens not only to kidnap but to "destroy" Toto. Still, something within Dorothy yearns for a richer life of the imagination, a yearning powerfully expressed in the lovely song that would become Judy Garland's signature, "Over the Rainbow."

In keeping with Mayer's own biography, Dorothy, though she grows up in a poor, home structured around duty and chores, is a dreamer who longs to visit that magic land that you cannot reach by boat or train. And when she reaches it, she pulls everyone else into her dream. By having the Scarecrow, Tin Man, and Cowardly Lion (not to mention the Wizard of Oz and the Wicked Witch) be played by actors who also appear in the Kansas sequences, the film does more than give itself an easy out to appease the skeptics in the audience (it was all a dream; Oz only exists in Dorothy's head). The doubling of actors, whether or not we decide the adventure was real or a dream, makes Dorothy's journey to Oz so compelling that it is able to assimilate and transform the characters that share her dreary, quotidian life in Kansas.

It is also significant that before she goes on her journey to Oz, Dorothy, like Tom and Huck, adopts the quintessentially American guise of the runaway orphan who seeks a kind of freedom she can't find on the farm. In her archetypal flight, she meets Professor Marvel (Frank Morgan), a sort of latter-day wandering minstrel who, in his own way, is living the bohemian life of the imagination. Unlike the people on the farm, Marvel sees right away that Dorothy feels misunderstood and longs to experience the wide world. Still, being a kindly man, he sends her home to her aunt and uncle, thus upholding, in true MGM/Mayer style, both the desire for adventure and the goodness of home and family.

Once she gets to Oz, the dichotomy between the life-crushing Miss Gulch and the life-affirming Professor Marvel will take on mythic proportions in the struggle between the Wicked Witch and the Wizard, who are played, it should come as no surprise, by the same set of actors. Oz will be the sound stage on which that struggle will be acted out. Modern audiences who watch the film carefully may be disappointed to discover that all the backdrops for Oz, from the fields to the forests to the mountains, are in reality huge matte paintings. Speaking for myself, I think the paintings add a greater degree of magic to Oz, making it seem as if Dorothy's imagination has created those colorful backdrops.

Speaking of color, I never get tired of watching that breathtaking moment when Dorothy opens the door of her cottage and walks out of her dull, sepia world into the dazzling Technicolor of Oz. The transition makes me catch my breath each time as it invites me to step into a world where the imagination has been set free and all things shimmer with wonder. If Dorothy is dreaming, then I'm happy to dream alongside her.

The Messianic Dorothy carries with her into Oz a sense of liberation that is infectious. In addition to bringing "political" liberation to the Munchkins by killing, if accidentally, the Wicked Witch of the East, her irrepressible faith, hope, and love draw otherwise timid characters into her quest. Inspired by Dorothy's simple strength and childlike courage, the Scarecrow (Ray Bolger), the Tin Man (Jack Haley), and the Cowardly Lion (Bert Lahr) join her, believing that the Wizard that she believes can send her home will also give them the brain, heart, and courage they lack.

After she sings and dances with the "safe" Munchkins, Dorothy is ready to move out into the unknown world. She is given some advice by

Glinda, the Good Witch of the North (Billie Burke), but it doesn't do her much good. Dorothy, in true self-reliant American fashion, will have to figure things out as she goes along, facing her deepest fears and learning to trust the insights of her three helpers/guides/mentors. Had *The Wizard of Oz* been made at Warner Brothers, Dorothy would have gotten by through wise-cracking cleverness and toughness; had it been made at Paramount, she would have relied on smooth sophistication and worldly savoir-faire. But this is the MGM of Louis B. Mayer, and so she remains a neophyte, an initiate who faces her tests and survives her rite of passage by clinging to her innocence, optimism, humility, and loyalty. Rather than make her weak, her innocence makes her strong and supple.

As they make their way to the Emerald City, Dorothy and her three companions must learn to work together, to use their individual gifts to complement and complete one another. That is to say, in good American style, they work cooperatively without losing their unique individuality. Team work, not socialism, collaboration, not communism is the American way. Not by losing themselves in the collective, but by strengthening one another and by focusing on their individual and group dreams, they achieve their goal.

But it won't be easy. In order to meet with the Wizard, they must walk down a long, narrow, scary corridor that resembles the birth canal through which the newborn baby is pushed, crying, into the world. Without ever getting Freudian, the film reminds us that the passage into full maturity is often painful and frightening. Dorothy faces that passage with courage and resolve, but it is her admission that she is Dorothy the weak and the small and the innocent tears she sheds that melt the Wizard's heart. Dorothy is worthy, but she cannot return home until she and her friends perform a task, stealing the Witch's broomstick, that is as archetypally resonant as the quest for the Holy Grail.

As part of that task, she must endure the terror and dread of a group of flying monkeys that have induced nightmares in four generations of movie viewers. Every thing about the Wicked Witch, from her green face to her monkeys, her forbidding castle to her robotic guards, plays on our numinous fears. Who cannot shiver with fright and anxiety when the

Witch locks Dorothy in a room and places before her a twisted hourglass? If she does not surrender her ruby slippers by the time the sand has run through the glass, her life will be forfeit. Alone and frightened, Dorothy gazes into the hourglass and sees, in sepia, her Aunt Em back on the farm looking for her. She calls out to her, only to watch in horror as Em's black and white face morphs into the green scowl of the Witch. Who shall prove to be Dorothy's mother figure? In whose footsteps will she follow?

It is powerfully significant that Dorothy kills the Wicked Witch, not with a sword or ax or dagger, but with a bucket of simple, clean water. As the Witch melts, she shrieks her dying words: "Who would have thought a good little girl like you could destroy my beautiful wickedness." The struggle here goes deeper than good vs. evil; it is really about innocence vs. corruption. In L. Frank Baum's novel, Dorothy throws the water on the Witch when she steals one of her slippers; in the film, she throws it to save Scarecrow from being burned by the Witch's fire. When the innocent Dorothy of the film acts, she almost always does so out of loyalty to her friends rather than out of self-preservation. She not only refuses to model herself on the Witch; she will not think or react like her.

After the Witch melts, Dorothy and her friends fear that the guards, the Winkies, will turn against them, but they are wrong. The Winkies who have been enslaved by the Witch, hail Dorothy as a liberator. Once again, the film teaches us that goodness and innocence are infectious, spreading hope and freedom in their wake. The scene in which the Wizard gives the Scarecrow, Tin Man, and Lion their brain, heart, and courage offers a memorable example of MGM gently poking fun at academics, philanthropists, and veterans while yet affirming the kindness and decency at the heart of Middle America.

But what of Dorothy's wish to go home to Kansas and Aunt Em? Alas, there is nothing in the Wizard's magic bag to help her do that. A bungled attempt to take Dorothy home on a hot air balloon proves equally ineffective. No, in good American optimistic fashion, it turns out that Dorothy herself has possessed within her all along the power to return home; she just needed to learn it for herself, to gain, on her feet, the maturity, wisdom, and insight to realize who she is and what she is capable of. What then must she do? Glinda gives her the instructions that she couldn't give her earlier, because, at that point, Dorothy would not have understood or appreciated them: "Close your eyes and tap your heels together three times. And think to yourself, there's no place like home."

In the novel, Dorothy says "take me home." By altering that to "there's no place like home," the film affirms MGM and Mayer's embrace of family values. Yes, Oz is a wonderful place where dreams come true and the imagination is liberated, but we also have duties to our family that must be upheld. Dorothy herself explains to us the moral of the story: "If ever I go looking for my heart's desire again, I won't look any further than my own back yard, because if it isn't there, I never really lost it to begin with."

Let's face it, Kansas is a dreary place and Aunt Em is hardly a bundle of maternal nurture, but it is home and she is family, and that's as much a part of the American dream as the wish to travel over the rainbow. The two may seem contradictory but not when we realize the power of dreams (and movies) to carry us to Oz without ever leaving Kansas.

Fun Facts for the Fans

- *The Wizard of Oz* was nominated for best picture and art direction; it took best song ("Over the Rainbow") and music direction and won Garland a special Oscar.
- MGM desperately wanted Shirley Temple for the role of Dorothy, but Twentieth Century Fox would not release her to do the picture. To make it up to her, Fox later produced an Oz-like Technicolor fantasy for Temple titled *The Blue Bird*.
- *The Wizard of Oz* was the kind of Prestige Picture Thalberg used to oversee (it cost 2.6 million). His death in 1936 freed Mayer to make the film his own way.
- Amazingly, the "Over the Rainbow" scene was almost cut from the film because it slowed down the picture, delaying Dorothy's arrival in Oz.

- The catchy, clever songs were written by Harold Arlen and E. Y. Harburg. Arlen would be responsible for writing the tunes for such standard American songs as "I've Got the World on a String," "Paper Moon," "Blues in the Night," "Come Rain or Come Shine," "Let's Fall in Love," "The Man That Got Away," "One for My Baby," "Stormy Weather," "That Old Black Magic," and "Get Happy."
- Buddy Ebsen was originally cast as the Scarecrow, then switched to the Tin Man, then had to back out due to an allergic reaction to the Tin Man's aluminum paint.
- The special edition DVD of *The Wizard of Oz* includes an energetic dance by the Scarecrow that was cut from the film; I highly recommend watching it.
- L. Frank Baum's 1900 novel had previously been filmed as a silent in 1925.
- In the novel, Dorothy's journey is real; the film suggests it might be a dream.
- In the novel, the Witch has one eye; the film gives her a green face instead.
- The novel's emerald slippers were changed to ruby to highlight the Technicolor.

Other Films to Watch

Here are some of my favorite non-horror/non-sci-fi fantasy films: *Lost Horizon*, *The Thief of Baghdad* (the best Arabian Nights tale put on film, starring Indian child actor Sabu), *All that Money Can Buy* (man sells his soul to the devil and then holds trial to get it back), *Cabin in the Sky* (all-black comedy-musical in which God and Satan fight for a soul), *Heaven Can Wait* (a man's life is reviewed after he dies), *Here Comes Mr. Jordan* (a man dies too soon and is sent back in another body), *Angel on my Shoulder* (a man in hell is given the chance to do a good deed on earth),

The Ghost and Mrs. Muir (romance between a young widow and the ghost of a sea captain; later a TV series), *Portrait of Jennie* (artist meets a mysterious girl who keeps ageing), *A Matter of Life and Death* (a man dies too soon and a trial is held in heaven to bring him back), *The Picture of Dorian Gray* (from the Oscar Wilde novel), *Gabriel Over the White House* (a Depression/New Deal fantasy), *The Man who Could Work Miracles* (mild-mannered man gets powers; based on an H. G. Wells story), *Things to Come* (futuristic utopia; based on a Wells novel), *The Time Machine* (Wells again, with good special effects), *Enchantment* (a house tells the tale of its owners), *Time after Time* (Wells chases Jack the Ripper into the future), *Somewhere in Time* (time-travel romance), *Topper, The Ghost Breakers, I Married a Witch, The Ghost Goes West,* and *Blithe Spririt* (all comedies with ghosts), *Carousel* (Rodgers and Hammerstein musical where dead man returns to visit his family).

Here are some that are perfect for kids and discerning adults of all ages. From Disney's animation studios: *Snow White and the Seven Dwarves, Pinocchio, Cinderella, Peter Pan, Sleeping Beauty, Alice in Wonderland, The Little Mermaid, Beauty and the Beast,* and *Aladdin*. Live action: *The Bluebird* (with Shirley Temple), *Miracle on 34th Street* (Santa Claus visits NYC), *Mary Poppins* (best live-action Disney film), *Chitty Chitty Bang Bang* (featuring a flying car), *Bednobs and Broomsticks* (featuring a flying bed), *Willy Wonka and the Chocolate Factory* (fantasy with a moral edge), *Jason and the Argonauts* (the best of the Greek mythology films, though *Clash of the Titans* is also quite good), *Tom Thumb* (has wonderful choreography and special effects), *Jack the Giant Killer* (truly magical), and Ray Harryhausen's *The Seventh Voyage of Sinbad, The Golden Voyage of Sinbad,* and *Sinbad and the Eye of the Tiger*.

And here are a few fantasies from other countries: *Siegfried* and *Metropolis* (German silent films from Fritz Lang), *The Seventh Seal* (Swedish; knight plays chess game with death), *Miracle in Milan* (Italian; magic child brings joy and hope with him), *La Belle et la Bete* and *Orphee* (French; Jean Cocteau's take on the Beauty and the Beast fairytale and the Orpheus myth), *Black Orpheus* (Brazil; Orpheus myth set during Carnival), *Kwaidan, Ugetsu,* and *Akira Kurosawa's Dreams* (collections of Japanese ghost stories).

M-G-M's MEET ME IN ST. LOUIS

GLORIOUS LOVE STORY WITH MUSIC

Starring JUDY Garland

With MARGARET O'BRIEN

MARY ASTOR LUCILLE BREMER

TOM DRAKE MARJORIE MAIN

SCREEN PLAY BY IRVING BRECHER AND FRED F. FINKLEHOFFE

A METRO-GOLDWYN-MAYER PICTURE

BASED ON THE BOOK BY SALLY BENSON

DIRECTED BY VINCENTE MINNELLI

PRODUCED BY ARTHUR FREED

Photographed in TECHNICOLOR

MEET ME IN ST. LOUIS

(MGM; 1944; VINCENTE MINNELLI)

Although five years and a World War separate *The Wizard of Oz* from *Meet Me in St. Louis,* both films end with the same MGM-Mayer affirmation that there's no place like home. The difference is that *Meet Me in St. Louis* introduces us to an ideal, small-town family that combines the duty and responsibility of Aunt Em and the Kansas farm with the rich imaginative life of Oz. Thus, when Esther Smith (Judy Garland) realizes that everything she really wants and needs is right there in her home town of St. Louis, she does not have to give up, as Dorothy seemingly has to give up, the joy, freedom, color, and song that she has yearned for and learned to value over the course of the film.

Meet Me in St. Louis is set in 1903, the year that the World's Fair came to St. Louis, and takes its viewers through four seasons in the life of an old-fashioned, all-American family. Lawyer Alonzo Smith (Leon Ames) and his perfect bourgeois wife Anna (Mary Astor) live in a big, but genteel house with their three older teenaged children, Lon, Rose (Lucille Bremer) and Esther, and their two young daughters, Agnes and Tootie (Margaret O'Brien). Grandpa (Harry Davenport) also lives with them, and they have a cook, Katie (Marjorie Main), who is practically one of the family.

Oddly, the film is at once episodic and seamlessly integrated. It is episodic in the sense that it moves from one carefully-framed snapshot to the next, each of which brings the family, or one of its members, into clear relief. As viewers, we watch the film over the shoulders of the Smith clan, catching them off guard as they reveal their hopes and fears, joys and sorrows, triumphs and disappointments. What unites these cameo-like episodes into a unified whole are the lovely, nostalgic songs by Hugh Martin and Ralph Blane, songs which Judy does not belt out in her usual fashion—she was known as the little girl with the big voice—but sings gently and sensitively, using her "inside voice."

Just one year earlier, Broadway had been revolutionized by Rodgers and Hammerstein's first show, *Oklahoma!* Whereas most previous Broadway musicals had really been reviews, stories interrupted by show-stopping numbers, *Oklahoma!* was a fully integrated musical in which each song carried forward the plot and aided in character development. Such is the case with *Meet Me in St. Louis,* where the songs rise up naturally out of the dreams and aspiration of Esther and her family.

In fact director Vincente Minnelli uses the title song, "Meet Me in St. Louis," not only to establish the exact time frame—the film begins seven months before the Fair—but to introduce us to the various members of the Smith family and to their home. The two young girls sing it with an abandon and bravado that sum up their free spirits, while the two older ones sing it with a kind of sophisticated romanticism that highlights their own yearnings for love and romance. Brother Lon is better at hiding his enthusiasm. Mother is happy to see her children excited by the coming Fair, while Father is sick and tired of the whole ordeal, annoyed that the song should even be invading his home. As for grandpa, he sings like one who has drunk from the fountain of youth. As the song passes infectiously from character to character, the audience too is drawn into the fun. To make the scene even more genuine and spontaneous, Minnelli even has Agnes sneeze on beat.

But the moment at which the film truly comes alive for me is when Esther shares with Rose her settled plan that their next-door neighbor John Truitt (Tom Drake) will fall in love with her and marry her. Her determination gives way, in a natural, unforced manner, to her singing "The Boy Next Door" as she gazes longingly out the window. Slowly, the camera shifts its perspective, allowing us in the audience to watch as the hopeful Esther, framed by lace curtains, sings of her heartfelt desire to be noticed and appreciated by the boy she has chosen. In this overheard, but non-voyeuristic moment of timid but passionate song, Esther's heart is laid bare. Yes, it's a star solo, an MGM photo-op to promote Judy Garland, but it's also real and authentic and deeply intimate.

Later in the film, after successfully luring John to her home for a party, Esther convinces him to accompany her as she turns off, one by one, the gas lights in each of the downstairs rooms. What ensues is one of the tenderest evocations of budding young love put on film. I can't watch this scene without involuntarily slowing my breathing and the beating of my heart. On the surface, all that happens is that a number of gas cocks are turned from the on to the off position, causing the lights to go out in each successive room. Beneath the surface, the eager hearts of a girl and a boy are mystically united by and through a ritual that has been lost forever in our fast-paced electrical age. The scene hangs frozen in time, a memento to a less-complicated world when people still had time to pause and contemplate the slow dimming of a gas light.

Which is not to say that the world of Esther Smith is anti-technology or bereft of high-octane energy and exhilaration. One of the film's most memorable sequences takes place on a trolley car as Esther sings to herself and those around her about the love-at-first-sight she experienced when she met John. In a burst of lyricism that seems to flow directly out of her without forethought or premeditation, she pictures that fateful meeting taking place on a busy, noisy trolley car: "'Clang, clang, clang,' went the trolley, / 'Ding, ding, ding,' went the bell, / 'Zing, zing, zing,' went my heartstrings, / From the moment I saw him I fell." Sound, color, and movement all work together to sweep the viewer up into her innocent fantasy, uniting the power of young love with that of wheels and gears.

Technology, it seems, *can* assist young love, but only when it operates in sync with the beating of the human heart. The new world, which will eventually be summed up in the Fair's façade of electric lights, need not sound the death knell of the old. In true MGM-American style, we can progress and advance without sacrificing traditional family values; if anything, that progress, properly harnessed, can aid in the preservation and integrity of those values. We just need to get our priorities straight.

At first sight, *Meet Me in St. Louis* seems to be dramatically hampered by its lack of a villain. We think, for a moment, that Lucille Ballard (June Lockhart), a supposed Eastern snob, will be the antagonist who will break up the proper loves of Lon and Rose; but we in the audience turn out to be as wrong about Lucille as Rose and Esther. Miss Ballard is actually a sweet young lady who does the right thing at just the right moment. No, if we are to correctly locate the villain, we must shift our sights away from the human characters that populate the film. Only then will we see that the real "bad guy" is New York City, the place to which Alonzo Smith announces he will be moving his family for the sake of upward mobility and a larger pay check that will benefit them all.

The scene in which Alonzo makes his announcement offers an object lesson in how a Judeo-Christian family grounded in a biblical understanding of the healthy and proper relationship between husbands and wives, parents and children should operate. When Alonzo shares his news, he fully expects that his family will be overjoyed by the chance to move to the big, progressive city of New York. For a second, they *are* excited, until they start realizing what the move would mean to each of them: smaller living quarters with no room for pets and sentimental possessions; the loss of friends and community; the marginalizing of grandpa. Even Katie throws in her two cents, warning them about the inferior ovens in New York City. For a terrible moment, communication breaks down and tempers start to flare. Though they all respect Alonzo, they have all worked a bit too hard to keep him out of the loop. This don't-tell-daddy strategy makes for much humor in the film, but it too often leaves him ignorant of what is going on in the lives of his wife and children, inevitably leading to a conflict like this one

As each individual member of the family excuses himself from the table, even turning down cake and ice cream to do so, the delicate unity of the Smith family seems poised to unravel. But the weave does not come undone! Though upset, Anna won't turn against her husband or compromise his authority as head of the household. She goes to the piano and begins to play. Soon, Alonzo comes beside her and begins to sing, not in the seasoned voice of a performer, but in the realistic, somewhat gruff voice of a tired patriarch. Anna quickly notices that she is playing out of his range and adjusts the key lower to accommodate his voice. As mother and father make music together, the children are drawn back into the sitting room. One by one, they take up their cake and ice cream and begin to sing, to converse, and to laugh.

Wife and children obey their father, not out of fear, but out of love and trust and respect. They know what kind of a man he is, that he will not act unless he believes his actions will benefit the family as a whole. Alonzo is strengthened by their support, and, in the end, he makes the right decision to forsake the opportunities promised by New York and remain in St. Louis. He does so because he comes to understand how disruptive the move would be to his family, and for another, subtler reason that is conveyed, as so much of the thematic message of the film is conveyed, through song. As Alonzo stands, God-like, on a dark stairway and surveys the pain he is causing to Esther and Tootie, we hear, quietly, the first four measures of "Meet Me in St. Louis," the very song that Alonzo found so nerve-wracking in the opening scene. Then, we hear it again, slightly louder, and a third time, blaring like a battle trumpet.

Though it is not stated directly, I believe that Alonzo actually hears the music in his head. It has sunk into his psyche and now plays out at full volume, provoking and inspiring an epiphany in the staid, pragmatic Alonzo Smith. He immediately calls his family together and announces that they are going to stay in St. Louis, stay until they rot! After all, New York doesn't have everything; St. Louis is poised to be a very important city, and they have a chance to be a part of it.

Such is the narrative core of *Meet Me in St. Louis*—well, with one important factor that I have thus far left out. Though the film celebrates masculinity and femininity in a beautiful and affirming way, it does place at the center of the film and of the Smith family a little girl whose outward sweetness (sugar and spice and everything nice) masks a macabre, hoodlum spirit rife with snips and snails and puppy dogs' tails. I mean Tootie, whose obsession with death and blood and fatal diseases greets us in the opening scene. One never knows what will come out of that child's mouth, as when she asks Esther if she can sing a song at her party, and then proceeds to belt out, while swaying on her little legs, "I was drunk last night, dear mother!"

Tootie is truly adorable, but her presence in the film never lets us forget that there is a dark side to humanity that must be understood and kept in check if civilization is to survive and thrive. In the Middle Ages, the Catholic Church wisely handled that dark side by allowing it to surface in bits and pieces without overwhelming the community. They did this in great part by setting up a seasonal calendar that included fasts as well as feasts, times of sober reflection as well as times of revelry. The best known example of the latter is Mardi Gras, Latin for "Fat Tuesday": the day before Ash Wednesday and the severities of Lent. Mardis Gras is also known as Carnival, Latin for "farewell to flesh." By means of the topsy-turvydom of Carnival, a time of riotous dancing, excessive carousing, and cross-dressing between the classes and the sexes, society was supplied with a sort of emotional safety valve to help people from all walks of life let off steam.

Meet Me in St. Louis, one of the greatest family films ever made, factors into its nostalgic snapshots just such a Carnival scene. The setting is All-Hallows Eve, but the people who give themselves over to madness are the children rather than the adults. Dressed in bizarre and frightening costumes, the child revelers build bonfires out of old and broken furniture and run riot in the streets. They then play a perfectly ghoulish game in which they "kill" neighbors they don't like by knocking on their door and, when they open it, throwing flour in their shocked faces. Tootie, who is overjoyed to learn that, in her costume, she looks the most horrible, volunteers to "kill" the one neighbor whom everyone fears and who is purported to own a wild, flesh-eating dog! Every numinous dread, every nameless anxiety felt by child or adult can be read in Tootie's face as she makes her way down a lane that looked innocent and quaint in the daylight scenes but is now transformed into nightmare alley. For a second, we see it all through the terrified but resolute eyes of Tootie—a world of dark shapes and sharp angles more appropriate to a noir film than an old-fashioned musical.

For the most part, this dark side of the human psyche is confined to the Halloween scene, but it does break out at one other point in the film. As the Smith family celebrate what they believe will be their last Christmas in St. Louis, Esther tries to cheer up the despairing Tootie by singing her a song that would become a standard yuletide carol: "Have Yourself a Merry Little Christmas." When the song is sung today by happy people gathered around the tree with their loved ones, they sing the cheery line, "Hang a shining star upon the highest bough"; when Esther sings it to Tootie, she uses the sadder, more poignant line: "Until then we'll have to muddle through somehow." This Christmas does not signify for the Smith children a time of joy and hope, but a farewell to the home and city they love.

As Esther finishes her song, something remarkable happens that takes me by surprise every time I watch the film. In a burst of tears, Tootie runs down the stairs and outside the house to a group of snowpeople that she had helped to make. As Esther and we look on helplessly from the window, Tootie takes up a bat and begins to smash off the heads of the snowpeople. She would rather kill them than let them stay behind in St. Louis without her. The savagery of her attack is truly disturbing to watch, partly because we as viewers have no categories in which to file this intense display of anger, grief, and confusion. Tootie expresses the emotions that no one else has the courage to express: partly because they are not willing to act in so anti-social a manner; partly because they don't understand the emotions they are feeling.

But her *cri de coeur*, her passionate cry of the heart, is heard by the patriarch who watches from the darkened stairs. He hears and he sees and he acts to restore balance and order to his family. The twenty-first century has unfortunately demonized the word patriarchy, but that is only because we have lost a sense of how it was meant to work, in the Bible, in the days of Christendom, in Victorian England, and in that portion of the American dream that MGM and Louis B. Mayer helped capture for all time in such classic family films as *Meet Me in St. Louis*.

Fun Facts for the Fans

- *Meet Me in St. Louis* was nominated for best script, photography, music direction, and song ("The Trolley Song"); Margaret O'Brien was awarded a special Oscar.
- Twenty-one-year-old Garland did not want to play the role of Esther; she had finally grown out of juvenile roles and did not want to play another teen. Luckily, Mayer forced her to do it, leading to one of her best loved screen performances.
- Garland never looked more beautiful than she did in this film; that is partly because director Vincente Minnelli, who was nineteen years older, was falling in love with her. He would marry her the following year and the two would give birth to Liza Minnelli, who would inherit her mother's vocal and dramatic talents.
- Minnelli was born in 1903, the year that the film takes place.
- Before the success of the Technicolor *Meet Me in St. Louis,* all of MGM's musicals (except the fantasy-musical *Wizard of Oz*) were shot in black and white. After its success, all future MGM musicals were shot in expensive Technicolor.
- Lionel Barrymore once said of the precocious O'Brien: "If that child had been born in the Middle Ages, she'd have been burned as a witch."
- The script was based on stories by Sally Benson that appeared in the New Yorker; to increase Garland's role, the film added in the character of the boy next door.
- "The Trolley Song" was written in a burst of inspiration after the composer and lyricist opened a children's book in the library to find a large picture of a trolley car with the caption: "Clang, clang, clang goes the Trolley."
- To give the film a warm, homey feel, the orchestra used was 1/3 the normal size.

- Due to wartime rationing, building material was in short supply. Knowing how vital the house was to the film, Minnelli spent nearly all his material on the house. That is why the glimpse we get of the World's Fair at the end is so sparse.
- Though Judy Garland married five times and Mickey Rooney eight times, they oddly never married each other!

Other Films to Watch

With the death of Irving Thalberg in 1936, MGM, under the firm hand and tastes of Louis B. Mayer, turned with full force to the kinds of films Mayer would want his daughters to see (with an * by those that starred Mayer's favorite boy wonder, Mickey Rooney): **Ah Wilderness* (based on a Eugene O'Neill play, this was MGM's first attempt at small-town USA; it's quite good and was remade as a musical, *Summer Holiday*), **A Family Affair* (first in a long line of Andy Hardy films that personified the American family; these were the sentimental Mayer's favorite films and dripped with sweetness and light), **Captains Courageous* (a moving coming-of-age sea tale from Rudyard Kipling), **Boys' Town* (real life Fr. Flanagan runs a school for juvenile delinquents), **The Adventures of Huckleberry Finn* (good rendition of Twaine's novel), **Babes in Arms* (first teaming of Mickey Rooney and Judy Garland, who join forces to put-on-a-show; followed by **Strike up the Band*, **Babes on Broadway*, and **Girl Crazy*), *The Wizard of Oz*, **The Human Comedy* (small-town boy comes of age; sad *and* funny), *The Clock* (GI meets and marries Judy Garland on a twenty-four-hour leave), **National Velvet* (young Elizabeth Taylor wins horse race), *The Secret Garden* (splendid Victorian family film with a dark house hiding a dark secret; offers three of the finest child performances on film), *Father of the Bride* (warm, funny film with Taylor as the bride; remade in 1991).

Judy Garland made many other fine musicals, including *Ziegfeld Girl* (as an aspiring singer), *For Me and My Gal* (with Gene Kelly) *Harvey Girls* (as an adventurous girl heading West), *The Pirate* (with Kelly again), *Easter Parade* (with Fred Astaire), *In the Good Old Summertime* (musical remake of *The Shop Around the Corner*), *Summer Stock* (with Kelly), and *A Star is Born* (that features both her singing and dramatic talents). At the end of her life, she gave strong performances in three dramatic films: *Judgment at Nuremburg, A Child is Waiting,* and *I Could Go on Singing.*

In addition to his musicals, Minnelli made some excellent non-musical films: *The Clock, Madame Bovary* (a good rendition of the Flaubert novel), *Father of the Bride, The Bad and the Beautiful* (one of the best films about Hollywood), *The Long, Long Trailer* (hilarious Lucille Ball comedy) *Lust for Life* (powerful biopic of Van Gogh in brilliant color), *Two Weeks in Another Town* (sequel to *Bad and the Beautiful*). He also made many melodramas with powerful scenes that have not aged as well: *The Cobweb, Tea and Sympathy, The Sandpiper,* etc.

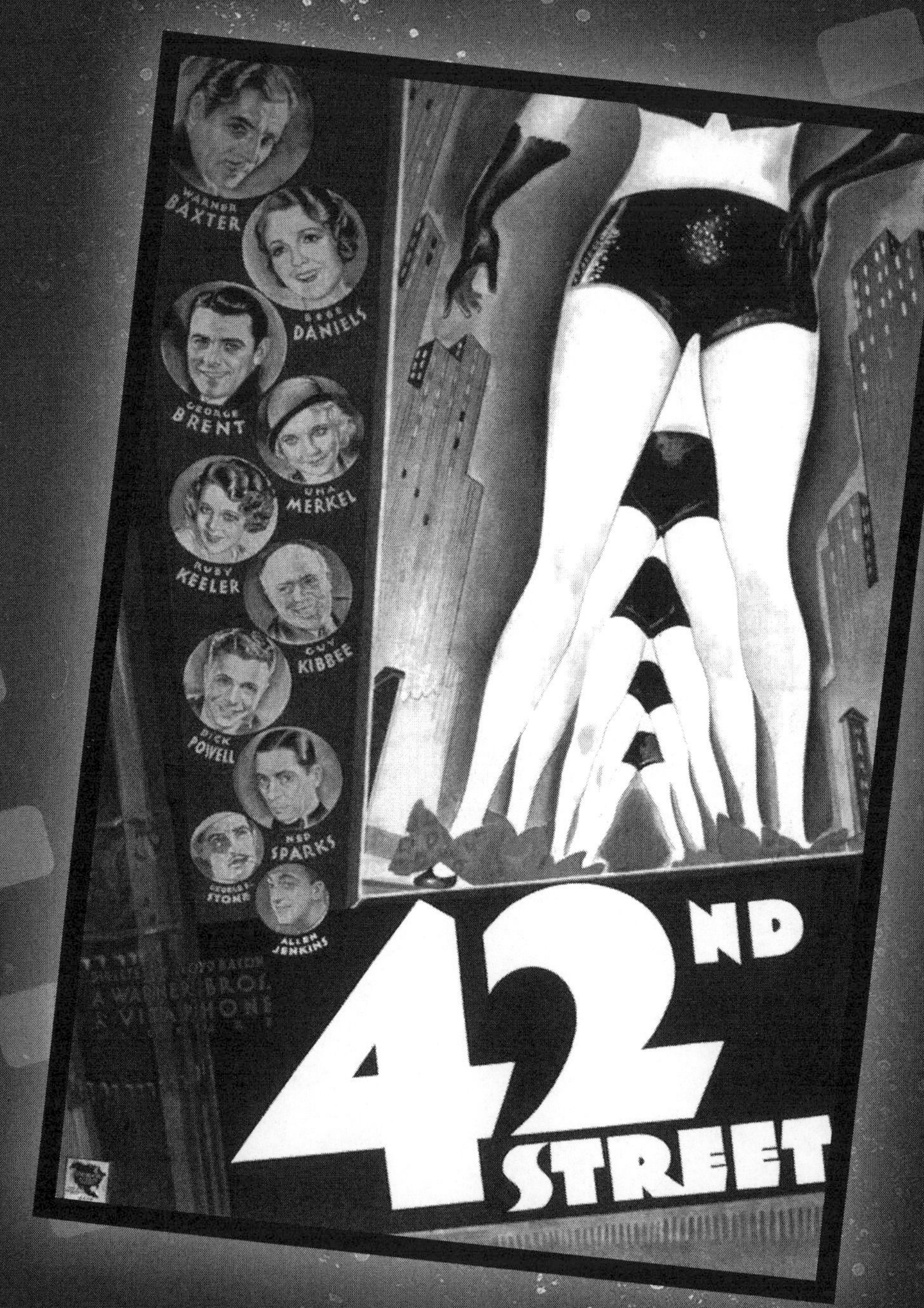
WARNER BAXTER
BEBE DANIELS
GEORGE BRENT
UNA MERKEL
RUBY KEELER
GUY KIBBEE
DICK POWELL
NED SPARKS
GEORGE E. STONE
ALLEN JENKINS
42ND STREET

42ND STREET

(WB; 1933; LLOYD BACON)

MGM's 1944 *Meet Me in St. Louis* is about a family. Warner Brothers' 1933 *42nd Street* is also about a family, but of a very different kind. But then Warner Brothers was itself a very different kind of studio, birthed and sustained by an actual, real-life family.

Patriarch Ben Warner had taught his four sons (Harry, Jack, Abe, and Sam) to stick together no matter what. He had even rendered that lesson concrete by handing each boy a stick and instructing him to snap it in half. Then, after each of them had snapped their stick with little to no strain, he gathered four new sticks and tied them together in a bundle. He then passed the bundle of sticks from one brother to the next, smiling on as each tried, unsuccessfully, to snap the bundle in half. The lesson was plain; as long as they stuck together as a family, nobody could tear them apart.

Two of the four sons are less known today, with Abe playing the role of salesman and Sam tinkering away until he helped perfect the transition from silent films to sound—only to die suddenly a mere twenty-four hours before the success of *The Jazz Singer*, Hollywood's first sound film, catapulted WB from a minor to a major studio. The other two retain their legendary status, with Harry taking care of the business end in New York City and Jack running the studio in California.

Harry, who was never comfortable around stars, led a simple life; he possessed a strong social conscience and wanted to make message-driven films that would enlighten and educate as well as entertain. Jack, in sharp contrast, was a womanizer who was ever unfaithful to his wife and who caused constant scandals that upset and embarrassed big brother Harry. As Chief of Production, he whose last name was blazoned across the WB water tower, Jack demanded complete submission to his rule, often fighting tooth-and-nail with such major stars as James Cagney and Bette Davis. Unlike Harry, Jack was not interested in educating or enlightening. "If I want to send a message," he was (in) famous for saying, "I'll call Western Union!"

And yet, for all the strife between Jack and Harry and Jack and his stars, and despite the fact that WB spent many long years on Poverty Row, the studio that the brothers Warner built retained its cohesion against all the odds. WB seemed always to have its back against the wall, yet they somehow always overcame the obstacles thrown in their path. They were underdogs who never gave up the fight. That is perhaps why WB was the only Jewish-run studio that maintained its Jewish identity. They never lost a sense of their immigrant-proletarian background, preferring to celebrate the scrappers who lived out their lives in a tough urban world where they teetered precariously on the edge of the gutter. While MGM and Paramount films acted as if the Great Depression were a million miles away, the WB films of the 1930s stared that grim reality in the face.

That is because the characters that inhabit MGM and Paramount films never have to worry about money. Whether or not the Smith family goes to New York or remains in St. Louis, none of the children is going to have to face eviction; neither Tom nor Gerry, that madcap couple from *The Palm Beach Story*, are ever in any real danger of starving in the street. Not so at WB, where one wrong move will send our hard-working, go-getting hero or heroine into the poor house or the brothel, the asylum or the jail. Even when, as in *42nd Street*, the film takes place on Broadway, the gangsters are only a phone call away and the prospect of having to spend the night on a park bench is an ever-present one. *42nd Street* is a musical, but it takes place in the same film noir world of back alleys and fly-by-night apartments as *The Maltese Falcon*. True, it boasts a happy ending, but that happy ending is hard fought, tenuous, and decidedly unglamorous.

Indeed, the film does not end, as it would have at MGM or Paramount with the happy wedding of our more mature couple or a passionate embrace and kiss by our young and perky couple, but with the underdog producer of the show sitting alone in the dark on the back stairs of the theater while the enthusiastic audience hails the new star, ignoring him and his contribution to the success of the show.

But now I am getting ahead of myself—an easy thing to do when writing about a film that moves forward at such a hectic pace that the viewer can barely catch his breath. Here are the bare bones of a plot which, though composed completely of cardboard characters and conventional cinema clichés, miraculously manages to transcend them.

Julian Marsh (Warner Baxter), one of the most successful producers on Broadway has lost all of his money in the Stock Market crash. Though his doctor has warned him against it, the driven Julian pushes forward to produce a new review show, *Pretty Lady*, which will get its backing from Abner Dillon (Guy Kibbee), a sugar daddy enamored of the show's temperamental star Dorothy Brock (Bebe Daniels). Unfortunately for the show, Dorothy is in love with Pat Denning (George Brent), who gave her her start in Vaudeville but whose star has since declined while hers has risen. If Abner finds out, he will surely pull his backing from the show.

Meanwhile, Peggy Sawyer (Ruby Keeler), an eager, wide-eyed innocent from the sticks has come to New York City to become a dancer. She quickly falls for the young singer Billy Lawler (Dick Powell), though Pat, upset by the way Dorothy has been brushing him aside for Abner, also takes interest in the guileless Peggy. Rounding out the ensemble cast are two wise-cracking chorus girls, Lorraine Fleming (Una Merkel) and Anytime Annie (Ginger Rogers), who are given the lion's share of the film's zippy one-liners. Things come to a head while the cast gives a preview show in Philadelphia. When Dorothy sees Pat with Peggy, she turns on Abner, jeopardizing the future of the show. An argument takes place in Dorothy's room with Pat and Peggy that causes Dorothy to stumble and fracture her ankle. Unable to open in New York City without Dorothy, Julian turns to Peggy who rises to the occasion and saves the show. While Dorothy leaves to marry Pat, Peggy, after cementing her affection for Billy, goes on to become Broadway's newest star.

And yet, as mentioned above, the final image of the film is not Pat and Dorothy's wedding or Peggy and Billy's climactic kiss—neither of which we see on screen—but the exhausted Julian sitting alone on a back staircase. But then that is pure WB. Though most of the characters in the film are underdogs, the one with whom we begin and end the film is Julian Marsh, the haggard, high-strung father of a dysfunctional family of performers who stick together against the forces that threaten to tear them all apart.

In my own life and life-choices, I have always come closer to Mayer's MGM vision. Still, I have learned a great deal from WB films like *42nd Street*. I have found their energy, their realism, and their camaraderie in the face of catastrophe to be thrilling and instructive. Before we meet a single character, the frantic, lurching camera carves out the urban microcosm in which the film will take place through a montage of street signs: 42nd and 7th, 42nd and 9th, 42nd and 11th, etc. These signs mark the boundaries of the world in which Julian, Dorothy, Peggy, and all the others will try to do two different things that, in this world, rarely seem compatible: survive and live out their dreams. But there's no time to worry whether the two can be joined; the film, like life, keeps hustling and bustling along, and we have to do the best we can to keep up.

The montage of street signs is followed by a montage of operators and reporters who spread the news that Julian Marsh is planning to put on a new show. These two montages capture perfectly the quick pace of Manhattan; through them we hear the city music that has called Julian and company to Broadway with their hearts on their sleeves but their feet on the ground. Yes, their feet on the ground, as we realize in the opening scene between the lascivious Abner and the gold-digging Dorothy. This show will be financed by a patron who loves, not dancing, but the shapely legs of dancers. Sex, not art, is oiling the machine. If we ever forget it, we are reminded by the constant stream of sexual innuendos that fall from the well-curled lips of Lorraine and Anytime Annie: she who got her nickname, we are told, because "she only said 'no' once, and then she didn't hear the question."

The film moves very quickly into the theater where the chorus and stars will hammer out their numbers and where most of the scenes in the film will be shot. It is a big, drab, cavernous space, but WB fills it with so much motion and emotion that we never feel like we're being cheated. Who needs those expensive Paramount and MGM sets when WB's cheap, serviceable set is overflowing with such a raw and tumultuous sea of humanity? Besides, the camera doesn't stop spinning and swirling long enough for us to study the details. We are all jumbled together with the stars and the chorines alike; not much aristocracy in this proletarian world. This is the urban jungle, after all, and, as such, it is subject to a Darwinian, survival-of-the-fittest ethos.

We catch sight of that ethos again and again: when Julian convinces a gangster friend of his to rough up Pat and scare him away from Dorothy; when Peggy is thrown out of her apartment when the landlady catches her with Pat, even though they have done nothing wrong; when it appears, for a brief, terrifying moment, that Pat will try to rape the evicted Peggy when he invites her to sleep at his place. There actually is a moment in *Meet Me in St. Louis* when the audience thinks that John Truitt, the boy next door, has molested Tootie. But we don't *really* fear it happened, for we know such a thing could not even be thought in the MGM-Mayer world. But we *do* sincerely fear, as Peggy herself fears, that Pat might rape her. Indeed, even though he doesn't, the possibility of such an act is reflected twice later in the film: when Peggy is first handled and then chased by a drunk guy from the chorus; when, during the 42nd Street number, we see a girl jump out of a window to escape being raped, only to be stabbed in the back after she lands safely on the street.

42nd Street, as the lyrics of the title song make clear, is a place where sweet and innocent nifties stand side by side with sexy, indiscreet ladies, a place "where the underworld can meet the elite," a naughty, haughty, gaudy place where one hears, day and night, "the rhapsody of laughter and tears." This jumbling together of people is, in one sense, quite liberating, but it ever threatens to reduce the characters to a mass of faceless automatons. I must admit that I have a love-hate relationship with Busby Berkeley, the brilliant choreographer of *42nd Street* and many other films. On the one hand, his kaleidoscopic numbers, that create vast, geometric shapes out of the lockstep movements of his dancers, are ingenious and exhilarating.

On the other, they tend to so press down the individual chorus members that they become nothing more than cogs in a machine. Yes, Berkeley sets the camera free, giving us every conceivable perspective on his precisely-staged routines, but at the expense of the freedom and distinctness of his performers. I am enraptured by the results, but I also find them disturbingly totalitarian.

I feel somewhat the same about the nature of 42nd *Street* as a musical. Unlike the integrated approach taken by Minnelli in *Meet Me in St. Louis*, where the songs rise up naturally out of the emotions and desires of the characters, the songs in 42nd *Street* are confined to the stage. No one breaks out in heartfelt song because they are in love; they only sing when they are performing: and nearly all of those performances are saved for the last fifteen minutes of the film. Two of the memorable songs that are sung on stage are "You're Getting to be a Habit with Me" and "Young and Healthy." Given the plot, characters, and song lyrics, it would be completely natural for Dorothy to sing the former song to Pat and Billy to sing the latter to Peggy. But that does not happen, not even in the numbers themselves, where Dorothy sings her song to a group of men from the chorus we don't know, and Billy sings his to a random chorus girl. In this musical, song represents a job and a skill rather than a means of expressing what is in one's heart or soul.

Still, this is the Golden Age of Hollywood, and even the tough, proletarian Jack Warner will not allow for a totalitarian vision that effaces the spirit, the dreams, and the self-sacrifice of the individual. WB is, after all, the studio of the underdog! Conformity to the mass is again and again subverted by two elements that would seem to stand in opposition to one another: wisecracks and warmth.

The former is best embodied by Lorraine and Annie, who act as a sort of satirical Greek chorus commenting on the actions and people around them. Nobody can force those two wisecracking gals to fit either a fascist or communist mold. They're just too wonderfully idiosyncratic and nonconformist. During the "Shuffle Off to Buffalo" number, which focuses on a newlywed couple taking the train to Buffalo (that is, Niagara Falls) for their honeymoon, Lorraine and Annie are on hand to inject a dose of sarcasm into the otherwise romantic proceedings. Like Mercutio shooting off his cynical and ribald jokes in the background while Juliet calls out to Romeo from her balcony, Lorraine and Annie offer us their own version of the song lyrics: "Matrimony is baloney, / She'll be wanting alimony / In a year or so" and "When she knows as much as we know / She'll be on her way to Reno / While he still has dough." They then follow the second line with their own version of the song's repeated refrain: not "Off we're gonna shuffle, shuffle off to Buffalo" but "She'll give him the shuffle, when they're back from Buffalo."

As for warmth, it is sprinkled liberally throughout the film in the way the company supports and encourages each other during the endless, exhausting rehearsals. Watching the chorus react in those scenes is like watching college students band together for an all-night study session. The gangsters may live next door and the landlady may be eyeing all of them like a hawk, but they will remain loyal to one another, the troupe-as-family, if you will.

This familial warmth that continually breaks through the egos and the infighting is most often directed toward the new kid on the block, the wide-eyed Miss Sawyer. When the naïve Peggy walks in, everyone plays tricks on her and imitates her open-mouthed stare. But it is not long before Lorraine, Annie, and Billy start sticking up for her. They recognize her sincerity and her lack of airs and graces and try to shield her as much as they can. In fact, after Dorothy angers Abner and breaks her ankle, and the savvy Annie swoops in to take over management of Abner, something surprising happens. Rather than take the place of Dorothy, which Abner insists upon, Annie confesses that she doesn't have what it takes, but that Peggy does. It is this altruistic act that gives Peggy her chance to become a star.

Better yet, as Peggy prepares for opening night, Dorothy shows up and, to everyone's surprise, wishes Peggy luck. Rather than envy her, Dorothy moves aside and gives her the chance she has been waiting for. She assures her that the audience *wants* to like her and that she has the talent and the drive to be a star. As she leaves to pursue the real love of her life, Pat Denning, she speaks her last line to Peggy, a line that should be corny but that somehow comes through with passion and sincerity: "Be so swell that you'll make me hate you."

A few moments later, Julian regales the nervous Peggy with a spirited pep talk composed of a series of clichés spoken in a staccato delivery that conveys conviction without sentimentality: "Sawyer, you listen to me, and you listen hard. 200 people, 200 jobs, 200 thousand dollars, five weeks of grind and blood and sweat depend upon you. It's the lives of all these people who've worked with you. You've go to go on, and you've got to give and give and give. They've got to like you. Got to. Do you understand? You can't fall down. You can't because your future's in it, my future and everything all of us have is staked on you. All right, now I'm through, but you keep your feet on the ground and your head on those shoulders of yours and go out, and Sawyer, you're going out a youngster but you've got to come back a star!"

Needless to say, the pep talk works, and Peggy goes on to be a star: which is quite ironic given the fact that Ruby Keeler is not particularly pretty or a particularly good actress or singer. She can hoof with the big boys, but she's rather heavy on her feet. And yet, somehow or other, we believe that she is a star. But then this is Warner Brothers, where stars are played by underdogs rather than serene immortals. If Keeler can make it big, anyone can. That's WB's version of the Hollywood Dream: it may not be MGM's apple-pie-and-picket-fence version, but it *is* quintessentially American, and it has, in its own way, shaped me as much as the bourgeois family values of the Smiths of St. Louis.

Fun Facts for the Fans

- *42nd Street* was nominated for best picture; it helped save WB from bankruptcy.
- It featured the following songs from composer Harry Warren and lyricist Al Dubin: "42nd Street" "You're Getting to Be a Habit with Me," "Young and Healthy," "It Must Be June," and "Shuffle Off to Buffalo."

- Harry Warren also wrote the following song standards: "I Found a Million Dollar Baby," "I Only Have Eyes for You," "Shadow Waltz," "We're in the Money," "The Boulevard of Broken Dreams," "Jeepers Creepers," "You Must Have Been a Beautiful Baby," "September in the Rain," "There Will Never Be Another You," "The More I See You," "You'll Never Know," and "I Had the Craziest Dream."
- A full half century later, *42nd Street* was turned into a full-blown integrated Broadway musical, with additional songs from the Harry Warren songbook.
- In 1933, the hard-working Ginger Rogers made nine films, including *Flying Down to Rio,* in which she performs a dance number with Fred Astaire.
- In the 1940s, Warner Baxter, in Julian Marsh fashion, had a nervous breakdown.
- Busby Berkley, who was married six times, invented a monorail for his camera to allow him to film scenes from directly overhead.
- Ruby Keeler married Al Jolson, the star of WB's *The Jazz Singer,* who was twenty-three years her senior; the marriage lasted for twelve years.
- Though Hal B. Wallis was the producer of the film, he worked under Darryl F. Zanuck, who later left to run Fox when Jack Warner refused to raise the salaries of his workers after imposing an eight-week pay cut on account of the Depression.
- Although Vincente Minnelli respected Berkeley's ingenuity, he criticized him for making backstage pictures where the songs were not integral to the plot.
- After making a number of pictures for WB, Berkeley was lured to MGM to direct the Judy Garland-Mickey Rooney putting-on-a-show musicals.

Other Films to Watch

In the same year as *42nd Street,* WB made two other top-notch back-stage musicals: *Gold Diggers of 1933* (Ruby Keeler, Joan Blondell, and Ginger Rogers as chorus girls in search of rich husbands) and *Footlight Parade* (James Cagney as a tough producer who puts on pre-movie musical numbers). Other good backstage musicals include *Dames, Boy Meets Girl, The Gold Diggers of 1935,* and *The Gold Diggers of 1937.* In 1942, Cagney won an Oscar for his portrayal of George M. Cohan in the rousing *Yankee Doodle Dandy.*

As with film noir, the backstagers were influenced by WB's gangster films: *Little Caesar* (Edward G. Robinson as a violent gangster who rises to fame but ends up in the gutter, saying to himself with disbelief: "Mother of mercy, is this the end of Rico"), *Public Enemy* (James Cagney as another gangster who rises and falls, saying, as he dies, "I ain't so tough"), *I Am a Fugitive from a Chain Gang* (a harrowing social expose in which an innocent man is thrown in prison and learns to be bad), *G-Men* (in answer to the public outcry over the charismatic gangsters portrayed in WB films, Cagney was cast as a charismatic good guy tracking down the hoodlums with violent glee). Humphrey Bogart got to play the central gangster in *The Petrified Forest, Dead End* (for Samuel Goldwyn) and *High Sierra.* In *Angels with Dirty Faces* and *The Roaring Twenties,* he played an irredeemable gangster over against Cagney's gangster with redeemable qualities. Later in their careers, Edward G. Robinson and Cagney each played older, more psychotic thugs in *Key Largo* and *White Heat,* respectively.

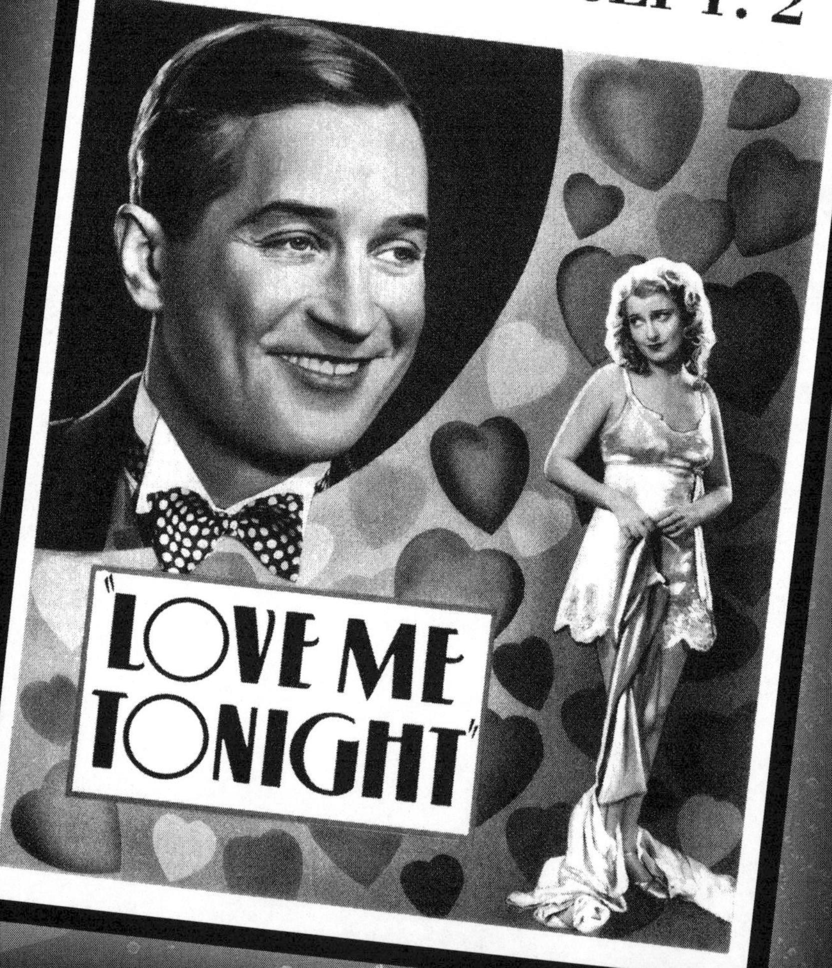
CIRCLE
INDIANAPOLIS
One Week Starting
SEPT. 2
"LOVE ME TONIGHT"

LOVE ME TONIGHT

(PARAMOUNT; 1932; ROUBEN MAMOULIAN)

In Chapter 16, I celebrated MGM's 1944 *Meet Me in St. Louis* for its integrated approach to the genre of the musical. Though it deserves that praise, it was by no means the first Hollywood musical to attempt an integration of story and song. During the early years of the Depression, Paramount's star director Ernst Lubitsch made a series of musicals that are overwhelmingly fluid, elegant, and graceful. In *The Love Parade* (1929), *Monte Carlo* (30), *The Smiling Lieutenant* (31), and *One Hour With You* (32), Lubitsch created a unique filmic world in which the songs not only rise up naturally from the plot and the characters, but are conveyed cinematically through experimental camera movements and editing. Influenced by all four of these films, and their charismatic stars Maurice Chevalier and Jeanette MacDonald, Rouben Mamoulian set himself the seemingly-impossible task of out-Lubitsching Lubitsch—and succeeded!

It took Hollywood several years to successfully transition from silent to sound pictures after the 1927 success of *The Jazz Singer*. The majority of films made between 1927 and 1930 are painful to watch, with their stiff, artificial dialogue and their leaden direction. As they struggled with the new medium of sound, the studios seemed to forget all the cinematic craft they had learned over the last few decades. Slowly, however, some adventurous directors figured out how to use sound in fresh, effective ways. The horror films made at Universal (*Frankenstein, Dracula, The Mummy, The Invisible Man*) and the gangster films at Warner Brothers (*Little Caesar, Public Enemy*) invigorated the medium, but it was Paramount who proved most successful due to her willingness to allow creative freedom to her stable of gifted producer-directors: Cecil B. DeMille, Josef von Sternberg, Ernst Lubitsch, and Rouben Mamoulian.

Just as *42nd Street* opened my ears to the brash, bustling city music of New York and *Meet Me in St. Louis* to the folksy, optimistic sounds of small town USA, so *Love Me Tonight* introduced me to the at-once earthier and more continental sounds of the Paris that was. After coaxing us in with actual footage of the City of Lights, Mamoulian quickly moves us into a sound stage where he recreates a Paris of the imagination that is, in its own way, as magical as Oz. Of this blessed kingdom, Maurice the Tailor (Maurice Chevalier) is the uncrowned monarch. Our first vision of him is of his straw hat, the immediately recognizable icon for which the real-life Chevalier, the acclaimed music-hall entertainer and Man of the Boulevard, was famous.

Maurice the Tailor is a caricature of Maurice Chevalier, but he is a caricature that has come to life and taken on flesh and blood. Music surrounds him; yet he is also the source of the music—it bubbles out of him, infecting everyone and everything that comes in his path. As he struts and glides through the city streets he loves, the camera pans and sways with him. The catchy tune he sings ("That's the Song of Paree") is really a duet that begins with random sounds generated by the street sweepers, cobblers, and cabbies who work in Maurice's neighborhood. Those sounds wake up Maurice who responds by channeling them into a song that he uses to rouse his city into shimmering life.

As he sings and strolls, Maurice greets his neighbors in turn. Though some of the husbands are clearly annoyed by him, the wives and young maids alike are swept away by his charm and charisma. One even cries out passionately, "Oh, what a man!" Maurice is a sort of James Bond of Parisian tailors, who can switch effortlessly from wearing the clothes of a roguish, street-smart lady-killer to those of a chic and debonair gentleman. Like the best of Paramount's light and dapper leading men, he can be a well-dressed lover of all things beautiful without sacrificing a jot of his masculinity.

Maurice, we soon learn, is far more than a blue-collar tailor; he is an artist who loves his craft and who can sew magic and romance with his needle, especially when the camera and the music join him in his weaving. In the verse to "Isn't it Romantic"—a character-driven, character-defining verse which one can only hear in this film, and not in any of the dozens of recordings of the song by later artists—Maurice shares with us his personal manifesto and creed:

> My face is glowing, I'm energetic.
> The art of sewing I find poetic.
> My needle punctuates the rhythm of romance.
> I don't give a stitch if I don't get rich.
> A custom tailor who has no custom
> Is like a sailor, no one will trust 'em.
> But there is magic in the music of my shears.
> I shed no tears, lend me your ears.

Paramount, with its continental, old-world charm, was fascinated by the aristocracy; yet, it also knew that the highest form of aristocracy resides in the heart. It is Maurice who possesses the true blue blood, who can live out the poetic life of the imagination equally well in a castle or a shop, who adheres at all times to a high code of honor and romance.

MGM idolized the rich, WB despised them. Paramount found them charming and amusing, feeling a bit sorry for their life-denying, spirit-stifling ways and therefore happy to send spontaneous, free-spirited natural aristocrats like Maurice to shake up them and their artificial world. And shake them up he does! But first, how is a connection to be made between the petit-bourgeois shop of Maurice and the lofty castle of Princess Jeanette (Jeanette MacDonald)? At MGM, the connection would likely have been made through a melodramatic plot twist; at WB, the impersonal forces of fate and destiny would have forged the link. At Paramount, only the power of song and the fluidity of the camera can bridge the gap between low and high, the working man and the idle rich.

After Maurice sings "Isn't it Romantic" to one of his customers, the elated customer leaves the shop humming the catchy tune. A taxi driver overhears him and begins to hum the tune himself, which is picked up, in turn, by a musician who takes a ride in his cab. The musician jots down the notes in his journal and begins to write some words. He continues his labors on a train, only to be overheard by a group of soldiers. As the troop exits the train and marches across the countryside, they sing the song lustily and in unison while the breathless camera does all it can to keep up with them. As they pass under a tree, a young gypsy resting in the shade hears them and tries out the melody on his violin. Exuberant, he carries it back to his camp, where the gypsies improvise a passionate version by the fireside. As the music from their fervent voices and fiddles rises up in the air, the camera searches out the castle and finds Jeanette perched, Juliet-like, in her balcony. The music has called the lonely princess to her window, and she breathes it in as if it were a rich perfume.

The version of the refrain that Maurice sings in his tailor shop is comically practical, focusing on how his future wife will scrub the floor, scratch his back, make him onion soup, and provide him with an army of children. Jeanette, in sharp contrast, sings a highly romantic and idealized refrain about knights in armor suing for her hand. Their visions of marriage and romance, not to mention musical styles—Folies Bergère for the two Maurices; Opera House for the two Jeanettes—are as diametrically opposed as the worlds in which they live, but the power of song and of Mamoulian's unleashed camera draws them together into an aesthetic neutral territory where they can meet and fall in love. True, fate and a few nice plot twists *will* play a hand in bringing Maurice to the castle, but we can not and must not forget that it was the barrier-breaking forces of cinema and song that paved the way for their union.

In keeping with one of Paramount's favorite running jokes–the thrifty servant has more cash at his disposal than the spendthrift, constantly-broke aristocrat—the film sends our brave little tailor off to the residence of a prodigal viscount (Charles Ruggles) who owes money to all the jewelers and clothes-makers in Maurice's beloved quarter of Paris. On the way, he collides with Jeanette who, as she bounces up and down on her horse, sings, distractedly and discontentedly, the song "Lover." Although in her version of "Isn't it Romantic" she says that her knight will be a slave to her, in this song, she says that she will be a slave to her lover who will wake her heart and make it beat faster. The lovable but egocentric Maurice immediately takes for granted that the pretty lady on the horse is singing the song to and for him. She denies it, but he will not accept her denial.

Instead, the besotted Maurice, who has fallen in love with Jeanette at first sight, asks if he may sing "Mimi" to her. When she protests that her name is not Mimi, he brushes the protest aside and sings:

> Mimi, you funny little good-for-nothing Mimi, am I the guy?
> Mimi, you sunny little honey of a Mimi, I'm aiming high.
> Mimi, you've got me sad and dreamy—you could free me—if you'd see me.
> Mimi, you know I'd like to have a little son of a Mimi by and by.

As he sings, the camera edits back and forth between their faces. At first, Jeanette smiles at the cuteness and quirkiness of the song, until Maurice sings the final, innuendo-rich line, causing her to shut down her heart and put up her defenses. Meanwhile, we watch Maurice's grinning, smirking, winking face as he stares deep into the heart of the stuffy and sexually-repressed Jeanette.

From this point forward, we are on Maurice's side and rout for him to get the girl, even though we know she's way out of his league. His singing and joie de vivre are so infectious that we feel assured that he will be able to overcome any obstacle to their love. Indeed, on the morning after he arrives at the castle where the cash-poor viscount and the lovelorn princess live, the camera lets us eavesdrop on the various aristocrats who share the castle with Jeanette, each of whom sings the song "Mimi" in a faux Chevalier accent! In this most scintillating of cinematic concoctions, art equals life, beauty equals freedom, and music equals love. We are in a world where the phrase "making love" has not yet been reduced to the sexual act. Here, to make love means to woo and to pursue, to seduce with sweet words and gestures, to transform a conversation between a boy and a girl into a mystical mingling of two hearts and souls.

The zaniness that ensues as Maurice—whom the viscount, needing time to mooch money off the duke (C. Aubrey Smith), convinces everyone is a nobleman in disguise—turns the castle and its traditions upside down is a pure pleasure to watch. But it serves a purpose beyond entertainment. When Jeanette scolds Maurice for mocking the tradition of the hunt by trying to save the fox ("There are things," she insists, that are "too fine and too sacred to be made ridiculous."), she is wrong and he is right. Without ever getting political or suggesting anything resembling a classless society, *Love Me Tonight* calls for some needed undressing. Everyone needs to have their façade torn down and their inner desires revealed—not through Freudian psychoanalysis, but through humility and laughter and vulnerability. Love is, after all, as ridiculous as the naughty, naked little cherub who inspires it with his bow and arrows.

Near the beginning of the film, a doctor comes to examine the listless twenty-two-year-old Jeanette who has been having fainting spells. At sixteen, she was married off to a now-deceased nobleman of seventy-two-years. At present, her only acceptable options for a second husband are aged twelve and eighty five. The unnaturalness of all this cries out for the intrusion of the hot-blooded Maurice. Jeanette needs sex, and she needs it badly! The doctor realizes this right away. After instructing her to undress and letting the camera—and us!—check her out from head to toe, the doctor gives his prognosis in a deadpan imitation of Groucho Marx: "You're not wasted away; you're just wasted!"

Ultimately, sex is the answer to all problems in the Paramount world. While sex is something to be denied and hidden away in the MGM world of *Meet Me in St. Louis*, and to be used as a tool, or weapon, for survival in the WB world of *42nd Street*, in the hands of a Lubitsch or a Mamoulian it becomes a gift to enjoy and be thankful for. In one of the film's funniest lines, Maurice the Tailor, alone in a cabin with a poorly-accoutered Jeanette, closes his eyes and puts his fingers to his forehead. When she asks him what he is doing, he tells her, "I'm trying to imagine you without these clothes." Well, yes, so are we, but not in a low or prurient way. We want to see her let down her hair and realize how desperately she needs the love and life and joy that Maurice can offer her.

In Lubitsch's *One Hour with You,* the film most like *Love Me Tonight,* Chevalier and MacDonald play a married couple, but we are initially unaware of that fact. We first meet them kissing on a Parisian park bench and falling foul of a police raid meant to chase lovers out of the free park and in to the money-generating cafes. When Chevalier tells the officer that they are married, he refuses to believe him. The couple leaves in a huff and returns to their home. After another kiss, MacDonald walks into the bedroom, but Chevalier does not follow her.

Instead, he shuts the door and turns toward the camera. Then, four decades before Woody Allen and a full half century before Ferris Bueller, he cavalierly tears down the fourth wall and addresses the audience directly. "Ladies and gentlemen," he says to us with a twinkle in his eye, "I must talk to you. This is a very delicate situation. There is Colette, and here am I. And I know what you think. Oh! I know. How *dare* you. You remember that policeman? He was wrong. And so are you. Believe it or not, we *are* married. I am her husband, and she is my wife.... In other words, I am married, and I like it. I'm sorry to disappoint you."

That is a speech that no one at MGM or WB could have conceived, much less written and shot. To take love making so casually, to suggest that a husband and wife would still be so erotically in love with each other that they would spend their evenings necking on a public bench! Unthinkable! But that is what Chevalier says; after which, he enters the bedroom, and he and MacDonald sing a song about what a little thing like a wedding ring can do. What that *thing* turns out to be is the unfettered permission to make love (in *both* senses of the phrase) whenever the spirit takes them!

Not wanting to be undone by Lubitsch, Mamoulian plays his own cinematic game in the sparkling, effervescent scene when Jeanette and Maurice confess their love for each other in a garden. Finally giving in to her passion, Jeanette tells Maurice that his "arms need never be empty of me" and promises that "whoever you are, whatever you are, wherever you are, I love you." The walls have all come tumbling down, and Maurice cries out that he fears he has gone mad, but that if he is, then he is "the luckiest madman in the world." With that, the title song begins, and the camera cuts to the smiling Maurice in his bed and the enraptured Jeanette in *her* bed. From there, we expect a fade to black, but Mamoulian has not finished playing his game. By splitting the screen so that the reclining Jeanette and Maurice appear on either side of the same screen, he cinematically puts the couple in bed together!

Playful, shocking, a bit scandalous—but never dirty or crudely sexual. These two are destined to spend their lives together, and the camera gives us a glimpse of that marital bliss with its magic, passion-unlocking ring. After all, as the closing lines of the song cry out so ardently and insistently: "Who knows what tomorrow brings, with the morning light. / Dear, I am here with a heart that sings—love me tonight."

And then, as in all the best romantic comedies, the dream (temporarily) explodes. Maurice's true identity as a tailor is exposed, not by the aristocrats, but by Maurice himself, whose love for his craft impels him to make a new riding outfit for Jeanette that will properly complement her figure and her beauty. Jeanette loves the new outfit, but it is too good; only a professional tailor could make something so chic and elegant.

As the aristocrats and servants alike exclaim in song that "the son-of-a-gun is nothing but a tailor"—the washer women are particularly incensed that they have been scrubbing the undergarments of a commoner—Maurice leaves the castle and heads for the train. But their (cinematic) night together was too strong, and the title song calls rhythmically and incessantly to Jeanette as she watches the departing Maurice from her window. Her own words come back to her: "whoever you are, whatever you are, wherever you are, I love you." She cannot let this man escape from her life. She mounts her horse and rides off to overtake Maurice's train.

What ensues is a thrilling example of cross-cutting/parallel editing that would put D. W. Griffith, Frank Capra, and Alfred Hitchcock to shame. Back and forth the camera cuts from the train speeding down the track and billowing smoke to the horse galloping like mad across the countryside. The music swells as whistles blow, pistons fire, and hooves beat against the earth. The train is powerful and seemingly unstoppable, but love is stronger. Managing to drive her horse ahead of the train, Jeanette dismounts, stands defiantly on the track, and reaches out her arm toward the oncoming engine. Whether or not the conductor stops, she will not budge from her post. Love has made her fearless, and, for a moment, she looks like a giant, a force of nature that cannot be moved.

The train screeches to a halt, and Jeanette and Maurice rush together for an embrace, only to be covered in a cloud of steam. The picture then dissolves to a huge tapestry in which Jeanette and Maurice are depicted as a knight on a horse and a lady in a high tower. And that is where the movie ends, not with a wedding scene but with a woven work of art that provides what may be the only neutral territory where a tailor and a princess can find true love together. That is the Paramount world: beautiful and finely-crafted, but fragile and apt to fray.

The gay Paree that was, depicted so lovingly in *One Hour with You*, *Love Me Tonight*, and many other Paramount pictures, had disappeared long before the 1930s—it died in the bloody crucible of World War I—but it lives on in those films, and for that I am eternally grateful. We live in an increasingly noisy and ill-mannered society; whenever the din and the ugliness get too strong, I happily turn back to Maurice and Jeanette for a much needed dose of class, charm, and savoir-faire.

Fun Facts for the Fans

- Although *Love Me Tonight* did not win any Oscar nominations, it set a high bar for future musicals. Realizing this, MGM wooed away Lubitsch, Chevalier, and MacDonald to make *The Merry Widow* in the manner of a Paramount musical.

- Mamoulian helped stage *Porgy and Bess*, inserting an original number, "Morning on Catfish Row," that mirrors the "That's the Song of Paree" number. A similar concept, where the waking of a community is conveyed through the sounds and cries of hawkers, is used in the "Who Will Buy?" number of *Oliver!*

- Even though the cartoon character Pepe Le Pew was directly inspired by Charles Boyer's character Pepe Le Moko in the movie *Algiers*, he also embodies the accent and mannerisms of Maurice Chevalier.

- In the French Revolution episode from Mel Brooks's *History of the World—Part I,* one of the revolutionaries complains that they are so poor that they cannot even afford their own language: all they have is a stupid accent that makes them sound like Maurice Chevalier!
- MGM toned down MacDonald's Paramount eroticism and teamed her up with Nelson Eddy for a series of fondly-remembered operatic musicals: *Naughty Marietta* (1935), *Rose Marie, Maytime, The Girl of the Golden West, Sweethearts, The New Moon, Bitter Sweet,* and *I Married an Angel* (1942). An unfriendly critic compared them to a mad rocking horse making love to a piece of rawhide leather.
- Chevalier and MacDonald were forty four and twenty nine when they made *Love Me Tonight;* both look *much* younger in the film.
- The cast includes a young Myrna Loy before her image shifted to the perfect wife.
- The songs were written by Richard Rodgers and Lorenz Hart; after Hart's early death in 1951, Rodgers teamed up with Oscar Hammerstein II.
- Here are some additional standards from Rodgers and Hart: "Bewitched," "Blue Moon," "Blue Room," "Dancing on the Ceiling," "Falling in Love with Love," "Glad to Be Unhappy," "Have You Met Miss Jones?" "I Could Write a Book," "I Didn't Know What Time it Was," "It Never Entered My Mind," "The Lady Is a Tramp," "Little Girl Blue," "Manhattan," "The Most Beautiful Girl in the World," "My Funny Valentine," "My Heart Stood Still," "My Romance," "Quiet Night," "A Ship Without a Sail," "Spring Is Here," "There's a Small Hotel," "Where or When," "Thou Swell," "You Are Too Beautiful," "You Took Advantage of Me."
- The old Paris of Paramount took two last gasps in two best-picture films directed by Vincente Minnelli for MGM: *An American in Paris* (1951) and *Gigi* (1958).

- Hollywood censorship did not kick in with full strength until 1934; that is why many of the films made between 1930 and 1934 have a charged kind of eroticism that would not be seen in Hollywood for several more decades.

Other Films to Watch

Before directing *Love Me Tonight*, Rouben Mamoulian made three visually inventive films at Paramount: *Applause* (about a vaudeville star), *Dr Jekyll and Mr. Hyde* (an extremely cinematic horror film with a brilliant, Oscar-winning performance by Fredric March), and *City Streets* (a stylish gangster picture with Gary Cooper). Afterwards, he graced the screen with such classics as *Song of Songs* (about a Pygmalion relationship between an artist and his sexy model, played by Marlene Dietrich), *Queen Cristina* (Greta Garbo's greatest film), *We Live Again* (from a Tolstoy novel), *Becky Sharp* (first film in three-color Technicolor; based on Thackeray's *Vanity Fair*), *The Gay Desperado* (a fun, lightly comic musical), *Golden Boy* (melodramatic Clifford Odets play about a young man who must choose between boxing and the violin), *The Mark of Zorro* (the most cinematic of all swashbucklers), *Blood and Sand* (the rise and fall of a bullfighter with a good use of color), *Summer Holiday* (smooth musical remake of *Ah Wilderness*), *Silk Stockings* (musical remake of the Garbo film *Ninotchka*).

Ernst Lubitsch directed Paramount's smoothest and most elegant romantic comedy, *Trouble in Paradise*, in 1932. After he moved to MGM to make *The Merry Widow*, his cinematic playfulness died down but the sophisticated charm and wit remained. The best of these films are *Ninotchka*, *The Shop Around the Corner*, *To Be Or not to Be*, *Heaven Can Wait*, and *Cluny Brown*.

Paramount kept alive the charm and sophistication of Lubitsch and Mamoulian in the 1934–44 romantic comedies and melodramas of director Mitchell Leisen. All of these films show a fascination with the rich, though often the poor guy gets the girl. They sparkle with wit and sexual innuendo and are ever class-conscious but never political: *Death Takes a Holiday* (death, played by Fredric March, takes vacation to learn why men fear him and ends up falling in love; remade as *Meet Joe Black*); *Hands Across the Table* (a manicurist must chose between a rich man and a poor but tough one; she chooses the poor one), *Swing High, Swing Low* (a trumpeter heads for the tropics), *Easy Living* (classic madcap rich family; script by Preston Sturges), *Midnight* (sparkling Cinderella story amongst the idle rich; script by Billy Wilder), *Remember the Night* (DA falls in love with a lady shoplifter; an intelligent, adult comedy), *Arise My Love* (love among foreign correspondents; script by Wilder), *Hold Back the Dawn* (a Mexican gigolo romances a schoolteacher in order to get into America; script by Wilder); *Take a Letter, Darling* (love between a lady executive and her male secretary), *No Time for Love* (lady photographer falls for a tough foreman), *Lady in the Dark* (the lady editor of a fashion magazine is psychoanalyzed), *Frenchman's Creek* (married lady falls for pirate but stays for her kids), *Kitty* (an aristocrat turns a tramp, Pygmalion style, into a courtesan).

After leaving for Europe in 1935, the seventy-year-old Chevalier returned to America to make a number of well-loved films: *Love in the Afternoon* (as a divorce detective), *Gigi* (as an old ladies man who is glad he is no longer young), *Can Can* (Cole Porter musical set in Paris), *Fanny* (in Marseilles with Charles Boyer and Leslie Caron), *In Search of the Castaways* (Disney adventure film). He also sang the title song for Disney's *Aristocats*.

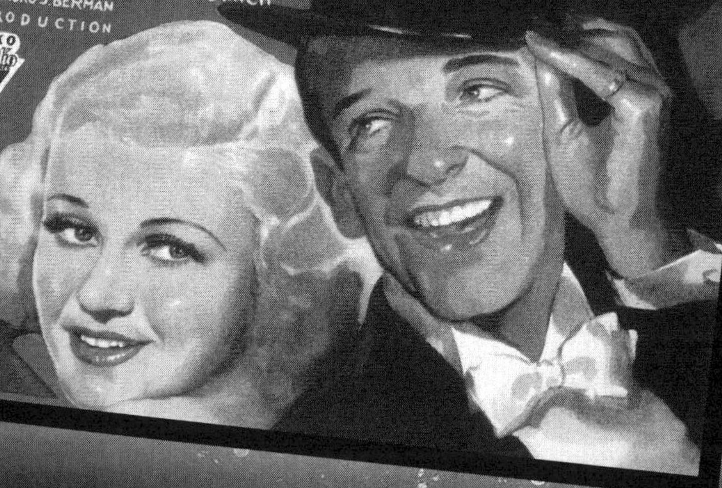
FRED ASTAIRE
Ginger ROGERS
IN
TOP HAT
MUSIC AND LYRICS BY
IRVING BERLIN
with
Edward Everett HORTON
HELEN BRODERICK
Erik RHODES • Eric BLORE
Directed by MARK SANDRICH
A PANDRO S. BERMAN
PRODUCTION
RKO Radio

TOP HAT

(RKO; 1935; MARK SANDRICH)

RKO, which stands for Radio-Keith-Orpheum, was the smallest of the major Hollywood studios. Like MGM and Paramount, it went for sophistication; however, unlike the lavish sophistication of MGM or the European sophistication of Paramount, RKO gravitated toward a New York/Art Deco look (think: Empire State Building), that sometimes gave it the urban bite of a WB film. RKO might not have been remembered for its musicals if it had not been lucky enough to pair up Fred Astaire and Ginger Rogers for a dance number in *Flying Down to Rio*. Audiences demanded more, and the couple would go on to make eight films between 1934 and 1939: *The Gay Divorcee, Roberta, Top Hat, Follow the Fleet, Swing Time, Shall We Dance, Carefree, The Story of Vernon and Irene Castle*; almost a decade later, they would reunite one last time to make their only color film together, *The Barkleys of Broadway* (1948), for MGM.

Whereas the proletarian, tough-guy Gene Kelly would light up the screen with his unique blend of tap dancing and ballet, the aristocratic, refined Astaire combined tap with ballroom dancing. Kelly would make a joyous and exuberant use of the camera, dancing with it as much as with his partner; Astaire instructed the directors of his films to put the camera on him and let him fill the space with his dancing. Still, even if the Astaire-Rogers films make a less flamboyant use of the camera, they sparkle with a New York kind of wit that is part Broadway comedy, part farce, and part vaudeville.

Top Hat, arguably the best of the Astaire-Rogers films, begins with a scene that is reminiscent of *Love Me Tonight.* Instead of Maurice the Tailor invading the stuffy castle with his warmth and passion for life, we have a mischievous Jerry Travers (Astaire) disrupting the funereal silence of an exclusive British club. While waiters walk on tiptoe, mortified lest they clink the glasses they are filling, Jerry grins at us from behind the newspaper he has just crinkled too loudly. Needless to say, we like him immediately and are hopeful that he, like Maurice, will stir up these aristocratic waxworks. And that's exactly what he does, by letting loose with a wild burst of tapping feet before rushing out of the club for safety.

And yet, as with Maurice, his real challenge will not be to melt the frozen facades of the upper class, but to warm the chilly, barricaded heart of the girl he falls in love with, Dale Tremont (Rogers). Here, as in most of the Astaire-Rogers films, Fred must teach Ginger to relax and enjoy herself, while she must teach him to be more responsible—in a word, domesticate him. It was Fred and Ginger, together with the films of Frank Capra, that taught me the important lesson that men are more often the romantic, idealistic ones and women the practical, realistic ones. He must soften her up, and she must clip his wings: not as a way of eradicating their true personalities, but of releasing them.

All the Astaire-Rogers films are built around a battle of the sexes that is really an extended courtship. Through that courtship, they both learn how to be more human, to leave behind their fears and anxieties over commitment (Fred) and intimacy (Ginger). It was said of Fred and Ginger that he gave her class while she gave him sex. That may seem to contradict what I just wrote about Ginger fearing intimacy, but it does not. The class that Fred gives her is a kind of romance that demands, a la Paramount, a surrender to the imagination The sex that Ginger gives him is a reality check that forces Fred, a la WB, to make a decision, to embrace life as it actually is on the ground and not ten feet in the air where he has so far lived his life.

Speaking of sex, it is a peculiarity of the Astaire-Rogers films that we never see them kiss (at last not until *Carefree,* when audience demand forced RKO to include an actual on-screen kiss). The reason we never see them join their lips is because they do their kissing through their dancing. Far more than impressive routines, their dances are exercises in seducing, flirting, competing, retreating, and letting go. Their dances are a form of poetry that transports us to a realm where all hypocrisy is torn down and the true heart—by which I mean both the emotions and the will—emerges to engage in dialogue with another human being. I often despair that any of us can really know another person; how *could* we unless we were able to switch places with them for a day and see the world through their eyes? When Fred and Ginger dance, that biological egocentrism in which we are all trapped seems to slip away and what Shakespeare called "the marriage of true minds" is realized in space and time. For a mystical, suspended moment, they move and think and feel as one. When Jerry and Dale finish dancing to Irving Berlin's "Cheek to Cheek," a strange hush falls about them, a breathless calm as if they have just arisen from their marriage bed. A Freudian might call this sublimation; I call it consummation.

There is nothing quite like an Astaire-Rogers film.

Locating a middle ground between the WB backstager and the MGM integrated musical, their films cast Fred (and often Ginger, as well) as an actual performer, thus offering a natural, logical reason for including staged numbers in the film. Thus, in *Top Hat*, we get to watch Jerry perform a rousing interpretation of Berlin's "Top Hat, White Tie and Tails" without ever leaving the confines of the well-constructed plot. Still, the public, professional numbers are balanced with private, non-professional numbers in which Fred, Ginger, or both sing a song that expresses their personal creed, their feelings about the other, or their struggles with their emotions. The first such song in *Top Hat* is Berlin's wonderfully jumpy "No Strings," the lyrics of which boldly assert Jerry's refusal to be tied down: "No strings and no connections, / No ties to my affections. / I'm fancy free and free for anything fancy."

No marriage knot for this playboy, nothing to hold him down. As he sings, Jerry pours himself a drink, for it is essential to any and all Astaire numbers that even the most mundane of movements be transfigured into dance. I love watching Astaire do such things, but they also frustrate me.

Why doesn't the physical world respond to my touch in the effortless way it does for him? He tosses something in the air, spins around, and it is always there for him to catch—as if he could compel gravity to do his will. All I'm left with when I try to imitate his manipulation of objects is broken glasses, shattered plates, and small knick knacks that fall into inaccessible crevices of my home. It is my firm belief that pre-fallen Adam was not only stronger, faster, and smarter than we are; he could move and dance like Fred Astaire.

As Jerry sings and pours, taps and spins, the camera tracks down to reveal Miss Tremont. She is trying to sleep, but cannot do so because of the noise that Jerry's dancing is making. She turns in bed, and we see her lovely face for the first time; but it is not so lovely now, for it is twisted into a disapproving look. Yes, here is an uptight, humorless, persnickety lady—OK, let's just use the forbidden word: bitch—who needs to be taught to relax by the fancy free dancer upstairs. Even though Jerry has no idea that his dancing is disturbing Dale, we can't help feeling that he is doing it on purpose to annoy her: step one in his taming of the shrew. Little does he know that while he is taming her, she will be tying up his strings. Here, as in all of their pictures, Fred and Ginger are quite evenly matched, sparring partners who will grow and mature in the process.

I have always loved watching them spar with each other, especially when they do it to music. Just as the camera pans down from Jerry's dancing to reveal Dale in bed, so, later in the film, when Dale gets in a horse-drawn carriage, the camera pans up to reveal that Jerry has changed places with the cabbie. "When dealing with a girl or horse," he advises, "Always let nature take its course." And it does, for nature generally takes Fred's side when he is actively wooing the stand-offish Ginger. In *Top Hat,* a sudden and very convenient rainstorm forces the two of them to take shelter in a gazebo, where Jerry sings to her one of Berlin's most clever lyrics, "Isn't This a Lovely Day (to Be Caught in the Rain)." The two then begin to dance, but in a rather competitive manner, with Dale being careful not to embrace Jerry or even join hands with him. That is, until a clap of thunder cuts through the air, and the tempo of the music doubles. Suddenly, they are in each others arms, dipping and spinning in joyful abandon. How wonderful if the wall between the sexes could always be torn down so simply and smoothly!

This thrilling game of pursuit and conquest by which the masculine and feminine realize their need for each other is played out in the midst of Hollywood's best character actors and farcical situations. The film even allows us to leave behind the fairly realistic London set and travel to a fully artificial, fairy-land Venice. To make it all the more appealing, Jerry and Dale, while clearly not belonging to the aristocracy, stay in the finest hotels without worrying a stitch about money. Here we have another iteration of the American dream: a classless society where everybody is rich and can visit exotic places at the drop of a hat. And, as at MGM and Paramount, there isn't a hint of the Depression.

I am grateful for films like *The Grapes of Wrath*, for the dark and painful side of life must be acknowledged and struggled with. But there is nothing wrong with flying away now and then to Venice (or Rio) with Fred and Ginger. How we deal with love and life and joy should certainly be as important as how we deal with war and death and pain. If I had my way, I would dismantle all the computer dating sites and replace them with mandatory showings of Astaire-Rogers films in high schools across America. Maybe then our young people would have the chance to see true masculinity and femininity in action and yearn for a rich, complementarian marriage with the power to unite the warring sexes in a higher harmony. If Fred and Ginger can do it, so can we!

Fun Facts for the Fans

- *Top Hat* was nominated for best picture, song ("Cheek to Cheek"), choreography (Hermes Pan), and art direction. Pan and Astaire strongly resembled each other.
- Fred Astaire's first dance partner was his sister Adele, but he lost her when she married Lord Charles Cavendish. *Royal Wedding* is partly based on the Astaires.

- Though Astaire became one of Hollywood's greatest stars and would introduce more hit songs than any other singer, the first talent scout to see him had this to say of his screen test: "Can't act. Can't sing. Slightly bald. Can dance a little."
- Astaire was a very good drummer, a testament to his flawless sense of rhythm.
- This film set the image of Astaire as a dapper man in a top hat, white tie, and tails.
- Ginger Rogers, like Judy Garland, was raised by a tough Broadway mom.
- Two of Hollywood's funniest and most beloved character actors, Edward Everett Horton and Eric Blore, appeared in this and many other Astaire-Rogers films.
- Look quick for a young Lucille Ball playing a flower clerk.
- For the Venice set, RKO built a canal and bridges between two sound stages.
- The imposition of the Hays Code in 1934 toned down the risqué subject matter in films like *Love Me Tonight* and *42nd Street*. *Top Hat* originally included a funny line where one of the more flamboyant characters exclaims: "For the men the sword, for the women the whip." RKO was forced to change it to "For the women the kiss, for the men the sword."
- Here are some other Berlin standards (also see below): "Always," "Be Careful, it's My Heart," "Better Luck Next Time," "Blue Skies," "Count Your Blessings Instead of Sheep," "A Couple of Swells," "Doin' What Comes Naturally," "Easter Parade," "The Girl that I Marry," "God Bless America," "How Deep Is the Ocean," "I Got the Sun in the Morning," "I've Got My Love to Keep Me Warm," "It Only Happens When I Dance With You," "It's a Lovely Day Today," "A Pretty Girl Is like a Melody," "Puttin' On the Ritz," "Remember,"

"Steppin' Out with My Baby," "They Say it's Wonderful," "What'll I Do," "White Christmas."

- The Astaire-Rogers films introduced a number of great standards. Here are some of the best known: *The Gay Divorcee* ("Night and Day" by Cole Porter), *Roberta* ("I Won't Dance," "Lovely to Look At," and "Smoke Gets in Your Eyes" by Jerome Kern), *Follow the Fleet* ("I'm Putting All My Eggs in One Basket," "Let's Face the Music and Dance," and "Let Yourself Go" by Irving Berlin) *Swing Time* ("Pick Yourself Up," "A Fine Romance," and "The Way You Look Tonight" by Jerome Kern), *Shall We Dance* ("Shall We Dance," "Let's Call the Whole Thing Off," "I've Got Beginner's Luck," "They All Laughed," and "They Can't Take that Away from Me" by the Gershwins), *Carefree* ("Change Partners" by Berlin).

Other Films to Watch

Without Ginger, Fred would go on to make *You'll Never Get Rich* (with Rita Hayworth), *Holiday Inn* (with Bing Crosby and a Berlin score), *You Were Never Lovelier* (Hayworth again, whom many consider his best dance partner), *Yolanda and the Thief* (odd but with good numbers), *Ziegfeld Follies* (includes only number he did with Gene Kelly), *Blue Skies* (with Bing and a Berlin score), *Easter Parade* (with Judy Garland and a Berlin score), *Royal Wedding* (where he dances on the ceiling), *The Band Wagon* (contains some of his best dance numbers), *Daddy Long Legs* (with Leslie Caron), *Funny Face* (with Audrey Hepburn and a Gershwin score), *Silk Stockings* (Cole Porter score), *On the Beach* (a dramatic role), *The Pleasures of His Company* (another dramatic role), *Finian's Rainbow* (his last musical role), *The Towering Inferno,* and *Ghost Story.*

Without Fred, Ginger made some excellent comedy-drama-romances: *Stage Door* (she and Katherine Hepburn are aspiring actresses), *Vivacious Lady* (with James Stewart), *Bachelor Mother* (playing, as she often did, a shop girl with grit and heart), *Fifth Avenue Girl* (poses as a gold digger), *Lucky Partners* (with Ronald Colman), *Kitty Foyle* (for which she won best actress), *Roxie Hart* (turned in to the musical *Chicago*), *The Major and the Minor* (first American film directed by Billy Wilder), *Lady in the Dark* (must choose between three men), *I'll Be Seeing You* (with Joseph Cotten), and many more.

The five major studios were MGM, WB, Paramount, RKO, and Twentieth Century Fox. Though Fox was known for making serious social pictures like *The Grapes of Wrath,* its musicals tended to be light and frothy. True, nearly all of them are about vaudeville type performers who are trying to struggle their way to the top; however, unlike the WB musicals, our would-be stars don't have to deal with gangsters, and there is little real danger of their ending up in the gutter. The key dilemma that characters must face in Fox musicals is the choice between love and career; often bad timing sets in and our lovers find to their dismay that one of them has achieved fame while the other has lagged behind. As in the WB backstage and the Astaire-Rogers musicals, Fox heroes and heroines are often performers. There is little attempt to integrate songs into the plot; the songs rise up when the characters sing them on stage. Fox musicals generally featured lots of songs/acts with little discernible plot. Instead of commissioning a set of new songs, they generally rehashed existing songs, and then added one or two new ones.

Other than Shirley Temple, who made Fox a considerable amount of money during the Depression, and who starred in both comedy-dramas and musicals, the two essential Fox musical heroines were Alice Faye and Betty Grable. The two starred together in *Tin Pan Alley,* probably the best of the musicals, but more often acted alone in films fashioned around them—with Grable's career shooting up as Faye's slowly sank down. Faye was famous for her wry little smile and her mix of resoluteness and vulnerability. While both actresses were good singers, Grable was more famous as a dancer—her legs were legendary—and for being more happy-go-lucky in her parts than the melancholy Faye. During World War II, Grable was the most famous pin-up girl and the love of all GI's.

Faye's best pictures: *In Old Chicago, Alexander's Ragtime Band, Rose of Washington Square, Hollywood Cavalcade, Lillian Russell, That Night in Rio,* and *Hello, Frisco, Hello.* Grable's best: *Down Argentine Way, Moon over Miami, I Wake up Screaming, Footlight Serenade, Springtime in the Rockies, Coney Island, The Dolly Sisters, Mother Wore Tights,* and *How to Marry a Millionaire* (which also starred Marilyn Monroe).

Faye's first three musicals starred Tyrone Power; however, as he could not sing, he was soon replaced by John Payne, who looked like Power but could sing, and who would star with both Faye and Grable. Fox's other key male lead was the versatile Don Ameche. Still, Fox musicals were defined by their heroines and their vaudeville backdrop. They were at their best when recreating the feel of old Broadway, and they made generous use of character actors and exotic acts. None of their musicals were profound or innovative, but they were well mounted, had lots of zip, and passed the time pleasantly enough.

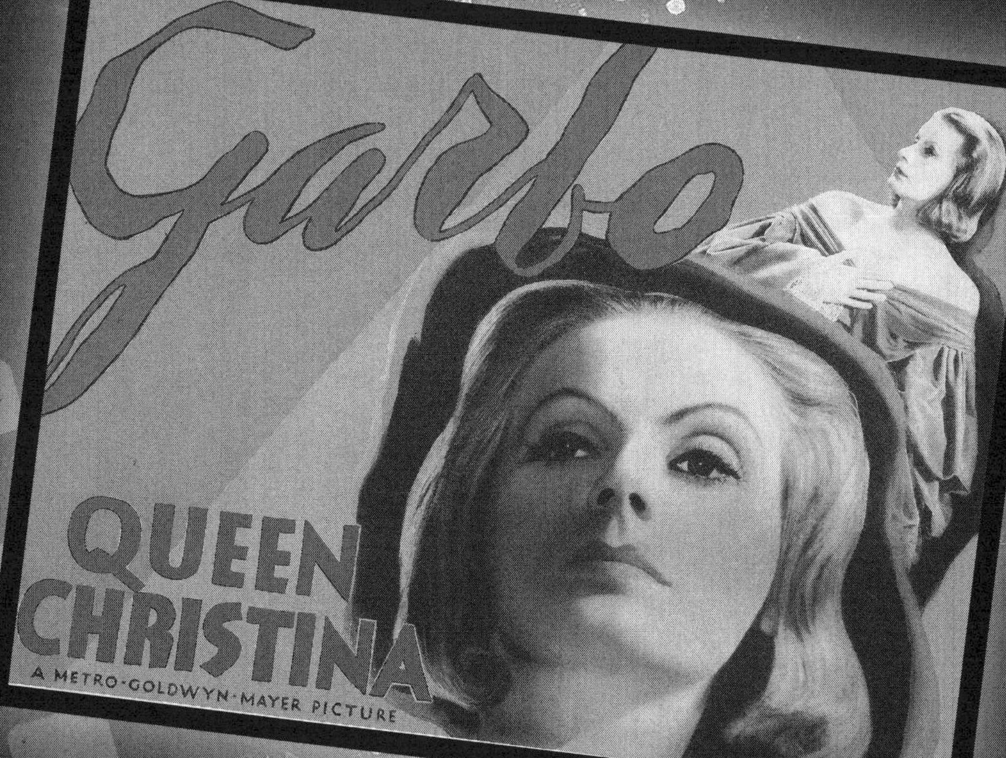
Garbo
QUEEN
CHRISTINA
A METRO-GOLDWYN-MAYER PICTURE

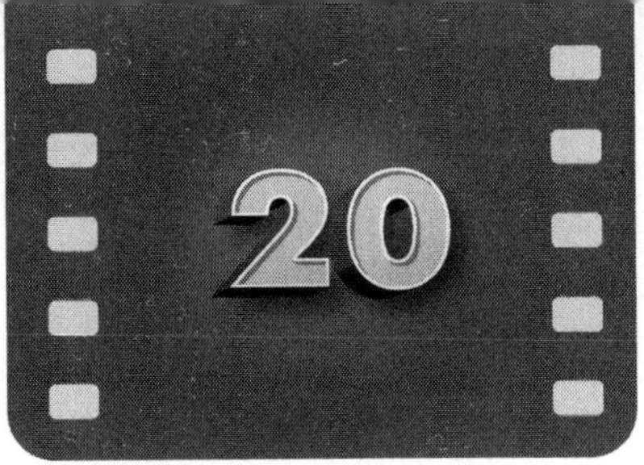

QUEEN CHRISTINA

(MGM; 1933; ROUBEN MAMOULIAN)

Here I am in my final chapter, and I've not yet addressed directly one of the essential pillars of the studio system and the Golden Age: its stars. Hollywood's reigning gods (Clark Gable, Humphrey Bogart, Cary Grant, Gary Cooper, John Wayne) and goddesses (Greta Garbo, Bette Davis, Joan Crawford, Katherine Hepburn, Marlene Dietrich) became the very embodiment of the public's desires and fantasies. Thousands of fan letters poured in every day, and the biggest stars soon became icons, almost religious images or symbols that stood for some abstract virtue or quality: Beauty, Courage, Energy, Passion, etc. The biggest stars would not just act in movies; the movies would be written to fit their particular charisma. More than that, the studios—MGM in particular, who claimed to house more stars than there are in the heavens—would spend millions of dollars creating, building-up, and exhibiting their stars.

The publicity departments of each studio, which were as vital to the machine as the writers or directors, would carefully groom the image of each star to fit public tastes and to emphasize their inner star-quality. (They would also orchestrate elaborate cover ups when one of their stars did something scandalous!) The studios were dream factories, and it was through the aura of their stars that we in the audience joined in the dream. However, though the stars commanded high salaries and virtual adoration, most of them were not free agents; they were, in fact, employees. Even the greatest stars had to sign long-term contracts, usually seven years, with their studios that left them very much at the whim of the moguls, who often put them in routine roles or pictures they despised and made them work long hours on multiple films. But there was a good side to this. Unlike many actors today, who only do films that will "further their career," the studio actors worked, and, as they did, they honed their craft.

Of all the stars of the Golden Age, the one that shined the brightest while remaining perpetually shrouded in mystery was MGM's Swedish Sphinx, Greta Garbo. She made her start in silent films, where she mesmerized the masses with her intense and passionate eyes set in the cold perfection of her face. The world had never seen anything like her tempestuous love scenes with John Gilbert in *Flesh and the Devil* and *Love*, a version of Tolstoy's *Anna Karenina*. For a while, it seemed as if Garbo and Gilbert would marry, but the pressures of her stardom pushed Garbo away from one of the few men, if not the *only* man, she ever loved. After she retired in 1941, rejecting all pleas to return to Hollywood, she moved to New York City where she lived the life of a private recluse until her death in 1990. The fact that she never married and that she continually refused to do any interviews only magnified her mystery.

When sound hit Hollywood in 1927, MGM, terrified that the fans would not like Garbo's voice, did not put her in a film until 1930. They needn't have worried. Unlike John Gilbert, whose weak voice and silent-movie mannerisms (big arm gestures, rising eyebrows, etc.) did not transfer well to the medium of sound, Garbo's husky, world-weary voice matched perfectly her silent screen persona. And yet, as her star rose higher and higher, Garbo isolated herself more and more from her fans, unwilling to take upon herself the burdensome duties and responsibilities that come with stardom. As her secretive, reclusive nature only inflamed the interest of her fans, Mayer and Thalberg allowed her to remain out of the public's eye, keeping up her star campaign without actually putting her on display. She remained at the very top of the MGM aristocracy while yet remaining as cold, distant, and aloof as the stars in the night sky. She was allowed to retain her privacy, but she had to sacrifice much of her freedom and self-determination, particularly in matters of the heart.

I offer these details about the life and career of Garbo because *Queen Christina*, a movie I never tire of watching, is as much about the

Queen of Sweden as it is about the Queen of MGM. The character in the film, like the star who plays her, has power, wealth, and prestige, but she lacks love and passion and joy. Had Mamoulian made the movie at Paramount, he might have allowed Garbo to have both: to get the love she yearns for while holding on to the reins of power. But this is MGM, where power always brings with it a heavy weight of duty. If she wants to get the desires of her heart, including and especially sex, then she will have to pay for it in the end. Love at Paramount is a game; at MGM it is serious business: it cannot be indulged in without consequences.

Though the inventive camera he had unleashed one year earlier in *Love Me Tonight* is here rendered less mobile and energetic, Mamoulian *did* get to avail himself of MGM's love of pageantry, and its willingness to build lavish set pieces to show off its stars. Nothing in this picture is small; when Christina spends the night in a country inn, her room is as big as a suite at the Waldorf. More to the point, the lavish throne room of her castle, with its huge interior space and its glossy décor, embodies the enormity of Christina's role, and responsibilities, as Queen of Sweden. The words of Shakespeare's Henry V ring true for the lonely Christina: "Uneasy lies the head that wears a crown."

The film presents Christina as a good diplomat and a brave leader, one who works hard and cares deeply for her people and her country. In good MGM-American style, she speaks up, not only for political liberty, but for freedom of thought and of religion as well. Sick and tired of war and death, she wants to help build a civilized Europe where swords can be beaten into plowshares. What good will it do Sweden to allow her Viking lust for blood to leave her "an island in a dead sea."

Still, despite her success as a monarch, she is empty inside, hungry for something more. She has given all for her people, but she will not give herself. Against the advice of her counselors, she refuses to be married off to the patriotic soldier Charles (Reginald Owen) or even to the scheming courtier Magnus (Ian Keith), for whom she at one time had feelings. She will work and slave for Sweden, but she will not sacrifice the heart that she only barely understands. From an early age, Christina has been raised as a boy, taught to hold back her tears and repress her emotions.

Most of the fun she has known has come from her long rides on horseback with her father figure Aage (C. Aubrey Smith). Early in the picture, she escapes with him for just such a ride through the snow, going out, as she often does, dressed as a boy. The snow, she explains, appeals to her melancholy soul: it is "like a wide sea; one can go out and get lost in it and forget the world."

But fate has something in store for her, a chance meeting with a Spanish diplomat named Antonio (John Gilbert), who, when he meets the disguised Christina, thinks she is a boy. Christina enjoys the ruse greatly, as do we in the audience, and she continues to play it, even when they end up stranded at an inn and overhear customers betting how many lovers the aloof Queen Christina has. Since the inclement weather has caused the inn to be packed with clients needing shelter for the night, Christina and Antonio are asked by the proprietor if they would be willing to share a room. Christina does all that she can to avoid sharing the room, but when Antonio interprets her hesitation as an insult to himself, she gives in, much to the shock of Aage!

Even before they head upstairs, tension has been mounting between Antonio and Christina, with the Spaniard praising love as an elegant, subtle, artistic thing that must be nourished, and the Swede dismissing it as a simple, elemental urge about which one should not foster illusions. The dialogue continues as they ascend to the room, with the audience holding its breath, wondering how and when Christina's true identity will be revealed and how Antonio will react when he learns she is a woman. "It's all a question of climate," Antonio explains to the romance-deprived Christina, "You cannot serenade a woman in a snowstorm. All the graces in the art of love—elaborate approaches that will make the game of love amusing—can only be practiced in those countries that quiver in the heat of the sun."

Well, as it so happens, Antonio and Christina do meet in a snowstorm, but the long-awaited undressing does not occur until they are in the upstairs room by a roaring fire. When Christina finally takes off enough of her outer garments to reveal her female figure, she adopts a vulnerable feminine pose, the first time we have seen her do so in the film. This first undressing will lead, as it must in MGM's world of duty and consequence, to a second undressing—that of her royal robes and her crown—but at this point in the story, we can only cheer that Christina has finally found the struggling woman deep within her. The rough cocoon has split open, and the lovely butterfly emerges.

What follows is an intoxicatingly sensuous scene that transcends the physical boundaries of the merely sensual. With a breathless intensity that is almost sacramental, Antonio feeds the supine Christina grapes that have been "warmed and ripened in the Spanish sun," in that mystical land of passion and romance where the "air smells purple." As Antonio luxuriates in the blessed improbability of discovering such rare beauty in the frozen wilderness of Sweden, Christina reflects on the new world that has been opened to her: "This is how the Lord must have felt when he first beheld the finished world with all his creatures living, breathing."

But Mamoulian is not yet done. After they have indulged in love, Christina rises from the bed and walks—or, rather, glides—around the room. As she does so, she touches—or, better, caresses—all the soft, curved surfaces in her new Eden. Mamoulian had Garbo act out this scene to the beating of a metronome, giving her movements a stately, ritualistic quality that is at once solemn and joyous. What is happening in this wordless, purely cinematic scene is that Christina is awakening to her own femininity, to the tenderness and warmth she has buried within herself for so long. Confused by her strange behavior, Antonio asks Christina what she is doing. "I have been memorizing this room," she responds, "In the future, in my memory, I shall live a great deal in this room."

I have long considered her response to be one of the top ten best lines in movie history, for it touches on the essence of what it means to be conscious creatures who are in great part defined by their memories. It also embodies film's power to layer images in our mind to which we can return in times of trouble or sorrow or confusion. Christina has found the happiness that she has been seeking all her life, and she will grasp on to it now with all that is within her. It is precious because it has been sought for, but it is even more precious because she knows it cannot last.

As the scene in the inn comes to a close, Antonio says to Christina, "I don't believe in you. You're an illusion. You'll vanish before my eyes."

Christina laughs, but then a shadow comes over her, and she is gone. After all, she, like Garbo herself, is finally nothing more than a flickering image on the screen—something unreal and insubstantial that cannot be held on to or owned.

In the next scene, we see Christina in a beautiful gown that shocks her courtiers and arouses the scheming Magnus. Love has transformed her, but, back in the cold palace with its imposing throne room, her love will not be able to survive. When Antonio comes to court and realizes the woman he has fallen in love with is the queen, he is at first embarrassed and angry, but he comes in time to forgive her. Still, from this point on, Antonio slowly diminishes, eclipsed both by the political power of Christina and the star power of Garbo. Garbo insisted, against the wishes of Mayer and MGM, that Gilbert be cast as Antonio, perhaps because she knew that the story of Christina was her own story, that her sincere love for Gilbert, like Christina's for Antonio, could not survive the royal demands put upon her and her screen incarnation.

As Christina throws caution to the wind and allows her affair with Antonio to be made public, Magnus rouses up the people against her. At one point, a Swedish mob assaults Antonio's carriage, threatening to tear him to pieces for daring to steal away, and monopolize, the heart of their beloved queen. But Christina, merely by the power of her voice and her eyes, saves Antonio and wins back the affections of her people. "Do I peer into the lives of my subjects?" she asks. If you want to understand the overwhelming magnetism of Golden Age Hollywood's greatest stars, then watch this scene a few times. It is not just Garbo's beauty or her skill at delivering the lines; it is her serene presence, her charisma, her ability to radiate a sense of complete self-possession.

Still, this is MGM, and a sacrifice must be made if Christina is to have Antonio. Though her people and her nobles alike beg her not to do it, Christina removes her crown and gives up her throne. There is "a voice in our soul," she explains to her heartbroken people, "that tells us what to do and we must obey." With that, she walks out of the palace, gently brushing off the hands that grasp on to her, imploring her to remain. Garbo's millions of fans would feel the same way when she retired in

1941, but she would brush off their insistent pleas with the same firm but melancholy air of abdication.

She will choose her heart over her duty, will go off to the "islands of the moon" with her lover, to "the house on the cliff" that Antonio has promised her in the misty never land of Spain. But even this is to be denied her. To be a star, a symbol, a living icon is to be alone. Even the removal of the crown cannot save her from isolation. As she rushes to the pier to board the ship to Spain, Antonio is drawn into a duel with Magnus that robs him of the life he would have shared with Christina. Her dreams shattered, we think for a moment that she will return to her throne. But no, she can no longer go back to her old life. She can only go forward, can only take the boat to Spain and find that promised "house on the cliff." Perhaps there she will find happiness and contentment.

In the final moment of the film, Christina walks swiftly to the front of the boat and stands, erect and alone against the sky, on the jutting prow. As she stands there, her face expressionless, the camera zooms in for Hollywood's most famous star close-up. When Garbo asked Mamoulian what she should be thinking of in that final moment, he told her to think of nothing. And he was right to do so. For Garbo, the ultimate Golden Age star, is finally a cipher, a blank slate onto which four generations of movie audiences have projected their hopes and their fears, their agonies and their ecstasies. What makes a star a star is our willingness to live vicariously through them, to make their dreams and triumphs and tragedies our own. A small portion of my own heart will forever remain with Christina-Garbo on the prow of that ship looking off into an uncertain future.

Fun Facts for the Fans

- Surprisingly, *Queen Christina* was not awarded any Oscar nominations; more surprisingly, Garbo herself, despite four nominations, never won an Oscar.
- *Queen Christina* is best watched alongside *The Private Lives of Elizabeth and Essex*, where WB's reigning queen, Bette Davis, plays Elizabeth I as a tough-as-nails, paranoid underdog, and *The Scarlet*

Empress, where Paramount's reigning queen, Marlene Dietrich, plays Catherine the Great as an innocent transformed into a highly-eroticized courtesan photographed through silken curtains.

- The historical Queen Christina moved to Rome, converted to Catholicism, and gathered around her a literary and scientific coterie of friends and admirers!
- A delightfully quirky film came out in 1984, *Garbo Talks,* in which a loyal son tracks down Garbo in NYC to fulfill his mother's dying wish to meet the star. Many New Yorkers scanned the streets for sightings of the reclusive celebrity.
- John Gilbert was MGM's greatest silent heart throb. His most successful silent pictures were *The Merry Widow* (directed by Erich von Stroheim) and *The Big Parade* (an epic film about World War I that is still highly entertaining).
- Though his voice and mannerisms were unsuitable to sound, Gilbert's career was also hurt by the death of Irving Thalberg, who had long protected him from the enmity of Louis B. Mayer and his threat to ruin Gilbert's Hollywood's career.
- MGM wanted to cast Laurence Olivier in the role of Antonio, but Garbo, still loyal to her old flame, said she would not do the picture without Gilbert. Sadly, Garbo's insistence delayed Olivier's Hollywood career by six years.
- In his last film, *Silk Stockings,* Mamoulian has Cyd Charisse—who plays the role of the cold-Soviet-warmed-by-love originated by Garbo in *Ninotchka*—perform a dance number that mimics the scene of awakening femininity in *Queen Christina.*

Other Films to Watch

Garbo's best sound pictures are: *Anna Christie* (her first talkie; she plays a waterfront prostitute in the Eugene O'Neill play), *Susan Lennox* (her only film with Clark Gable; in it, she dramatically and cinematically rises and falls), *Mata Hari* (as the sexy, femme-fatale World War I spy), *Grand Hotel* (as a sad ballerina who wants to be alone until she falls in love with cat burglar John Barrymore), *As You Desire Me* (as an amnesiac), *The Painted Veil* (from a Somerset Maugham novel), *Anna Karenina* (second stab at Tolstoy's classic, with Fredric March as her soldier lover), *Camille* (as a French courtesan who loses her bid for love; a classic weepy directed by George Cukor), *Conquest* (as the mistress of Napoleon, who is played, excellently, by Charles Boyer), *Ninotchka* (a rare comic role, directed by Paramount's Ernst Lubitsch, that allows her to have sex *and* a happy ending), *Two-Faced Woman* (a frivolous, ill-judged comic role that ended her career).

Garbo was one of three MGM queens whose images were carefully cultivated by Irving Thalberg: the other two are Joan Crawford and Norma Shearer (the later Mrs. Thalberg).

Crawford was the ultimate proletarian shop-girl—tough, aggressive, determined—who made it big. She began her career playing opposite Gable's dangerous man (eight times!) in such films as *Possessed, Dancing Lady,* and *Strange Cargo,* but she made better films without him. She checked in along with Garbo to the *Grand Hotel,* played a reformed prostitute in *Rain,* the mistress of Andrew Jackson in *The Gorgeous Hussy,* a husband-stealing home-wrecker in *The Women,* and a disfigured woman who turns to crime in *A Woman's Face.* But oddly, or not so oddly, she gave some of her best performances at the proletarian Warner Brothers: especially *Mildred Pierce* (for which she won her Oscar), *Humoresque,* and *Possessed,* all of which possess film noir elements.

Shearer played the ultimate lady, refined, sensitive, and whimsical with a touch of flirtatiousness. Her best sound roles include a flirtatious but finally noble wife in *The Divorcee* (for which she won her Oscar), a similar role in Noel Coward's *Private Lives,* a tragic Victorian lady in *Smilin' Through,* Elizabeth Barrett Browning in *The Barretts of Wimpole Street,*

Juliet in *Romeo and Juliet,* the title role in *Marie Antoinette,* and a noble. long-suffering wife who almost loses her man to Crawford in *The Women.*

FURTHER READING

If you are serious about diving into classic movies, then you must purchase a copy of *Halliwell's Film and Video Guide* and *Halliwell's Who's Who in the Movies*. Though there are many guides out there, these are the best when it comes to the Golden Age of Hollywood. The first gives synopses and reviews of some 20,000 movies, including silent and foreign films, together with major credits and other fascinating bits of information. The second is an encyclopedia of the stars, directors, writers, and other key people; it also has entries on major characters and themes. Both are available in numerous editions, the later ones edited by John Walker. You should be able to pick up an older edition for next to nothing in a good used bookstore. I have also found Leonard Maltin's *Movie Guide* and Ephraim Katz's *Film Encyclopedia* helpful; both are available in numerous editions.

There are many film textbooks out there. The one I would recommend is *Understanding Movies* by Louis Giannetti. Giannetti's *Flashback: A Brief History of Film* (which he co-wrote with Scott Eyman) is also quite good. Both are available in many editions; I would personally go with the older editions, since they tend to be less trendy and politicized.

Also make sure to visit the Internet Movie Data Base (imdb.com) which allows you to search by titles, stars, directors, writers, etc. It also offers a wealth of trivia on each film, together with professional and amateur reviews. The site is extremely well constructed and cross-referenced. Once you get on it, you may find yourself there for hours. Also make sure to watch Turner Classic Movies as often as you can; it's good for your soul!

Below are a list of books that will help increase your enjoyment of and appreciation for the films of Hollywood's Golden Age. I have put an * by my dozen favorites.

Ackroyd, Peter. *Alfred Hitchcock: A Brief Life* (Nan Talese, 2015). Good brief biography.

Anobile, Richard J., editor. *Michael Curtiz's Casablanca.* This entry in the Film Classics Library offers frame by frame blowups of the entire film with all the dialogue in caption form. A delight to browse through. The FCL has also done this for *Frankenstein, Psycho, The Maltese Falcon, Stagecoach, Dr. Jekyll and Mr. Hyde,* and *Ninotchka.*

Behlmer, Rudy. *Inside Warner Bros.: 1935–1951* (Fireside, 1985). History come alive.

Behlmer, Rudy, editor. *Memo from David O. Selznick* (Viking, 1972). A wonderful, often hilarious selection from Selznick's endless, brilliant, maddening memos.

Bergman, Andrew. *We're in the Money: Depression America and Its Films* (Harper, 1971). Seminal study, essential for understanding WB films and the early Capra.

Bordwell, David, Janet Staigner, and Kristin Thompson. *The Classical Hollywood Cinema: Film Style & Mode of Production to 1960* (Columbia UP, 1985). Though a bit on the technical side, this is the seminal textbook for the subject.

Brady, Frank. *Citizen Welles: A Biography of Orson Welles* (Anchor, 1989). Good, readable biography of the larger-than-life Welles.

* Capra, Frank *The Name Above the Title* (Da Capo, 1997). The best and most essential of all Hollywood autobiographies. A delight to read and packed with insight.

Carney, Ray. *American Vision: The Films of Frank Capra* (Wesleyan UP, 1996). Offers a unique analysis of the films and the vision of Frank Capra.

Cowie, Peter. *The Cinema of Orson Welles* (Da Capo, 1983). Accessible and well illustrated analysis of all his films and his acting career.

Croce, Arlene. *The Fred Astaire & Ginger Rogers Book* (Vintage, 1972). This has it all; a gift for the fans. It even allows you to watch them dance by flipping the page corners!

Davis, Ronald L. *John Ford: Hollywood's Old Master* (U of OK Press, 1995). A good study of the man and his films.

Eastman, John. *Retakes: Behind the Scenes of 500 Classic Movies* (Ballantine, 1989). A great source of movie trivia.

Ellis, Jack C. *A History of Film* (Prentice-Hall, 1979). A solid study of world cinema.

Everson, William K. *Hollywood Bedlam: Classic Screwball Comedies* (Citadel, 1994). Breezy, well-illustrated jaunt through the genre.

* Gabler, Neal. *An Empire of Their Own: How the Jews Invented Hollywood* (Doubleday, 1988). A seminal and engrossing book that proves its thesis while bringing its subject matter to life. All the major Jewish moguls are covered. A&E turned the book into a two-hour documentary titled *Hollywood: An Empire of Their Own.*

Grant, Barry Keith, editor. *Film Genre Reader* (U of TX Press Austin, 1986). A helpful collection of academic essays that are nevertheless quite accessible.

* Hamilton, Ian. *Writers in Hollywood: 1915–1951* (Carroll & Graf, 1990). One of the best and most accessible treatments of the subject.

Harmetz, Aljean. *The Making of the Wizard of Oz* (Hyperion, 1998). Definitive study.

Harvey, Stephen. *Directed by Vincente Minnelli* (Harper, 1989). Companion book to an exhibition at New York's Museum of Modern Art. Well-illustrated and incisive.

* Hay, Peter. *MGM: When the Lion Roars* (Turner Publishing, 1991). This beautiful, well-researched coffee table book was turned into a brilliant, six-hour documentary narrated by Patrick Stewart. The documentary offers the best introduction to the Golden Age.

Higham, Charles. *Merchant of Dreams: Louis B. Mayer, MGM and the Secret of Hollywood* (Dutton, 1993). Good biography of Mayer and the studio he built.

Hirschhorn, Clive. *The Hollywood Musical: Every Hollywood Musical from 1927 to the Present Day* (Crown, 1981). If you love film musicals, this should be on your shelf.

* *Hitchcock Truffaut: The Definitive Study of Alfred Hitchcock by François Truffaut* (Touchstone, 1985). This book length interview of Hitchcock that covers his life and every one of his films must be on the shelf of all film lovers.

Hitt, Jim. *Words and Shadows: Literature on the Screen* (Citadel, 1992). Well-illustrated study that spans seventy years and that is helpfully organized by the major novelists.

Hyams, Joe. *Bogie* (Signet, 1966). Good standard biography of Humphrey Bogart.

* Kael, Pauline. *The Citizen Kane Book* (Bantam, 1971). Includes the shooting script illustrated with stills from the film along with Kael's excellent essay, "Raising Kane."

Kanin. Garson. *Hollywood* (Viking, 1974). Warm and funny insider look at Hollywood.

* Kendall, Elizabeth. *The Runaway Bride: Hollywood Romantic Comedy of the 1930s* (Doubleday, 1990). If you love these films, you will want to read this book that is helpfully organized in terms of the major directors and their leading ladies.

Knight, Arthur. *The Liveliest Art: A Panoramic History of the Movies* (Mentor, 1957). A classic study that is well worth having on your shelf.

Koszarski, Richard. *Hollywood Directors: 1941–1976* (Oxford UP, 1977). Helpful snapshots of directors and their contributions to film history.

Lawton, Richard. *A World of Movies: 70 Years of Film History* (Bonanza Books, 1974). My favorite picture book with clever captions by Hugo Leckey.

Lebo, Harlan. *Casablanca Behind the Scenes: The Illustrated History of One of the Favorite Films of All Time* (Fireside, 1992). A treasure trove of trivia.

* Leff, Leonard J. *Hitchcock and Selznick: The Rich and Strange Collaboration of Alfred Hitchcock and David O. Selznick in Hollywood* (U of CA P, 1987). An engrossing study of two larger than life personalities that helped define the Golden Age.

Levy, Emanuel. *George Cukor, Master of Elegance: Hollywood's Legendary Director and His Stars* (William Morrow and Company, 1994). Well-done biography.

MacBride, Joseph. *Frank Capra: The Catastrophe of Success* (Simon & Schuster, 1992). Good biography, but paints a picture that is perhaps too dark.

Mast, Gerald. *A Short History of the Movies* (Bobbs-Merrill, 1971). Good overview that is available in numerous editions.

* McGilligan, Pat, editor. *Six Screenplays by Robert Riskin* (U of CA Press, 1997). Includes six screenplays that Riskin wrote for Capra (*Platinum Blonde, American Madness, It Happened One Night, Mr. Deeds Goes to Town, Lost Horizon, Meet John Doe*), along with a very thorough introduction by the editor. A must for Capra fans.

* *Moguls & Movie Stars: A History of Hollywood.* A seven-hour documentary series from Turner Classic Movies that traces the rise of Hollywood through commentary and clips.

* Mordden, Ethan. *The Hollywood Studios: House Style in the Golden Age of Movies* (Fireside, 1988). A must-read book that is written with zest and style.

Mosley, Leonard. *Zanuck: The Rise and Fall of Hollywood's Last Tycoon* (Little, Brown, and Company, 1984). Good biography of Zanuck and the Hollywood he helped build.

Olivier, Laurence. *Confessions of an Actor* (Simon and Schuster, 1982). A compelling and entertaining autobiography of the greatest stage and screen actor.

Paul, William. *Ernst Lubitsch's American Comedy* (Columbia UP, 1983). Excellent analysis of his major films and his contribution to American comedy.

Sarris, Andrew. *The American Cinema: Directors and Directions 1929–1968* (Dutton, 1968). Includes incisive capsule biographies of over two-hundred directors.

* Schatz, Thomas. *Hollywood Genres: Formulas, Filmmaking, and the Studio System* (U of TX at Austin, 1981). Best textbook on the subject; accessible and well-illustrated.

Schatz, Thomas. *The Genius of the System: Hollywood Filmmaking in the Studio Era* (Pantheon, 1988). A seminal study of the subject with a wide vision.

Sennett, Ted. *Lunatics and Lovers: A Tribute to the Giddy and Glittering Era of the Screen's Screwball and Romantic Comedies* (Arlington House, 1973). A very fun read!

Sennett, Ted. *Masters of Menace: Greenstreet and Lorre* (Dutton, 1979). For the fans.

Sennett, Ted. *Warner Brothers Presents: The Most Exciting Years—from The Jazz Singer to White Heat* (Castle, 1971). Great overview of the glory days of WB.

Server, Lee, Ed Gorman, and Martin H. Greenberg. *The Big Book of Noir* (Carroll & Graf, 1998). A helpful compilation of essays on all aspects of noir.

Shipman, David. *Movie Talk: Who Said What About Whom in the Movies* (St. Martin's Press, 1988). A fun collection of over 4,000 Hollywood on Hollywood quotes.

Sklar, Robert. *Film: An International History of the Medium* (Thames & Hudson, 1993). A seminal study.

Sklar, Robert. *Movie-Made America: A Cultural History of American Movies* (Vintage, 1975). A socio-economic look at the rise of American films.

Smith, Dian G. *Great American Film Directors: From the Flickers Through Hollywood's Golden Age* (Julian Messner, 1987). Includes good overviews of Capra, Ford, Hitchcock, Cukor, Welles, and Huston.

Solomon, Stanley J. *Beyond Formula: American Film Genres* (HBJ, 1976). Classic study of westerns, gangster films, musicals, horror films, detective stories, and war pictures.

Sperling, Cass Warner and Cork Milner, with Jack Warner Jr. *Hollywood Be Thy Name: The Warner Brothers Story* (Prima, 1994). Good inside look at the Warners.

Spoto, Donald. *Madcap: The Life of Preston Sturges* (Little, Brown and Company, 1990). An entertaining and instructive biography of a truly original writer and director.

Spoto, Donald. *The Art of Alfred Hitchcock: Fifty Years of His Motion Pictures* (Anchor, 1991). The best film-by-film analysis of Hitchcock's 50+ films. Spoto has also written a controversial biography of Hitch: *The Dark Side of Genius: The Life of Alfred Hitchcock.*

Tornabene, Lyn. *Long Live the King: A Biography of Clark Gable* (Pocket, 1976). Fun exploration of a truly magnetic star.

Welles, Orson, Peter Bogdanovich, and Jonathan Rosenbaum (editor). *This is Orson Welles* (HarperPerennial, 1992). Conversations between a great actor-director and a great director-critic with a passion for Welles.

Wiley, Mason and Damien Bona. *Inside Oscar: The Unofficial History of the Academy Awards* (Ballantine, 1987). Lots of books like this out there; this one is a lot of fun.

You Must Remember This: The Warner Bros. Story. A five-hour documentary series narrated by Clint Eastwood; well done but not as good as *MGM: When the Lion Roars*.

Zierold, Norman. *The Moguls: Hollywood's Merchants of Myth* (Silman-James Press, 1969). Good capsule bios of each of the major moguls.

ABOUT THE AUTHOR

Louis Markos (PhD, University of Michigan), Professor of English and Scholar in Residence at Houston Christian University, holds the Robert H. Ray Chair in Humanities. His 25 books include *On the Shoulders of Hobbits: The Road to Virtue with Tolkien and Lewis, C. S. Lewis for Beginners, Tolkien for Beginners, Literature: A Student's Guide, The Myth Made Fact, From Plato to Christ,* and *Ancient Voices: An Insider's Guide to the Early Church.*

THE END